History of the

Lutheran Theological Seminary
at Philadelphia
1864-1964

History of the

Lutheran Theological Seminary
at Philadelphia
1864-1964

Theodore G. Tappert

Philadelphia
Lutheran Theological Seminary
1964

Library of Congress Catalogue Card Number: 64-22501

CONTENTS

PREFACE

THIS BRIEF HISTORY of the Lutheran Theological Seminary at Philadelphia is intended to be an honest and critical account. It has not been written merely for purposes of promotion. This is not to suggest that a review of the past hundred years will not provide occasion for gratitude as well as regret, for pride as well as humility, for praise as well as blame. Where each of these may be appropriate is left largely to the judgment of the reader, although the writer has not shirked his own responsibility of assessment.

Because the Philadelphia Seminary is a school, and more particularly a school of theology, more has been required than a relation of how the external fabric of grounds, buildings, and furnishings was acquired and how it was maintained and used. Within the limits of available space attention has been given to the social and intellectual life of students, to the atmosphere in which academic work was carried on, and to the directions which theological inquiry and instruction took.

The statistical studies in the appendix were prepared by Mr. Jules J. Auger, a member of the class of 1964. For additional information on the alumni of the seminary the reader is referred to the companion volume edited by John A. Kaufmann.

The costs of producing the book have been shared by the alumni and the seminary itself. The method of printing adopted has made it possible to illustrate the history more richly than letterpress would have allowed.

References to sources, relegated to the back of the book, were included to identify the location of quotations and to enable the interested reader to pursue some item of interest further. Antiquated forms of punctuation, capitalization, hyphenation, and occasionally word order were freely altered where it seemed that they might be more disturbing than helpful to the reader, and special attention has not been called to these changes. Most of the manuscript materials cited are in the archives in the seminary's library.

Readers who are intimately acquainted with the seminary may wonder why some things in its history are passed over in silence. Obviously everything could not be included. The writer is especially conscious of the fact that wives of members of the faculty are not referred to. The conclusion should not be drawn that their participation in the life of the seminary was negligible, for in the last analysis even the theology which their husbands taught did not remain uninfluenced by them. Since the writer lacks the temerity to specify and evaluate this influence, however, he dedicates this volume to the wives of his colleagues, and especially to his own wife who suffered more or less patiently through its writing, in the assurance that they can and will make their own judgments.

Chapter I

Predecessors of the Philadelphia Seminary

DURING THE COLONIAL PERIOD Lutheran inhabitants of North America were ecclesiastically dependent in many ways on their fellow believers in Europe. The Dutch-speaking Lutherans who settled along the Hudson River in the first half of the seventeenth century looked for assistance to the Lutheran Church in the Netherlands, and they and those who followed after them secured ministers from the consistory of Amsterdam and the ministerium of Hamburg to the eve of the American Revolution. The Swedish-speaking Lutherans on the Delaware River comprised a mission of the Church of Sweden, from which they received a long succession of ordained clergymen from 1642 to 1779. The German-speaking Lutherans who came to the New World in far larger numbers during the eighteenth century, and who came to be scattered along the entire Atlantic seaboard from Nova Scotia to Georgia, had no single ecclesiastical authority to which they could turn for ministers. Their homeland was ecclesiastically as well as politically divided, and a sense of colonial responsibility was absent because no German colony was ever established in North America like the colonies of the Dutch and Swedes or, for that matter, of the French, the Spaniards, and the English. Nevertheless, the Salzburg Lutherans in Georgia were supplied with a line of ministers through the personal intervention of the Rev. Samuel Urlsperger in Augsburg. Several ministers were sent to North Carolina by Professor John Velthusen, of the University of Helmstedt. A far larger number was sent — especially to Pennsylvania, New York, and New Jersey — by the directors of the Franckean Institutions in Halle, Saxony, and it was these men in particular who helped to give colonial Lutheranism its distinctively pietistic complexion.

The number of ministers who were officially sent to America by ecclesiastical authorities in Europe was not sufficient to meet the needs of the growing Lutheran population. In exceptional cases ordained clergymen voluntarily crossed the Atlantic Ocean with colonists and ministered to them in their new settlements. More often men who had been ordained in Germany found their way into American congregations after they had been suspended or dismissed from their office abroad. Others who had university training but lacked the recommendation of formal ordination responded to the pleas of shepherdless Lutherans and assumed the duties of preacher and pastor. Under the conditions which obtained it sometimes happened that neither the motives nor the abilities of the men who offered their services were of a high caliber. The German-speaking Lutherans in Pennsylvania alone had 20 ministers who had been sent from Europe by ecclesiastical authorities before the Revolution, 17 who had come from Europe as ordained clergymen without being officially sent, and 26 who served as ministers without benefit of theological education or formal ecclesiastical ordination.[1]

These last were sometimes incompetent men who "preached and administered the holy sacraments as if they were plying a trade, scattered congregations rather than gathered them, and were a disgrace to the church instead of an ornament."[2] They could be removed from office, however, only if better men were available to put in their places. Since Europe was not able to supply all the ministers who were needed in America, it was gradually recognized that a native ministry would have to be trained. A few clergymen therefore began to take promising young men into their homes, instruct them privately in languages and theology, and thus prepare them for eventual examination and ordination. Among the self-appointed tutors in theology during the eighteenth century were Henry Melchior Muhlenberg, the first of the ministers sent from Halle and the

Monument of Henry Melchior Muhlenberg Erected on the Seminary Campus in 1917

2

man who was responsible above all others for giving to colonial Lutheranism the shape it came to have; Charles Magnus Wrangel, dean (provost) of the Swedish Lutheran clergy on the Delaware River who advised and encouraged Muhlenberg; John C. Kunze, who succeeded Muhlenberg in Philadelphia and later moved to New York City; J. C. Henry Helmuth, who started his tutoring in Lancaster, Pa., and later continued it in Philadelphia; and Jacob Goering, who had a total of more than a score of students under his tutelage in York, Pa. The advantage of the system of private instruction was that it afforded a maximum of practical experience, for, while they were studying, young men assisted their tutors by teaching school, reading sermons, and engaging in pastoral work under close supervision. The disadvantage of the system was that it offered a minimum of academic equipment and stimulation, for a student had only one part-time teacher, and this a man who was so preoccupied with parish duties that as a rule he had all he could do to impart what he remembered from his studies long before.[3] A committee which examined the sermons of some of these privately tutored students in 1795 declared that "if they preach sermons like the outlines presented, their congregations are to be sincerely pitied."[4]

The shortage of ministers played a leading part in the formation in 1748 of the first permanent synodical organization of Lutherans in America. Six years after the arrival in Philadelphia of Henry Melchior Muhlenberg, what came to be called the Evangelical Lutheran Ministerium in North America was brought into being there by four German ministers, the dean of the Swedish clergy on the Delaware, and a candidate for ordination in the presence of lay representatives from one Swedish and ten German congregations. As the name "ministerium" suggests, the body was originally a union of ministers. The chief purpose for convening it was to provide some semblance of ecclesiastical authority for the examination and ordination of a candidate for the ministry, John Nicholas Kurtz, who had been educated in Europe.[5]

A year after the Ministerium was organized the first attempt was made to establish a school for the education of ministers. With funds sent by European patrons in Halle and London, and therefore in their names, Muhlenberg purchased forty-nine acres of land in the county of Philadelphia for £82 10s. The indenture, dated Oct. 20, 1749, declared that the land, "together with all and singular the Buildings, Improvements, Ways, Woods, Waters, Water-Courses, Rights, Liberties, Privileges, Hereditaments and Appurtenances whatsoever thereunto belonging," was held in trust "for the use, purpose and Intent of a protestant Christian School and Seminary, of a Burial place for deceased Christian people, of an Hospital for decrepit and faithful Ministers and their poor Widows that served in the united Lutheran Congregations in the County of Philadelphia and of the protestant Evangelical Society associating themselves to the House of divine Worship on the above demised Spot of Land . . . ."[6] Mention of a school, cemetery, and home for the aged suggests that Muhlenberg had in mind establishing a cluster of buildings similar to the Franckean Institutions with which he had become acquainted in Halle. A few years after this the congregation in Philadelphia erected a schoolhouse for elementary instruction and laid out a cemetery, but the dream of a theological seminary and a home for the aged was not realized at this time.

The notion of establishing a school of theology was not abandoned. It was mentioned again and again in correspondence with European patrons. It was explained that "the building of necessary churches requires so much money, and most of the congregations are so deeply in debt," that it was not possible to raise money for a seminary. Besides, "the preachers lack the necessary time to put this wholesome and useful proposal into effect." The want of re-

Partial View of the Franckean Institutions Established in Halle,
Saxony, in the Eighteenth Century

sources was obliquely alluded to when at a meeting of the Ministerium in 1769 the verse, "We have a little sister, and she has no breasts" (S. of Sol. 8:8), was quoted as a kind of toast to "the seminary which is to be established."[7] Muhlenberg believed that the growth of the Presbyterians was due, among other things, to their schools for the training of ministers, and he pointed with some envy to William Tennent's "log college," which was a forerunner of Princeton: "One old preacher, named Tennent, who lived in a log hut in the country, started with his own sons, and a large institution, the *Seminarium* in Jersey, has grown out of it."[8]

A concrete proposal to start a Lutheran seminary was discouraged by the authorities in Halle,[9] but Muhlenberg tried to make it clear to them that American expectations were very modest. "Oh, what a necessary, useful, and cheering thing would it not be to have a long wished for institution in which with divine help catechists could be trained and made competent and willing to teach school during the week and preach a sermon on Sundays and festival days! It would not be necessary to torment such candidates with foreign languages over a period of many years; it would be sufficient if they possess native intelligence, a compendious knowledge and experience of the marrow and sap of theology, the ability to write a tolerable hand, and understanding of the mother tongue and English and possibly also the declensions and conjugations of the Latin language, a robust constitution able to endure every kind of food and weather, and, pre-eminently, a heart that sincerely loves the Saviour of the world and his sheep and lambs."[10] The need for ministers was so great that it seemed unreasonable to insist on the kind of academic standards that prevailed in Europe. "As far as the oriental and occidental languages, with which the studious youth is so sorely detained and tormented, are concerned, we now have such an abundance of the most ingeniously contrived lexicons, paraphrases, critiques, expositions, translations from the basic languages, notes upon notes, etc., etc. in our mother tongue, high German, English, and Dutch, that even a moderately educated catechist and preacher can be profitable and pleasing to his Lord if he only does not lack righteousness of the heart and personal experience of repentance, faith, and devotion."11 Here a typical pietistic emphasis on experimental religion was combined with the pressing demands of the American frontier.

On the eve of the Revolution, in 1773, Muhlenberg once again raised the question, "Is it not time to consider seriously and carefully whether it is not practicable to establish an orphans' home and educational institution?" He made it plain that he was not interested in an elaborate and expensive school for the "manufacture of theoretical schoolmasters and clergymen." He proposed an institution "for worn out Evangelical preachers, for schoolmasters who have served faithfully, and for their widows and orphans." Such persons were not to spend their time in idleness but were to cultivate the fields and raise cattle and sheep. Widows and their daughters were to "spin, sew, knit, wash, and bleach" as well as keep house and raise vegetables. Meanwhile the retired preachers and schoolmasters, "no matter how bent they might be, could give the boys enough work for body and soul and, if they have aptitude, teach them to become schoolmasters or country preachers and catechists." It was suggested that silk culture might be undertaken on the side, and that the institution serve as a center for the sale of books and Halle medicines. Muhlenberg proposed that land be purchased for this purpose with funds to be provided through Halle. It seemed to him that it was not practicable to locate such an institution in the city of Philadelphia because land was too expensive there. On the other hand, it ought not be very far from the city because Philadelphia was central "for correspondence, travel, and trade." Muhlenberg proposed Barren Hill (the present Barren Lafayette Hill, about fifteen miles north of the center of Philadelphia) as a desirable location, where land would be available and the combined school and home for orphans and the aged would be accessible to a larger number of congregations.12

Although this plan remained a "pious wish," as it was called, a school was actually started in February of the same year 1773. It was conceived and brought into being by a younger colleague of Muhlenberg, John Christopher Kunze, who had from his youth "had a special inclination," as he put it, "to have something to do with a school in which the languages and sciences are taught." He organized a "Society for the Promotion of Christianity and Useful Knowledge among the Germans in America," a society which might in the future erect a home for orphans, establish a mission among American Indians, and support churches and parish schools as well as open the proposed "seminarium, that is, a Latin school." The society was formed by twenty-four members of the German Lutheran church in Philadelphia, each of whom contributed £10 to the treasury. It was hoped that additional contributions might be received from foreign patrons and from such American groups as the Lutheran Ministerium. Kunze found a teacher in the person of John Christian Leps, a former student in the University of Halle who had spent several years as a schoolmaster in the Danish West Indies before arriving at this opportune time in the port of Philadelphia. Equipped with a rented room, the school opened, with five boys enrolled, on Feb. 15, 1773. At its height there were forty-one students. Besides Leps, there were three part-time instructors, including the director Kunze himself, and the curriculum embraced such subjects as Latin, German, English, religion, mathematics, and physics. It is obvious that the purpose was to offer instruction on the level of an academy in preparation for later professional study in theology, law, medicine, and the like. In 1777, when the British occupied Philadelphia and

John Christopher Kunze, Founder of the Seminarium in Philadelphia in 1773

the life of the city was disrupted by the Revolution, the school was forced to close after an existence of only four years.[13]

Kunze's *seminarium* may be said to have received new life when the University of Pennsylvania was reorganized in 1779 after the end of the British occupation of Philadelphia. A new charter provided that the leading clergyman of each of the six principal denominations in the city should be a member of the university's board of trustees. John Christopher Kunze thus became the Lutheran representative, and in addition Frederick A. Muhlenberg, son of the patriarch, was named as one of twelve eminent citizens on the board. (From this time until 1898 the Lutheran Church was regularly represented on the university board.) On the ground that the inhabitants of many counties of Pennsylvania were Germans whose children did not speak a word of English, Kunze persuaded the board of trustees to establish a German department (or German Institute) and appoint a German professor of Philology, later called professor of German and Oriental Languages. It was Kunze's hope that students might proceed from the study of German, Greek, and Hebrew to the study of theology. In fact, he proposed to the board that professors of divinity be appointed and that a school of theology be made a part of the university, but his motion was "ordered to lie on the table for consideration" and was never taken up again. Kunze was himself appointed professor of German and Oriental Languages, and when he moved to New York he was succeeded by the Rev. J. C. Henry Helmuth until 1822. The so-called German Institute began auspiciously, at one time had more than seventy students, but soon dwindled in enrollment and significance.[14]

In 1784 Kunze accepted a call to the united churches in New York City. With his consuming interest in teaching, he was attracted by the opportunity to be associated with Columbia University. Originally called King's College, this school had been chartered in 1754, and from the beginning the pastor of the "ancient Lutheran church" in New York was an ex officio member of the board of governors. The Rev. John A. Weygand served in this capacity from 1755 until his death in 1770, and the Rev. Bernard M. Hausihl (or Hauseal) served from 1771 until he moved to Nova Scotia in 1783.[15] Kunze not only succeeded to the position of member of the board of governors (to 1807) but was also named professor of Oriental Languages, without salary until he had students. He attached great hopes to the provision of the university according to which any congregation or any members of a religious denomination guaranteeing the university at least 200 bushels of wheat annually toward the salary could nominate a professor of Theology.[16] Kunze was listed as professor of Oriental Languages in Columbia University from 1784 to 1787 and again from 1792 to 1799,[17] but he seldom had students, although he was reputed to have done more than any other man in his time to promote Semitic studies in America.[18]

Two years after his removal to New York from Philadelphia Kunze called a meeting of all the Lutheran ministers, nine in number, in the state of New York and in northern New Jersey. In response three of these ministers and two laymen met in Albany in October, 1786, and set in motion the organization of what was afterwards called the Lutheran Ministerium of New York and Adjacent States. This was not intended as a rival or competitor of the earlier Ministerium of North America. As a matter of fact, the organizers of the new body remained members of the older body as well as of the new one the rest of their lives. The hope was that the large territory in the Hudson and Mohawk Valleys might be cultivated more effectively through a separate union of ministers and congregations. Although the name "ministerium" was adopted from the earlier body, the new organization was in reality a synod from the very beginning, for lay delegates from congregations as well as ministers were given seats and votes. The older body, which now adopted the name Ministerium of Pennsylvania and Adjacent States, followed suit in 1792 and became a synod too. During the first decades of its life the Ministerium of New York, like its sister body, devoted a great deal of attention to the provision and regulation of ministers.

An opportunity presented itself to secure a better supply of ministers when resources for this purpose were unexpectedly made available. In 1796 the Rev. John Christopher Hartwick (or Hartwig), an eccentric bachelor who had participated in the organization of the original Ministerium in 1748, died in Clermont, N. Y. In the course of his ministry on the Hudson River he had bought thirty-six square miles of land in the present Otsego County, in central New York, from the Mowhawk Indians for $250. Some of this property was lost through mismanagement before Hartwick's death, but much of it remained and increased in value. In his curious will Hartwick appointed the Hon. Jeremiah van Rensselaer and the Hon. Frederick A. Muhlenberg as executors and stipulated that they, with the assistance of John C. Kunze, president of the New York Ministerium, and J. C. Henry Helmuth, president of the Pennsylvania Ministerium, use the estate of the deceased to establish an "Evangelical School for Ministers for the Propagation of the Christian Religion among the Heathen." A year after Hartwick's death the executors arranged that an elementary school be started in Otsego County, that an academy or preparatory school be opened in Albany, and that theological instruction be given in New York City by Kunze. Only Kunze began at once to tutor a few students in his home, and he continued to do so until his death in 1807. Not until 1815, after much of the original estate had been further dissipated, was a school actually founded in the village called Hartwick Seminary,

Hier ruhet
JOHANN C:HARTWICH
Prediger der Evangelifch
Lutherifchen Kirohe.
gebohren in Sax-Gotha
den 6Jenner 1714.
Geftorben
den 16 Julius 1796.
Seines alters
82 Jahre 6Monat

Das kurzgefleckte ziel der tage
Ift fiebenzig ift achtzig inhr
Ein innbegrif von muh und plage
Auch wennesnoch fokoftlich war.
Geflugelt eilt mit uns die zeit.
In eine lange ewigkeit.

Inscription on the Tombstone of John Christopher Hartwick

Otsego County, N. Y. According to the charter, granted the next year, two-thirds of the members of the board of trustees were chosen by the Ministerium of New York. The school was really an academy, and a theological department was attached to it. The Rev. Ernest L. Hazelius was the first principal of the school and also the sole professor of Theology, followed in 1830 by the Rev. George B. Miller. The location in the hinterlands of New York — proposals were often made to move it — and the want of financial support prevented the school from contributing significantly to alleviate the shortage of ministers.[19]

Meanwhile the Lutherans in Pennsylvania were not content with existing provisions for the training of men for the ministry. Three clerical members of the Ministerium of Pennsylvania were serving as trustees of Dickinson College (a Methodist school founded in Carlisle, Pa., in 1773) when it requested aid. In 1784 the Ministerium promised "assistance and support through contributions and recommendations," but there is no evidence of any real cooperation.[20] The major reason for this was that three years later the Lutherans and the Reformed combined their resources to establish a college of their own. The initiative for this enterprise came from J. C. H. Helmuth and Caspar Weiberg, respectively Lutheran and Reformed ministers in Philadelphia, and from Henry Ernest Muhlenberg and William Hendel, Lutheran and Reformed ministers in Lancaster, Pa. In 1784 Helmuth had recommended to the Ministerium of Pennsylvania a "thorough and scholarly education of our youth,"[21] and the following year the Reformed Coetus of Pennsylvania petitioned for help from Holland to establish "a school in the central part of the state of Pennsylvania in which young men might be prepared for the ministry." It was reported that the Reformed had declined to support Dickinson, the English Methodist college, on the ground that "we had reason to fear that this might tend to suppress the German language, and even our nationality, and might be to the disadvantage of our religion."[22] No help was forthcoming from Holland, and so the Reformed cooperated with the Lutherans in founding what Helmuth and Weiberg called "the first German college in America."[23]

It is estimated that at this time a fourth of the inhabitants of Pennsylvania was German-speaking. What united the Lutheran Ministerium and the Reformed Coetus in an educational project was not only their common need for ministers but also their common language and national background. The so-called "German Institute" in the University of Pennsylvania, in which Helmuth was teaching, was not meeting the needs of these churches. Philadelphia was not central to the heaviest concentrations of German-speaking people. Moreover, as a contributor to a German newspaper expressed it in 1785, "In a German college the Germans would not be discouraged by being termed Dutchman or Sour Crout, as has happened in the English colleges."[24] Lancaster, the largest inland town in America, situated in the heart of the German-speaking population of Pennsylvania, was chosen as the site of the new college, and Franklin (after Benjamin Franklin) was selected as its name. According to the charter, one-third of the members of the board of trustees was to be made up of Lutheran clergymen and laymen, one-third of Reformed clergymen and laymen, and "the remainder from any other society of Christians." It was agreed that the presidents should be alternately Lutheran and Reformed, and the first president was Henry Ernest Muhlenberg, youngest son of the patriarch. He already had a reputation as a botanist, and he continued to serve Trinity Lutheran Church in Lancaster as its pastor during his term as president of Franklin College, which extended from 1787 until his death in 1815. Under Muhlenberg's presidency the college was able to do little more than preserve a precarious existence, for neither the Lutherans nor the Reformed supported it adequately.[25]

G. Henry Ernest Muhlenberg, First President of Franklin College in Lancaster

The founding of Franklin College did not contribute materially to meeting the crying need for ministers. After all, it was a college and not a theological seminary. Moreover, its enrollment was very small. During the early decades of the nineteenth century — in fact, beyond the middle of the century — students therefore continued to be tutored privately in theology. Kunze, Helmuth, and the younger Muhlenberg, who devoted so much time and effort to college teaching, also took students of theology into their homes. They were succeeded by other tutors: Carl R. Demme in Philadelphia, George Lochman in Harrisburg, John G. Schmucker in York, Pa., John P. Hecht in Easton, Pa., F. W. Geissenhainer in New York City, Frederick H. Quitman in Rhinebeck, N. Y., and more than a score of others. Some idea of what was involved in the relation of tutor and student may be gained from this description by Emanuel Greenwald, a student of the Rev. David F. Schaeffer: "It was he that invited me to his study, that heard my recitations, that furnished me with the necessary textbooks, that admitted me even to his table, and that aided me in every possible way until I was duly admitted to the sacred office of the ministry. The distance from my father's house to the study of Dr. Schaeffer down town [in Frederick, Md.] was four miles. Going and coming was a daily walk of eight miles. This was made in all seasons, both summer and winter, and Sundays as well as weekdays, as I attended church regularly every Sunday. This was kept up for five years, making a walk for my education of more than fourteen thousand miles! "[26]

The demand for ministers was increased not only by the need for replacements and the growth of existing congregations but also by the establishment of new parishes, especially on the frontier. In 1804 the Ministerium of Pennsylvania adopted a plan for sending itinerant missionaries on annual tours to minister to migrating people and gather them into congregations.[27] Many of these people, it was pointed out, left congregations in the Ministerium to move to the frontier, and as their forefathers in the East had appealed to Europe for help a generation or two earlier, so these migrants were now asking the Ministerium for pastors.[28] A long succession of itinerants was sent out. Among them Paul Henkel (first sent out in 1806),[29] John Stauch (1807),[30] John Christian Frederick Heyer (1820),[31] Ezra Keller (1836),[32] and Frederick Wyneken (1839)[33] especially

Frederick Wyneken, one of the Western Missionaries in the Early Nineteenth Century

distinguished themselves. Such missionaries went to central and western Pennsylvania, to Ohio, and then beyond to what are now the states of Indiana, Illinois, Michigan, Wisconsin, and Missouri. Others traveled to the western parts of Virginia and the Carolinas, to Kentucky and Tennessee. Meanwhile the Ministerium of New York sent similar missionaries to Ontario and western New York.

During these years, especially after 1820, there was a resumption of German immigration, and the resulting further demand for ministers was met in part by the coming of clergymen from Germany. A few had continued to come before 1820, and among them were Frederick H. Quitman (1795) and Carl R. Demme (1819),[34] who have already been mentioned as tutors. The synodical minutes in Pennsylvania and New York indicate that not all who applied for admission as clergymen or for ordination were found worthy, but virtually every year at least one new arrival in America was received into the ranks of the ministry. Societies formed in Bremen and other cities of Germany to send missionaries to America, and especially to the Middle West, were thanked for their efforts, and they were assured that such ministers were welcome because too few were being trained in America.[35] They came from all parts of Germany — from Württemberg, Bavaria, Baden, Hesse, Hanover, Holstein, Prussia — and while some of them remained in the East, more of them were sent to minister to the increasing numbers of immigrants who were settling in the Middle West.

Some of the societies in Germany which sent missionaries to America tended to gloss over all confessional distinctions between Lutherans and Reformed.[36] There was precedent for this in the formation in 1817 of the so-called Prussian Union, the union of Lutheran and Reformed churches in Prussia, and then also elsewhere, under a common ecclesiastical administration. Long before this, as we have seen, Lutherans and Reformed in Pennsylvania had co-operated in the founding of Franklin College in 1787, although they had since allowed it to languish and virtually die. Helmuth, who participated in the founding of this college, began the publication of the short-lived *Evangelisches Magazin* in 1811 in the hope of uniting German-speaking Protestants in resistance against anglicization. In 1817 a union hymnal, the *Gemeinschaftliches Gesangbuch,* appeared from the press, was endorsed by the Lutheran Ministeriums of Pennsylvania and New York and the North Carolina and Ohio Synods as well as by the Reformed Synod (so called since 1792), and enjoyed extensive use for more than a generation. In the same year, the tercentenary of Luther's posting of the Ninety-five Theses, the Ministerium of Pennsylvania "resolved that the German Evangelical Reformed Synod, the Moravians, the English Episcopal and Presbyterian Churches . . . be invited by our president to celebrate the Reformation festival with us." The Rev. Frederick C. Schaeffer, of New York, in a

J. C. Henry Helmuth, Leader in Educational and Missionary Work after the American Revolution

11

letter addressed to the Ministerium of Pennsylvania urged "a closer union between the Lutheran and Reformed Churches in our states" and suggested that "in this laudable and truly evangelical cause our brethren in Germany have set us an excellent example."[37]

The temper of the times therefore seemed favorable to a proposal of the Reformed Synod in 1817 that, "because of the increase and growth of our congregations, efforts should be made to provide an institution for the education of young preachers" and that the Lutheran Ministerium of Pennsylvania should be invited to participate in establishing a joint theological seminary. In 1819 a plan for a "Theological Seminary for the Education of Pious Young Men for the Evangelical Ministry" was drafted which provided for one professor and nine board members from each denomination. Nothing came of the plan, for the projected seminary ran into conflict with internal problems which occupied the attention of both churches. In 1820 the Reformed Synod decided to establish a seminary of its own, and this was finally accomplished in 1825.[38] For many years the Reformed Seminary was located in Mercersburg, Pa., until in 1871 it was moved to Lancaster.

Since the opening of the nineteenth century the Lutheran Church, like the Reformed, had been growing internally and expanding geographically. In the case of the Lutherans such growth and expansion were marked and were accompanied by the formation of new synods in addition to the older Pennsylvania and New York Ministeriums, which had been embracing in their membership (at least nominally) ministers from Ontario to South Carolina and from the Atlantic coast to the farthest penetration of the western frontier. The Synod of North Carolina came into being in 1803, and some ministers and congregations withdrew from it in 1820 to form the Tennessee Synod, while others withdrew in 1824 to organize the Synod of South Carolina. Before this happened the Synod of Ohio was organized in 1818, and its territory was limited toward the east when the Pittsburgh Synod was established in 1845. The Synod of Maryland and Virginia was founded in 1820, and this was divided in 1829 into separate synods for each of the two states. For the most part the new synods were formed amicably and continued to look for leadership and assistance to the oldest and largest of the synods, the Ministerium of Pennsylvania, whose constitution they followed as a model for their own. A case in point is the appeal of the Synod of North Carolina to the practice of the Ministerium in the matter of licensing preachers and the decision in 1816 "to treat this matter in the same way as our honored ministerial brethren in Pennsylvania do."[39]

In response to a communication from the Ministerium of Pennsylvania in 1807,[40] which communication was mislaid for several years, the Synod of North Carolina in 1812 expressed "a fervent wish . . . to enter into nearer and more cordial connection with the brethren professing our faith in Pennsylvania."[41] When in the years which followed ministers and congregations in Ohio, Maryland, and Virginia began to loosen their ties with the Ministerium of Pennsylvania and prepare to form separate synods, the mother synod declared in 1818 that it thought it "desirable if the various Evangelical Lutheran synods in the United States were to stand in some way or other in closer connection with one another" and instructed its officers to inaugurate correspondence with a view "to bring about, wherever practicable, a union with the other Evangelical Lutheran synods in the United States."[42] Within a year a plan was proposed for an organization to be called the General Synod of the Evangelical Lutheran Church in the United States of North America.[43] The synods of Pennsylvania, New York, Maryland-Virginia, and North Carolina were represented in an organizing meeting in 1820, and in the following year all of these but New York elected delegates to the first convention of the General Synod. Ohio and Tennessee remained aloof, and in 1823 the Ministerium of Pennsylvania, which had initiated the union, withdrew under the combined pressure of those who still preferred closer relations with the Reformed and those who feared that connection with the General Synod would be detrimental to continued use of the German language. The New York Ministerium found it "inexpedient" to join at the time. In each of the last two bodies there were strong advocates of the General Synod. In 1825 ministers and churches west of the Susquehanna River withdrew from the Ministerium of Pennsylvania, organized the West Pennsylvania Synod, and promptly joined the General Synod.[44] In 1830 the western conference of the Ministerium of New York withdrew from that body, organized the Hartwick Synod, and promptly united with the General Synod.[45] Such schisms were naturally accompanied by a measure of bitterness which strengthened the opposition of those who remained outside the general organization.

At the first convention of the General Synod there was a proposal to establish a theological seminary, but it was decided that the matter be "deferred for several years." The Rev. Samuel S. Schmucker meanwhile gathered a group of students in his parsonage in New Market, Va., and urged that it be made the nucleus of an enlarged institution of the church. The idea found support in the Synod of Maryland and Virginia, which recommended that such a school "be officially put into operation" by the General Synod. At the meeting of the latter body in 1825 it was decided "that the General Synod will forthwith commence, in the name of the Triune God, and in humble reliance on his aid, the establishment of a theological seminary, . . . and that in this seminary shall be taught, in the

Samuel Simon Schmucker, Chief Founder of the Seminary in Gettysburg

German and English languages, the fundamental doctrines of the Sacred Scriptures, as contained in the Augsburg Confession." A board of directors was elected, Samuel S. Schmucker was chosen the first (and for a time only) professor, and steps were taken to select a site which might "offer the greatest advantages." If the Ministerium of Pennsylvania and the Ministerium of New York had then been members of the General Synod, the seminary would probably have been located in Philadelphia, where Muhlenberg had long since planned such a school and where Kunze, Helmuth, and more recently Carl R. Demme kept alive the tradition of scholarship and theological instruction. But Philadelphia was not on the territory of the General Synod at the time, nor was it central to the existing constituency of that body. The village of Gettysburg was finally chosen as the location for the seminary, partly because it offered $7,000 and the temporary use of a building and partly because important highways leading east and west, north and south, converged in Gettysburg and made it accessible. All these matters having been settled, the school opened in September, 1826, with a total enrollment during the first year of fifteen students.[46]

It soon appeared desirable to add a second man to the teaching staff of the Gettysburg Theological Seminary. In 1830 Ernest L. Hazelius, who had until this time been serving as principal and professor of Theology in Hartwick Seminary in central New York, was called as professor of Biblical and Oriental Literature and of the German Language. He remained only three years, resigning to accept a call to the Lutheran Theological Southern Seminary, established in 1830 in South Carolina. Hazelius was succeeded by Charles Philip Krauth, pastor of St. Matthew's Church in Philadelphia, who stayed in Gettysburg until his death in 1867. Actually the seminary did not have the benefit of two teachers of theology inasmuch as Schmucker, Hazelius, and Krauth spent much of their time in remedial instruction. They found that many of their students were deficient in their preparation, and they attempted to remedy this by private tutoring, then by establishing a "gymnasium" or academy, and finally by developing this into a college. It was in this way, largely under Schmucker's leadership, that Pennsylvania College (called Gettysburg College since 1921) came to be chartered in 1832. Krauth served as its president from 1834 to 1850, and only after this did he devote all of his time to teaching in the seminary. Beginning in 1844, Charles Augustus Hay, a native of York, Pa., who was graduated from the seminary just three years before, also became an instructor who divided his time between the two schools.[47]

Although, as has been suggested,[48] the Gettysburg Seminary's faculty was in its first generation manned entirely by men who were born and baptized in the Ministerium of Pennsylvania, its founding was greeted in that body with mixed feelings. Some welcomed it as an answer at long last to the problem of securing an adequate ministry and contributed to its support. Others opposed or ignored it because of its remote location, because it was not sufficiently German, or because of a suspicion of the General Synod.[49] In the Ministerium of New York the founding of the new seminary was greeted with general indifference not only on account of the greater geographical separation but also on account of the burden of maintaining the struggling Hartwick Seminary on its own territory. The uncertainty and the ambivalence in the Ministerium of Pennsylvania are reflected in the almost simultaneous actions to transfer the Frey legacy to Gettysburg for the support of students and to attempt to revive and strengthen Franklin College in Lancaster, which was a joint undertaking with the Reformed.[50]

There was no want of effort on the part of the faculty and board at Gettysburg to win friends and support in the Ministerium of Pennsylvania. Carl R. Demme, scholarly pastor of the influential St. Michael's and Zion Church in Philadelphia, was called to Gettysburg in 1840 with the understanding that he was to give part of his time to instruction in German. This conciliatory gesture was declined. In fact, John G. Morris, although a member of the Gettysburg board, advised his friend Demme not to accept the call and "condescend to be a schoolmaster and teach the elements of the German language." He told Demme that "life in a dead, out-of-the-way village, twenty-five miles from a railroad, as it was at that time, where there was no market, and other privations to contend with, would by no means suit his tastes or habits, or those of his family."[51]

Carl R. Demme, Scholarly Successor
to Helmuth in Philadelphia

Two years later the Ministerium of Pennsylvania indicated its recurring coolness toward Gettysburg by recommending another Lutheran theological seminary in distant Columbus, Ohio, as "worthy of our sympathy and support" and by appointing a committee to explore how the Ministerium "might enter into connection with said institution."[52] This was a young and struggling seminary established by the Synod of Ohio in 1830 in order, as it was put, "to have an institution for the education of our ministry within her own borders, where her interests might generally concentrate."[53] In the same year in which he was called to Gettysburg, Demme was called to be professor in Columbus. He declined this approach, too, but recommended his former student and brother-in-law, the Rev. Charles F. Schaeffer, who accepted and served as professor for two years. In 1843 a tentative agreement was made according to which the Ministerium of Pennsylvania would pay the salary of a professor in Columbus in return for one-third representation on the seminary's board of directors and the cooperation of the two synods in the publication of church papers. During a controversy over the use of German or English in theological instruction the Synod of Ohio postponed the amending of the seminary charter so as to admit representatives of the Ministerium of Pennsylvania to seats and votes on the board, and thus the rather curious negotiations come to an end.[54]

In 1843, while conversations with Columbus were in progress, the Homeopathic Institute in Allentown, Pa., offered "to sell or rent its buildings" to the Ministerium of Pennsylvania "for the use of a high school or seminary."[55] Three years later Lafayette College, a Presbyterian school which had been founded in Easton, Pa., in 1826, offered to appoint a professor of German, named by the Ministerium, if that body would send the college twenty or more students a year.[56] Neither of these proposals was favorably received, but looking forward to the centennial of the organization in 1748 of the Ministerium of Pennsylvania, it was suggested that it would be highly appropriate to mark the anniversary by gathering funds for a "theological institution." In 1846 it was decided to open such a school in Philadelphia in the fall of the following year, to make college training a prerequisite for admission, to spend $200 on theological textbooks, and to name Carl R. Demme professor. When Demme finally declined to serve, S. S. Schmucker appeared on the floor of the synodical convention to invite the Ministerium to enter, instead, into a connection with Gettysburg. The suggestion was taken up, and it was resolved to assemble funds to establish a German professorship in Gettysburg. Demme was nominated to this position but once again refused, and the post remained unoccupied for several years.[57] However, it was decided to transfer the synod's one-third interest in the assets of Franklin College to Gettysburg College and endow the Franklin professorship there.[58] This action ended the attempt to collaborate with the Reformed in higher education and turned the attention of the synod back to Gettysburg as the place where future ministers might receive their academic preparation.

The way was at the same time prepared for a return of the Ministerium of Pennsylvania to the General Synod, which it had helped create in 1820 and 1821 and then abandoned in 1823. The Ministerium of New York, which had participated in the planning of the general organization but had not joined it, became a member in 1836 with the cautious proviso "that the General Synod be regarded as an advisory body only." Shortly afterwards the New Yorkers "affectionately and earnestly" urged the Ministerium of Pennsylvania to unite with the General Synod.[59] At the time there was no disposition to follow the lead of New York. But the president of the Ministerium of New York correctly saw in the connection which the Ministerium of Pennsylvania was establishing with Gettysburg an evidence of "the tendency of the whole church to union and cooperation."[60] In fact, reunion with the General Synod was proposed in 1852 in view of the mother synod's new interest in the seminary and college in Gettysburg, and the synods of Ohio, Tennessee, and Missouri were encouraged to take a similar step. The encouragement bore no fruit, but in 1853, thirty years after its withdrawal, the Ministerium of Pennsylvania reunited with the General Synod in the interest of "the union of all parts of the whole Evangelical Lutheran Church," with the understanding that the General Synod was "simply an association" of synods adhering to the unaltered Augsburg Confession. It was also decided that, "should the General Synod violate its constitution and require of our synod or of any other synod, as a condition of admission or of continuation of membership, assent to anything conflicting with the old and long established faith of the Evangelical Lutheran Church, then our delegates are hereby required *to protest against such action,* to withdraw from its sessions, and to report to this body."[61]

It appeared, at least on the surface, that the long and tortuous quest for an adequate supply of qualified ministers had come to a happy and promising end. A large majority of the Lutherans in the eastern part of the United States were now associated with one another in the General Synod, under whose auspices the college and seminary in Gettysburg had been founded. There was reason to hope that these schools would be the major source of Lutheran ministers in America during the forseeable future.

Chapter II

Founding of the Seminary in Philadelphia
1864

THE MIDDLE THIRD of the nineteenth century was marked by controversy in the Lutheran Church in the United States. As a matter of fact, this was characteristic of all ecclesiastical bodies in America at the time, as it was also characteristic of political, social, and economic life in general. Controversy led to civil war in the state, and strife led to schisms in several churches. Although testiness and conflict pervaded almost every aspect of life, they took their own peculiar course among Lutherans.

In the first place, what came to be called "the language problem" assumed explosive proportions. From earliest colonial days Lutherans were confronted in the New World with the necessity of making adjustments in language. Lutheran settlers on the Hudson River in the seventeenth century included Germans, Norwegians, and Danes as well as Dutchmen, but all of them employed the Dutch language of the colony in their public worship. Lutheran settlers on the Delaware River during the same century included Finns as well as Swedes, but the Swedish language of the colony was uniformly used. In the course of the first half of the eighteenth century most of the descendents of the early colonists adopted English and were in time lost to the Lutheran Church. Meanwhile, during the eighteenth century, larger numbers of colonists came to America from Germany. Wherever they settled together, especially in rural areas, these colonists and their descendants clung to their mother tongue, but shortly after the Revolution those who lived among predominantly English-speaking people, especially in the cities, gradually adopted the predominant language of their environment. Since immigration came to a virtual standstill between the years 1775 and 1820 and linguistic as well as other contacts with Germany were consequently interrupted, the process of anglicization was rapid.[1]

Resistance to the inroads of English speech was natural, and it was particularly stubborn in the churches, partly because churches tend to be conservative and partly because the ministers, whether or not they had come from Europe, found it least burdensome to follow the accustomed path. English congregations were formed here and there in major cities during the first two decades of the nineteenth century, but elsewhere provisions were occasionally introduced into congregational constitutions which defiantly or optimistically declared that

17

"services and other pastoral acts in this church shall always, as long as grass grows in this world, be conducted in the German language," or, to take another example, "As long as the moon shines and water flows, only German preaching will be permitted in this church."[2] Language and religion, it was believed, are interdependent. An editorial in the first number of the *Evangelisches Magazin,* published in 1812 under the auspices of the Lutheran Ministerium of Pennsylvania, announced, "We wish to promote the German language as much as we can, for

Evangelisches

Magazin,

unter der Auffiðt der

Deutfð = Evangelifð = Lutherifðen Synode.

Erfter Band.

Philadelphia :

Gebruckt bey Conrad Zentler, in der Zweyten Straße, unterhalb der Rehs=Straße.

1812.

Title Page of the First Lutheran Periodical in America

we are convinced that if our church gives up its language, it will lose unspeakably much, if indeed it does not for the most part eventually sacrifice its very existence in America."[3] It was suggested that children brought up in English instead of German "will forever lose all the edification they could otherwise have had in German services — the beautiful German prayers, the splendid catechetical instruction, and the many devout hymns and songs with which our ancestors comforted themselves in time of trouble and death — for the English language is much too poor ever to make an adequate translation of these possible."[4] Convictions such as these played a decisive role in the proposal of 1819 to establish a joint Lutheran and Reformed theological seminary, for the use of a common language of devotion seemed more important than the differences in confession of faith.

Despite the propaganda, the erosion of German speech continued. By 1807 the minutes of the Ministerium of New York began to be printed in English. Not only in this synod but also in its daughter Hartwick Synod, organized in 1830, business was transacted in English. Anglicization was far less uniform and far less complete in the Ministerium of Pennsylvania, but even there the minutes began to be printed in English as well as German by 1828. By this time, however, a change was already in the making. A growing tide of new immigrants was coming from Germany. Congregations which had continued to employ the German language increased in membership, English congregations sometimes reintroduced German services, and many new congregations were founded to accommodate the immigrants. The Ministerium of New York once again became a German-speaking body, after the withdrawal from it in 1867 of many English-speaking ministers and congregations to form the Synod of New York.[5] Meanwhile the Ministerium of Pennsylvania tried in 1862 to keep a precarious balance between the two language groups by officially, if not actually, assuming a bilingual character.[6] "It is not many years since," it was reported, "that a young member, arising to address the synod in English, was cried down with the demand of 'Deutsch! Deutsch!'"[7]

So there was renewed tension between advocates of English and advocates of German. The former were right in insisting that in time German-speaking Lutherans would have to adopt English, although some went to the extreme of sharing the current nativist contempt for foreigners. On the other hand, advocates of German were right in insisting that people needed to be ministered to in their own tongue, although some went to the extreme of identifying true religion with that particular tongue. "I am persuaded," a pastor who had recently come to America declared, "that a Lutheran congregation whose preacher does not have a mastery of the German language is faced with the very great danger that its Evangelical Lutheran religion may gradually be corrupted by all sorts of accretions from Presbyterianism, Methodism, Catholicism, and Deism and in the end become a complete caricature, of which, unhappily, there are already many evidences in this country."[8] A similar fear was expressed by one who was presumably a descendant of eighteenth century colonists and who couched his complaint in the dialect of the so-called Pennsylvania Dutch: "Wer seine Sproch verlässt, der schämt sich doch sehner Eltern und verlässt noch sehne Religion und werd en Methodist. Und ist denn die englisch Sproch vornemmer und schenner, als die deitsch? Ich denk nätt. Unser alter Pharrer hett immer kesagt, dass die deitsche Sproch die vornehmst und best wär, und sell glob ich ooch. Aver sobald der Hochmut in die junge Leit fährt, wolle sie englisch seyn und schäme sich, deitsch zu schwätze, als of Sünd und Schand wär. So viel englisch wie sie breicht, lerne sie ännyhau uf der Stross."[9] This kind of sentiment helps to explain the action of the Ministerium of Pennsylvania in 1842 to seek connection with the seminary in far-away Columbus, Ohio, rather than support the seminary in Gettysburg. In Columbus, it was said, German was the *medium* of instruction while in Gettysburg it was merely an *object* of study.[10]

There was a second occasion for Lutheran controversy during the middle third of the nineteenth century in addition to that involving the language problem. This concerned the church's doctrine. In the colonial period the teaching and practice in Lutheran churches had been formally defined in constitutions and other official documents as conforming with "the unaltered Augsburg Confession and other symbolical books."[11] Since the attitudes of both clergy and laity had been largely shaped in the eighteenth century by Pietism, however, there was little sympathy, as Henry Melchior Muhlenberg expressed it, for orthodoxists "who adhered to the unaltered Augsburg Confession with unaltered hearts" or who forced exegesis of the Bible into a "mathematical corset in order that the consensus of the fathers might thereby be given a better form and figure."[12]

During the last decade of the eighteenth and the first two decades of the nineteenth century, even formal appeal to the Lutheran Confessions disappeared.

The pietistic insistence on "practical" rather than "theoretical" Christianity prepared the way for a neglect of, and even a contempt for, doctrine and doctrinal standards. The academic shortcomings of education for the ministry under private tutors contributed to widespread theological ignorance and indifference. The influence of the current deism, or rationalism, also made itself felt. Frederick H. Quitman, who served for many years as president of the Ministerium of New York, was asked by that synod in 1809 to prepare "a new catechism in the English language, adapted to the wants of the rising generation," and in response he published in 1814 a substitute for Luther's Catechism which breathed the rationalistic spirit of the time.[13] John August Propst, a pastor in Easton, Pa., could write: "All enlightened and informed preachers of Lutheran and Reformed faith are agreed that much in the hitherto existing Confessions must be deleted as obsolete and absurd and must be rewritten in conformity with the Bible, that one need subscribe neither Luther's, nor Zwingli's, nor Calvin's opinions, inasmuch as they are human, but that only one, Christ, is our teacher and master. No evangelical Christian is bound to either Luther's or Calvin's or anybody else's interpretation of the words of Christ, but he is entitled to expound them himself in the best light of his conscience . . . . Since much more reasonable and scriptural views now prevail among all educated Lutheran and Reformed preachers with respect to doctrines that were formerly disputed, why the continued separation between them?"[14] Similar conclusions were reached by George B. Miller, who succeeded Ernest L. Hazelius as principal of Hartwick Seminary. He declared in 1831 that all human creeds are but "shibboleths of a darker age" and "are no better than a Chinese shoe, by which the living foot, being cramped, never attains its proper shape and natural proportions."[15]

The significance of these criticisms of inherited doctrinal standards lies in the fact that they were expressed by prominent ministers and not merely by a few disgruntled men. The vast majority of Lutheran ministers appears to have supported the critics by apathetic indifference or by silent acquiescence. *The Lutheran Observer,* published in Baltimore since 1831 and edited for a generation by Benjamin Kurtz, threw its considerable weight behind the critics of the Lutheran Confessions.

Higher ground than most of his contemporaries was initially taken by Samuel S. Schmucker, who reported to his father in 1820 concerning a conversation he had had with the Rev. F. C. Schaeffer, of New York City, "We promised each other . . . that the Augsburg Confession should be brought up out of the dust."[16] When, in 1826, he was inaugurated as professor in the Gettysburg Seminary, Schmucker declared, "I believe the Augsburg Confession and the Catechism of Luther to be a summary and just exhibition of the fundamental doctrines of the Word of God . . . . I promise, by the aid of God, to vindicate and inculcate these doctrines and principles in opposition to the views of Atheists, Deists," etc.[17] In the early decades of the General Synod that body was gradually led to occupy a position similar to his, "that the fundamental doctrines of the Word of God are taught in a manner substantially correct in the doctrinal articles of the Augsburg Confession." Just how vague a commitment this really was appears from Schmucker's definition of its negative limits. "The General Synod of the Lutheran Church," he wrote in 1834, "has adopted only the 21 doctrinal articles, omitting even the condemnatory clauses of these, and also the entire catalogue of Abuses corrected. No minister, however, considers himself bound to believe every sentiment contained in these twenty-one articles, but only the fundamental doctrines."[18] Like many of his fellow-Lutherans, Schmucker was so eager to naturalize the Lutheran Church on American soil that he was ready to accommodate its teachings and practices to the dominant revivalistic Puritanism of its environment. He became a champion of "American Lutheranism" as distinguished from "European Lutheranism." Yet he contended for the right of the Lutheran Church to separate existence and was untiring in his efforts to strengthen it.

Although Schmucker gave a great impetus to the revival of denominational self-consciousness, he was not willing to go so far as increasing numbers of his fellow Lutherans soon wished him to go. He clung with perseverence to his original position while many of his contemporaries were moving beyond it. The middle third of the nineteenth century was a time of conservative reaction and partisan conflict in both European and American Christianity. It was a time when the Rev. David Henkel and others of his family, having withdrawn from the Synod of North Carolina to form the Tennessee Synod and consequently remaining out of sympathy with the General Synod, justified their separate existence by cultivating the distinctive teachings of Luther's Small Catechism and the Augsburg Confession.[19] Elsewhere too — notably but not exclusively in the Ministerium of Pennsylvania — some ministers who continued to employ German speech were by their language insulated against the views which were being disseminated in English. They were supported by immigrants from Germany who were settling in larger and larger numbers in the eastern as well as the middle western states and who carried with them attitudes and convictions which had been nurtured in the Confessional awakening in Europe.

Meanwhile English-speaking ministers, too, were adopting more traditional views. They were influenced by their own studies, by the conservative theological

THE

EVANGELICAL REVIEW.

EDITED BY WILLIAM M. REYNOLDS,
Professor in Pennsylvania College.

ASSISTED BY DR. J. G. MORRIS, PROF. H. I. SCHMIDT, REV. C. W. SCHAEFFER, AND REV. E. GREENWALD.

"Es sei denn, dass ich mit Zeugnissen der heiligen Schrift, oder mit offentlichen, klaren, und hellen Grunden und Ursachen uberwunden und uberweiset werde, so kann und will ich nichts widerrufen."—LUTHER.

VOL I.

GETTYSBURG:
PRINTED BY H. C. NEINSTEDT.
1849-50.

First Number of Theological Journal Later Called the Lutheran Quarterly

literature which was emanating from Europe, and by the example of the Mercersburg theology in the German Reformed Church.[20] In 1849 a theological quarterly, named *The Evangelical Review,* began to be published in Gettysburg and furnished these men with an organ of literary expression. Here John G. Morris, of Baltimore, criticized the neglect of the Lutheran heritage by men "who fashioned their theological garments after the ever-varying taste of the modern artiste and have adopted too many inventions and notions of the land as productive of both." Charles Philip Krauth, of Gettysburg, commended the increasing number of "men of talent, learning, and piety who regard the doctrines of the symbolical books not only as the truth of God but likewise as constituting the system which can alone entitle him who receives it to regard himself as a Lutheran." Charles F. Schaeffer, of Red Hook, N. Y., wrote "with sincere gratification" about "the renewed interest" in the Confessions and referred to the new quarterly as a channel "through which the English community in general can be made acquainted with important facts that have hitherto been known to those, chiefly, who read German or Latin."[21]

It is noteworthy that Morris was a member of the Gettysburg Seminary's board of directors, Krauth was a colleague of Schmucker on its faculty, and Schaeffer was shortly to join that faculty. The "very considerable diversity of views both as regards doctrine and practice" to which the editor of *The Evangelical Review* referred in his introduction to the new quarterly[22] was not so much between synods as within them and introduced sharp division in Gettysburg Seminary itself.[23] For the sake of the outward unity of Lutherans every effort was made to keep the conflict off the floor of the General Synod. When at the convention in 1845 Frederick Wyneken proposed that this body either renounce the name "Lutheran" or repudiate the teachings of Schmucker, Kurtz, and others, the delegates were reported to have "listened good-naturedly to this funny notion and tabled it."[24] By this time the Ministerium of Pennsylvania was beginning to appeal to the Augsburg Confession as a standard of doctrine, and in 1853 it acknowledged that "the Evangelical Lutheran Church has of late arrived at clearer views of its doctrinal and other distinctive features" and officially declared its adherence to the Confessions included in the Book of Concord.[25] A similar position was taken, at first tentatively and then more positively, by new church

William A. Passavant, Editor and
Pioneer in Social Missions

papers like the *Lutherische Kirchenzeitung,* published since 1838 by Frederick Schmidt in Easton, Pa., and then in Pittsburgh; the *Lutheran Standard,* published in Ohio since 1843 under the editorial supervision of Emanuel Greenwald and others; *The Missionary,* published in Pittsburgh by William A. Passavant since 1848; and the *Lutherische Zeitschrift,* published in Allentown, Pa., since 1858 by Samuel K. Brobst.

In this time of growing conflict the issue was clearly drawn when, in 1855, Schmucker, at the urging of friends and supporters, prepared what he called a "Definite Synodical Platform." This included an "American recension of the Augsburg Confession," which he proposed as a doctrinal basis for the General Synod and its district synods. In keeping with the position he had championed for a generation, Schmucker's recension included only twenty-one of the twenty-eight articles of the Augsburg Confession, and these were reduced to less than half of their original length by omitting those things which especially distinguished Lutherans from other American Protestants.[26] The proposed changes in the doctrinal standard were widely deplored as an occasion for further controversy and a threat to Lutheran unity. The Ministerium of Pennsylvania declared its opposition to "every innovating attempt to lay violent hands on the ancient foundations of the faith" and reiterated its acceptance of the Lutheran Confessions "as a faithful exposition of the divine Word."[27] The Pittsburgh Synod recognized that some parts of the Augsburg Confession were "received in different degrees by different brethren" in the church, but it also asserted that it regarded this symbol "lovingly and reverently as the 'good confession' of our fathers, witnessed before heaven, earth, and hell."[28] The Ministerium of New York instructed its delegates "to vote against the adoption and sanction of the so-called Definite Synodical Platform" and two years later attempted to revise its own doctrinal affirmation in order to "show to the Christian public and to the world at large, clearly and unmistakably, what position we occupy."[29]

Even synods which were closely attached to Schmucker rejected his proposed American recension. The Synod of Central Pennsylvania, just organized, was an exception, and in 1857 Benjamin Kurtz led a minority in the Maryland Synod to separate from that body and form the Melanchthon Synod in protest against the former synod's rejection of the Definite Synodical Platform. The subsequent admission of the new synod to the General Synod was protested by the delegates of the Ministerium of Pennsylvania on the ground that the application for admission "was connected with a certain confession of faith which appeared to us to come into conflict with the unaltered Augsburg Confession."[30] The General Synod, which at this time embraced in its membership all the major district synods in the East, continued a precarious existence as the doctrinal controversy between the "New Lutherans," who supported Schmucker, and the "Old Lutherans," who opposed him, shook it to its foundations.

In addition to issues concerning language and doctrine, there was a third area of controversy, and this involved practice. There was repeated reference to "departure from the pure doctrines and forms of worship peculiar to our church" and to "essential differences in doctrine and cultus."[31] Some Lutherans who had accommodated themselves to the teachings of other churches in their environment also introduced the revivalistic procedures which were prevalent among their Protestant neighbors. Lutherans were prepared for this by their pietistic heritage, but the "new measures" which came to be employed were borrowed more than they were inherited.

At the end of the first decade of the nineteenth century the Rev. John George Butler reported from western Maryland about a revival in a congregation of his.

"God approached us in a special manner, and several of my hearers were powerfully affected . . . . The King of glory came to us and wrought a powerful awakening. In short, the following three days were blessed days during which, in the hearts of old and young, the Lord kindled a fire that burns still to the praise of his name."[32] More typical of later revivals is this account of a "protracted meeting" in Richmondville, N. Y., which lasted for four days in 1834: "On Friday there was a deep, solemn, and heart-melting season. Christians prayed and 'wrestled with God' and were awakened to a lively sense of their duties. Sinners were deeply impressed with the consciousness of their guilt — sin lay heavy upon them while they were enquiring the way to be saved. A call was made to the anxious seat, and many came forward, trembling beneath their load of sin; and so our meeting continued until Sunday evening, when between 35 and 40 had taken

Benjamin Kurtz, Editor of the Lutheran
Observer and Promoter of Revivals

the anxious seat."[33] Benjamin Kurtz, editor of *The Lutheran Observer* from 1833 to 1861, was the most persistent advocate of new measures. He spoke and wrote against "burthening the church with a multiplication of ritualistic forms and ceremonies" and employed his vigorous pen in support of revivals.[34]

It was claimed that before the middle of the eighteenth century more than half of the Lutheran ministers in America were in favor of the mourner's bench, but this was certainly an exaggeration.[35] While there were "seasons of spiritual refreshment," as they were called, in every state east of the Mississippi River at one time or another between 1800 and 1860, some geographical areas, like some ministers, were especially given to revival practices.[36] In central New York, it was claimed, "Our ministers have ever been the decided advocates of experimental religion and a holy ministry and the firm friends of revivals, temperance, and so on . . . . The first 'anxious seat' was opened among us in 1831, and has been used more or less ever since as a blessed means of calling out awakened and convicted sinners, and has been approbated of God to the conversion of thousands of souls."[37] It was reported in central Pennsylvania: "The Lord has visited many of our dear congregations since our last synod with revivals . . . . We are all, my dear Brethren, in favor of revivals, properly conducted."[38] The qualification "properly conducted" was not uncommon. The East

24

Pennsylvania Synod, for example, adopted a statement which declared, "We strongly disapprove of all avoidable noise, confusion, and disorder, . . . the praying of more than one person at a time, . . . clapping of hands, etc."[39]

Even such a "judicious" use of new measures was criticized by many ministers and congregations. Opposition to revivals was not always limited to those who continued to cling conservatively to the German language and to inherited standards of doctrine, for motives were mixed. An early protest in the Synod of Ohio against "new ways and measures which accommodate themselves to the fanatical spirit of the times"[40] was followed by a resolution in the Ministerium of Pennsylvania which expressed "decided disapprobation" of "disorderly measures which are in utter conflict with the old customs of our church."[41] Public worship according to "the old customs" was usually conducted in a church "with a high gallery and a high box pulpit, a communion table standing in isolated condition in front of the pulpit, surrounded by a circular railing."[42] As a rule the minister wore no gown. This was referred to as an "obsolete usage," but in 1860 the Ministerium of Pennsylvania recommended "a return to the good old usage," at least in city churches, of wearing clerical gowns.[43] The service itself was sober and dignified, consisting of hymns, free prayers, readings from the Scriptures, and a long sermon. It differed from the services of new measure preachers chiefly in the absence of an emotionally charged atmosphere, the want of spontaneity in lay participation, and the avoidance of such devices of revivalism as the protracted meeting and the anxious bench. Friction and conflict between advocates and opponents of new measures sometimes became so severe that congregations were split.[44]

The coming of new immigrants further complicated the problem. A few ministers who had come from parts of Germany in which such practices were required by state law introduced innovations into their congregations in America. These things included "burning tapers in the day time," placing crucifixes in churches, making the sign of the cross in connection with baptisms or benedictions, and even "chanting Latin hymns." Such practices were declared to be "unadvised, inexpedient, and exceedingly unbecoming." When parishioners complained about the innovations, the practices were adjudged "repulsive to the views and feelings of Christians in America."[45] Most of the immigrant ministers did not cause scandal by forcing alien or unwanted customs on their people, but as a rule the new churches founded by German immigrants were nevertheless more liturgical in practice than the older English Lutheran churches. This remained the case for decades, as an observer remarked about Philadelphia: "If you go into our German churches in this city and then into our English churches, you will see little or no similarity. In the German churches the pastor wears a gown, uses a liturgical service, and everything wears a churchly appearance; but in most of our English churches it is quite different . . . . When our German people come into an English church, . . . they find little difference between most of our English churches and those of the [other] denominations."[46] This situation simply accentuated the conflict between protagonists and opponents of new measures.

All three of these areas of controversy — concerning language, doctrine, and worship — played a part in the relation of the Ministerium of Pennsylvania to the seminary in Gettysburg.

When, in 1853, the Ministerium returned to the General Synod, it gave every appearance of returning in good faith and with the intention of cooperating fully in the general body's enterprises. It transferred the small amount of money raised earlier for its own projected school, and added about $16,000 to this sum, to endow a German professorship at Gettysburg.[47] The Rev. William J. Mann, successor of Demme in Philadelphia, was nominated by the Ministerium of Pennsylvania for this professorship in 1854, but he declined.[48] The next year the Rev. Charles F. Schaeffer, brother-in-law both of Demme and of S. S. Schmucker and at the time pastor of St. John's Church in Easton, Pa., was nominated. After some hesitation he was persuaded to accept on condition that he might give half of his time to teaching the German language in the college and the other half of his time to teaching "the various departments of theology" through the medium of German in the seminary.[49] When the seminary's board of directors elected the nominee, assenting to the condition, Schaeffer moved to Gettysburg in the summer of the year 1856. In his inaugural address, delivered during the debate over his brother-in-law's Definite Synodical Platform, Schaeffer frankly expressed the hope and expectation that all Lutherans in America would "accept the entire Book of Concord not only as a banner to be followed but also as a formative influence in the spiritual lives of its individual members."[50] Meanwhile, that the Ministerium of Pennsylvania was hopeful that the college and seminary in Gettysburg would ultimately answer its need for ministers is suggested in a resolution which ended private tutorship by disapproving "of any of its members instructing those who have the ministry in view, save in especial cases."[51]

The arrangement with Gettysburg did not prove to be satisfactory in the long run to either party. Schaeffer remarked upon "the difficulty inevitably attending a professorship divided between two institutions." A committee of the Ministerium of Pennsylvania thereupon directed attention to "the very trying position of our professor under existing circumstances" and asked that he be relieved of his duties in the college so as to enable him to devote all his time to the seminary. When Schaeffer was permitted to teach in German only those disciplines of theology which were not being taught in English, the Ministerium demanded that he be granted "liberty to give instruction in all the branches of theology to those students who do not understand the English language."[52] This was finally permitted, but other complaints were aired. Dissatisfaction was expressed concerning the small number of members on the seminary's board of directors which the Ministerium was allowed to elect. There was criticism of academic standards — the admission of students with inadequate preparation, the time given as a consequence to remedial work, the absence of students not only on long vacations but on frequent preaching assignments, and the compression of the whole course of study into two years or, more accurately, eighteen months. More serious was the cleavage in both faculty and student body between Old and New Lutheranism, between German and English.[53] In 1859 five students from the Ministerium withdrew from the seminary in protest against the conditions there, and it was proposed to transfer the Ministerium's professorship to "some other locality."[54]

The quantity as well as the quality of men for the ministry was distressing. There were not enough ministers to meet the needs of congregations, swelled by new immigrants as well as by natural increase. The president of the Ministerium of Pennsylvania declared in 1853 that he "sensibly experienced what a great want of ministers there is in the church, especially of those who preach in both languages." The president of the Ministerium of New York made a similar observation two years later, and shortly after this the president of the former body again called attention to "the many vacant charges which still exist within our synod" and to "those other destitute regions where multitudes of brethren, professing the same faith with ourselves, are scattered and go astray as sheep having no shepherd."[55] It was reported in 1860 that during the preceding dozen years only 18 men had been ordained by the Ministerium of Pennsylvania while 22 ministers were lost by death. At the time, it was added, only three students were studying theology under the German professor in Gettysburg, and two, and perhaps all three, of them were planning to serve congregations in the Middle West.[56] There was no want of interest in what was happening in the Middle West, for the synod was sending German-speaking missionaries to Iowa, Wisconsin, Minnesota, and Illinois. Visited by the Rev. Lars P. Esbjörn and the Rev. Paul Anderson, the synod also gathered funds to assist in the erection of Swedish Lutheran churches.[57] But there were also pressing needs nearby. For want of available ministers, and therefore also of churches, thousands of German and Pennsylvania German Lutherans in Scranton, Pa., were deprived of the services of their own church.[58] The same was reported to be true of a considerable number of Germans and descendants of Germans in such cities in New York as Buffalo, Syracuse, Troy, and Schenectady.[59] In New Jersey the situation was identical.[60]

When the Ministerium of Pennsylvania met in 1860 its president, C. F. Welden, declared in his annual report: "The number of young ministers which Gettysburg annually sends us is not sufficient to supply the congregations becoming vacant from year to year . . . . Various causes may have brought about this result, but the principal one is to be found . . . in the remoteness of the institution . . . . If we again afford a fair opportunity . . . within the bounds of our synod, where the great mass of our Lutheran population resides, from the Delaware to the country beyond the Schuylkill, it will be easy to supply this want . . . . In the absence of anything better, . . . I lay before you the following resolution: That immediate steps be taken to establish a theological school in some suitable place . . . ." President Welden added a warning concerning a too indulgent attitude toward questionable theological education. "We have no right to assume, in a good-natured manner, that a minister who has been educated amidst prejudice and false doctrine will gradually arrive at correct knowledge and true faith."[61]

Some "failed to see the propriety of the remedy proposed," but a committee was appointed to consider the matter. The report which the committee submitted the following year reflected the thinking especially of the Rev. S. K. Brobst, editor of the *Lutherische Zeitschrift* in Allentown. The committee recommended that Charles F. Schaeffer, the Ministerium's German professor in Gettysburg, be transferred to Allentown, "in the midst of the oldest, largest, and most wealthy German Lutheran congregations in America." There, with the possible part-time help of a few local ministers, the committee recommended that students be taught theology in English and German. The plan was neither imaginative nor academically adequate. It appears that it was these deficiencies as much as the outbreak of the Civil War that defeated the proposal. It was resolved "that the times and circumstances render it inadvisable for this body, at this time, to take any further action in the matter than to request the committee to keep it under consideration for another year." Similar action was taken the next year.[62] In May, 1864, the Rev. Charles W. Schaeffer, nephew of the German professor in Gettysburg and at the time president of the Ministerium of Pennsylvania, reported to that body once again about the continuing shortage of ministers. "Providence indeed seems to be forcing upon our attention," he wrote, "the duty of making more ample provision for the education of pastors . . . . The necessity for definite and liberal action is now upon us. If synod should longer delay, it may be too late. Men whose loyalty to our Confession is doubtful may gradually get possession of our churches."[63]

Samuel K. Brobst, Pastor in Allentown
and Advocate of Educational and Missionary Projects

The question may properly be asked, why prompt and urgent action seemed
now to be necessary when only two years before "the times and circumstances"
rendered it inadvisable to act. The Civil War was still in progress, and there
was no significant change in economic or social conditions which could explain
the sudden change in sentiment. In fact, it was a time of a "general advance of
prices," and the high cost of living might have suggested restraint. There were,
however, three ecclesiastical events which precipitated action.

The first of these was the weakening of the General Synod by the withdrawal
from it of the southern district synods. The outbreak of the Civil War led to sharp
criticisms in the North of southerners in general, and these were echoed in the
church. In 1862 the General Synod expressed "decided disapprobation of the
course of those synods and ministers, heretofore connected with this body, in the
open sympathy and active co-operation they have given to the cause of treason
and insurrection." The southern synods responded to this and to earlier, though
less official, condemnations by severing their relation with what now became
the "northern" General Synod and by forming, in 1863, the General Synod of the
Evangelical Lutheran Church in the Confederate States of America.[64] Thus the
unity and strength of the General Synod were broken, and a precedent was given
for further disruption.

The second event was the unforeseen eruption of strife between the Ministerium of Pennsylvania and the General Synod. At the York, Pa., convention of the
General Synod, May 5-12, 1864, the Franckean Synod was admitted to the general

body after a long and sharp debate. This synod had been formed in 1837 by separation from the Hartwick Synod in the state of New York. Not only had it avoided all reference to the Augsburg Confession in its official literature, but it had a declaration of its own which was in many respects in conflict with the Augsburg Confession. The delegation of the Ministerium of Pennsylvania, headed by Charles W. Schaeffer, protested the admission of the Franckean Synod as unconstitutional and withdrew from the convention. This was in accordance with the Ministerium's action at the time of its reunion with the General Synod in 1853, an action which required the delegates to protest and withdraw if the General Synod should "violate its constitution" or "assent to anything conflicting with the old and long established faith of the Evangelical Lutheran Church." The dramatic protest and retirement was commended by some delegates of other synods and was afterwards approved by the Ministerium of Pennsylvania. Although it was not until two years later that the Ministerium officially withdrew from the General Synod, the impact of the action at York exposed existing differences which were more than merely parliamentary.[65]

The third event was the resignation of Samuel S. Schmucker from the professorship in the Gettysburg Seminary after thirty-eight years of service. In his formal resignation, read to the board of directors on Aug. 9, 1864, he gave as his reasons "the gradual and natural increase of the infirmities of age" and "a desire to have more time at hand for the execution of some literary enterprises." He also expressed the conviction that this was "as favorable a time as would soon be offered to elect a successor who would carry on the work to which my life has been devoted in the same liberal spirit in which the institution was founded and has been thus far conducted."[66] The resignation was not unexpected. In fact,

The Seminary in Gettysburg as it Looked about 1864

there had for some time been speculation about a successor. "Many of us," the Rev. G. F. Krotel wrote, "had long waited for this change and hoped that the conservative element in the board at Gettysburg would be strong enough to put Dr. C. P. Krauth in S. S. Schmucker's place. He being in the theological seminary, we felt sure that Gettysburg might be made all right, little by little, and we meant that the Pennsylvania Synod should stick to it and to the General Synod." In the spring of 1864 the choice of Charles Porterfield Krauth, able and conservative son of Schmucker's colleague, became increasingly dubious. At the York convention, Krotel reported, the gossipy John G. Morris, who served many terms on the Gettysburg board before and after this, "doubted whether there was strength enough in the board to elect him."[67]

While it was a gross oversimplification to charge that Krauth started a new seminary when the old one did not elect him as its professor,[68] personal disappointment on the part of Krauth's friends and on his own part was a real factor. There was evidence of some pique as well as of some truth in the words which Krauth wrote just before Schmucker's resignation: "We might more safely send our sons to Princeton or Andover to imbue them with just ideas of Lutheran doctrine, and with love for it, than we can send them to any institution of our church within our reach in which doctrinal theology is taught in English."[69]

These three events — the secession of the southern synods, the controversy over the admission of the Franckean Synod, and the resignation of Schmucker — precipitated the proposal of Charles W. Schaeffer that a new seminary be founded at once. Also behind the proposal, of course, was the long festering friction over language, confession, and practice to which reference has already been made. The response to Schaeffer's proposal was the recommendation of a committee of the Ministerium of Pennsylvania that steps be taken immediately "towards establishing a theological seminary either by uniting Gettysburg Theological Seminary with it or by founding a new one." After some discussion, reference to Gettysburg's joining in the enterprise fell away, and it was resolved "that in the name of the Lord we now determine to undertake the establishment of a theological seminary." A series of carefully framed resolutions, which determined the character of the proposed school, was then adopted. The school was to be "devoted to the interests of the Evangelical Lutheran Church of the United States," not merely a part of it, and in its teaching it was to be "unreservedly and unalterably based on all the Confessions of the Evangelical Lutheran Church." The school was to have "due regard" for "all the wants of our church," and accordingly instruction was to be "imparted in both the English and German languages." The school was to be located in Philadelphia "temporarily, on account of the facilities which appear to offer themselves, and permanently, should our expectations be realized." At a special meeting of the Ministerium held two months after the regular meeting, a board of directors was elected and authorized to do whatever was necessary to put the proposed new seminary in operation. A faculty of three professors and two assistant professors was elected, and provisions were made for the endowment of professorships "by the gift or bequest of thirty thousand dollars, or by securing in perpetuity the annual income of that principal sum," for each. Other neighboring synods were "cordially invited" to cooperate, "with the assurance that they shall have a proper representation in the board of directors in proportion to the amount contributed by them to the endowment fund," and it was provided that any other synod which endowed a professorship would have "the right to nominate the incumbent."[70]

As the first professors, the Ministerium of Pennsylvania elected Charles F. Schaeffer, at the time the Ministerium's German professor in Gettysburg; William Julius Mann, pastor of St. Michael's-Zion Church in Philadelphia who had before declined a nomination to the same professorship in Gettysburg; and Charles Porterfield Krauth, since 1861 the editor of *The Lutheran and Missionary,* published in Philadelphia as the successor of the church paper previously published by William A. Passavant, and the man whom some had hoped to see in

Schmucker's chair in Gettysburg. Krauth was designated the English professor, Mann was called as the German professor, and Schaeffer was named "intermediate professor," which meant that he was to teach in both English and German. In addition, two assistant professors were elected: Charles W. Schaeffer, pastor of St. Michael's Church in Germantown and a nephew of the "intermediate" professor, and G. F. Krotel, pastor of St. Mark's Church in Philadelphia, where he had succeeded Krauth on the latter's resignation to become editor.

A few weeks after the election of these members of the faculty Krauth explained to readers of his paper why, in his view, a new seminary was needed. "It is needed for the sake of pure doctrine. There is no theological seminary in the United States in which are fully taught, in the English language, the doctrines of the Reformation as our church then held and now holds and confesses them.... We need it for the sake of internal homogeneousness among the men who are to be trained for our ministry. It will meet one grand want in training, in the same doctrine, love, and life, all our students. It is most unnatural and dangerous that in the same communion, and under the same roof [that is, at Gettysburg], one set of students should be taught to regard as Romish abominations and dangerous errors what others are taught to consider as the very truth of God . . . . We need it for the sake of the true co-ordinating and harmonious working of the two languages, English and German. It is one great want of our church that the two tongues should work in sisterly harmony."[71] Here once again language, doctrine, and practice were singled out as the issues which were at stake.

The steps which were taken to establish the new seminary in Philadelphia naturally invited criticism. When Schaeffer was called to Philadelphia, he at first intended to delay his removal from Gettysburg, and so assured the board of directors in Gettysburg, but then he changed his mind and hastily departed on the eve of a new academic year. This was of course deeply resented, and the Gettysburg authorities expressed "most decided disapprobation of a course so eminently reprehensible."[72] The move to start a new seminary was described as "virtually one of secession" and as "revolutionary." The selection of Philadelphia as the location was declared foolish. "Theological seminaries in cities have been failures. There is not a single instance of eminent success in this country." The future graduates of the new seminary were ridiculed as "antediluvian petrifactions or theological automatons" because they would be taught "symbolic orthodoxy" and "narrow, unfraternal, and denominational exclusivism," "formal ritualism," and "anti-revivalism." "There the Old Lutheran, obsolete doctrines . . . . are to be recalled from their grave."[73] Such bitter jibes reflected the deep feelings which were stirred on both sides. Gettysburg and Philadelphia were rivals and antagonists.

In some circles it was regarded as a foregone conclusion that the founding of the seminary in Philadelphia would lead to the final separation of the Ministerium of Pennsylvania from the General Synod. This finally happened in 1866. What especially evoked criticism, however, was the leadership of the Ministerium and of Charles Porterfield Krauth in calling into being, in 1867, the General Council of the Evangelical Lutheran Church in North America.[74] Some of the more conservative district synods withdrew from the General Synod to attach themselves to this new general body. A few independent synods in the Middle West, of Swedish and German provenance, also were attracted to the General Council. Some district synods of the General Synod were divided. For example, the Ministerium of New York joined the General Council, but a minority formed the new Synod of New York and retained membership in the General Synod. The Pittsburgh Synod experienced a similar disruption, the majority uniting with the

General Council and the minority adhering to the General Synod. These unhappy divisions had the effect of intensifying rather than relaxing the tensions in the church. The prospect of gradually resolving differences was ended by the withdrawal of many conservatives from the General Synod and by the hardening of the hearts of others. On both sides men agonized over the question of whether they ought to hold on to what they believed to be the truth and sacrifice the peace and unity of the church or preserve the peace and unity of the church at the expense of the truth. To be sure, the question was never quite so uncomplicated, for a multitude of personal and sociological factors was involved. "Our differences," Henry N. Pohlman, president of the Ministerium of New York, suggested, "arise not so much from variety of opinion as from variance of heart, not so much from theological idiosyncrasies as from unscrupulous partisanship. And the great and urgent want of the Lutheran Church in this country at present is not new organizations but more love and harmony in the old."[75] But, for good or ill, the die was cast.

Chapter III

Twenty-five Years in the Center of the City
1864-1889

THE HASTY DEPARTURE of Charles F. Schaeffer from Gettysburg compelled the provisional board of directors of the proposed seminary in Philadelphia to act more quickly than it otherwise might have. A faculty had been elected during the last week of July, 1864, but no serious financial or academic planning had been possible, nor had provision been made for a building to house the school. With Professor Schaeffer on the scene, however, makeshift arrangements had to be made. Permission was secured to use a couple of rooms in the rear of the Lutheran bookstore on Ninth Street, near Arch Street, and these were transformed into temporary classrooms. The neighborhood was scoured "to secure suitable boarding places for the students," and in this fashion the immediate physical needs seemed to be met.[1]

On the evening of October 4, 1864, the professors were formally installed in a public service in St. John's Church on Race Street. As secretary of the board of directors, the Rev. Beale M. Schmucker, who did not share the views of his father, S. S. Schmucker, delivered the "charge to the professors." The three hundred congregations of the Ministerium of Pennsylvania, he observed, "comprise nearly as many communicants as do all the congregations of all the synods, except our own, which have hitherto depended upon the seminary at Gettysburg for a supply of ministers." This alone offered some justification for the founding of a new seminary. But more emphasis was placed on the need for theological education in German as well as in English, not only in view of the fact that a large proportion of congregations in the Ministerium "use no other language in the services of public worship than the German," but also in view of "the immense work to be done before the German Lutheran immigrants, now resident in this country, shall be gathered into congregations and supplied with the ministrations of the gospel." Most important of all, Schmucker asserted, was the unreserved commitment of the seminary, for English-speaking and German-speaking students alike, to the Confessions of the Lutheran Church. "We are not disposed to undervalue the labors for the Redeemer's kingdom of any of the theological seminaries now in existence. We are animated by no spirit of opposition to them. We thank God for all the good they have wrought . . . . But as openly as many confess their rejection of some of the teachings of the Confessions of our church as inconsistent with the Word of God, and their disapproval of the order of wor-

The Lutheran Bookstore in which the First Classes of the Philadelphia Seminary were Held

ship of the Lutheran Church as tending to formality, thus openly do we confess and maintain our belief that the Confessions of the church are in accordance with the Word . . . ." Charles Porterfield Krauth was asked by his colleagues to speak for all of them, and he replied in an address in which he eloquently defended the church's need for a confession of faith which is taken seriously.[2]

The next day applicants for admission were interviewed by the faculty. Half of the fourteen applicants came directly from one or another college and were enrolled as Juniors. The rest had previously begun their theological education elsewhere — four in Gettysburg — and were admitted to advanced standing. Classes began the following day.[3] "When I reached the bookstore that day," Professor Mann later recalled, "I was conducted to the rear building of the house, and there, in a small room on the second floor, I found those students seated around an oval table and began my lecture. I recollect that it was the first lecture given in the seminary."[4] There was no library, and "no books but the few carried by the professors to their classes."[5] It was under such primitive conditions that the seminary began its existence.

The development of the school was in the hands of a provisional board, which was succeeded within a year by a regular board of directors. Its members, made up of equal numbers of ministers and laymen, were at first elected by the Ministerium of Pennsylvania. Later, when other synods participated in the support of the seminary, these bodies elected representatives of their own. The president of the permanent board of directors from 1865 until his death in 1905 was Joseph A. Seiss, pastor of St. John's Church and later of the Church of the Holy Communion in Philadelphia, who gave unstintingly of his time and effort. So did

Joseph Augustus Seiss, President of the Board of
Directors for almost Forty Years

the English secretary of the board (from 1864 to 1888), Beale M. Schmucker,
pastor in Easton and then in Pottstown, Pa., and the German secretary (1864 to
1879), J. T. Vogelbach, pastor of St. Jakobus Church in Philadelphia. Other
prominent ministers on the board were Samuel K. Brobst, of Allentown, Pa.;
Frederick W. Geissenhainer, of New York City; and John Kohler, of Trappe and
Stroudsburg, Pa. Among the most active laymen on the board were Mr. Lewis L.
Houpt, a lawyer; Dr. John Rommel, a physician; and Judge William H. Staake, all
of Philadelphia.

About two weeks before the seminary opened a somewhat informal meeting
"of persons disposed to cooperate in the endowment of the new seminary" was
held in Philadelphia. The results were disappointing, although several members
of the board of directors, like the Rev. F. W. Geissenhainer, Dr. H. H.
Muhlenberg, and Dr. John Rommel, subscribed substantial amounts. The day
before the opening of the seminary a so-called central committee was appointed
by the board of directors to prepare "a plan for securing the endowment of the
seminary," and now a serious effort was made to raise money. The interest of
Mr. Charles F. Norton, a wealthy coal merchant and faithful member of St.
Mark's Church in Philadelphia who was serving on the board of directors, had
been awakened by his father-in-law, the recently deceased Rev. Benjamin Keller,
and in November he promised in writing, "I agree to pay the sum of $30,000 as
the endowment of one professorship as soon as an equal amount shall have been
collected for the endowment of another professorship." This other professorship
was to be endowed by raising a similar sum in the congregations of the Ministerium of Pennsylvania, and it took several years to gather subscriptions for
the requisite amount for the professorship.[6]

A lively interest in the new seminary was expressed from the start in the
Ministerium of New York. This synod was committed at the time to support
Hartwick Seminary, although it repeatedly urged that Hartwick move "to some
more desirable locality."[7] As late as 1865 it decided to attempt to raise $20,000
to endow a professorship at Hartwick. The Pennsylvanians, it was reported,
"would fain have us unite with them" in support of the seminary in Philadelphia,
"but seeing we have an institution of our own which needs our fostering care, they
will make no such application."[8] The synod's official visitors to Hartwick
Seminary expressed dissatisfaction with that school the following year, and in
1867 the Ministerium ended its support of Hartwick.[9] However, it was not until
1872 that the Ministerium of New York entered into an official relation with the
Philadelphia Seminary. This happened when Mrs. Anna Burkhalter, a member of
Trinity Church in Manhattan, was persuaded by her pastor G. F. Krotel, who had
moved from Philadelphia to New York four years before, to endow a professorship
in the new seminary by a gift of $30,000. Krotel said that it was the hope of Mrs.
Burkhalter that her gift would encourage the Ministerium of New York to endow
an additional chair of its own.[10]

Charles F. Norton, the First to Endow a Professorship in the Philadelphia Seminary

Krotel had proposed just this the year before. At that time it was believed by some in New York that the growing demand for German-speaking ministers could be met by sending to Germany for them. Correspondence with responsible leaders of the church in Germany made it clear, however, that such an expectation was illusory; the church in America would have to educate its own ministry. "Inasmuch as all efforts to secure help from Germany have remained almost entirely fruitless, and according to an official report there is little prospect of securing adequate help from there in the future, the synod recognizes that it is its holy duty, which is no longer to be put off, to take immediate steps to meet these pressing needs in some measure at least." It was therefore decided to found two academies for preparatory schooling, one in eastern and the other in western New York, and to establish a German professorship in the Philadelphia Seminary.[11] Since it seemed impossible to raise $30,000 in the immediate future, the Ministerium of New York proposed, instead, to pay $2,000 annually for a professor's salary. This was satisfactory to the board of directors in Philadelphia, and so a new professorship was added in 1872. The following year still another professorship was established through the gradually accumulated gifts, totaling $24,820, of St. John's Church in Philadelphia.[12]

Within the first decade of its existence, therefore, five professorships were provided for. Three of them — the Norton, the Burkhalter, and the St. John's — were designated as English chairs, and those of the Ministerium of Pennsylvania and the Ministerium of New York were intended to be German. The Ministerium of New York was credited with two of the professorships and was given representation on the board of directors accordingly, but when Trinity Church, of which Mrs. Burkhalter was a member, transferred for a time from the New York to the Pennsylvania Ministerium, the representation was reduced.[13] Appeals for support were also made to the Pittsburgh Synod but bore no fruit at this time.[14]

Not less important than gathering endowments was the provision of adequate housing for the seminary. The space in the rear of the bookstore was hardly more adequate for classrooms than the rooming of students in the neighborhood was satisfactory. The school had no physical center. "The present arrangement and management, as far as the boarding of students and the rooms for lectures are concerned," Professor Mann reported in November, 1864, "is by no means satisfactory." He proposed that a building be rented in which students might live and study together, have access to a library, and receive their instruction. Such a building might be placed in the charge of "a decent Christian family" which could be expected to furnish board.[15] Mann's proposal was looked upon with favor by the board of directors, which acted with dispatch. A house was found at 216 Franklin Street (opposite the entrance to the present Benjamin Franklin Bridge), was purchased for $17,700, and was opened for use on Mar. 13, 1865. The building was not large enough to house more than twenty students comfortably. By September it was apparent that it could not accommodate all the applicants for the second academic year. Four students instead of two were placed in many rooms. "The seminary building is now overcrowded with boarders," the secretary of the faculty recorded, "and inconvenience and dissatisfaction, calculated to affect the institution injuriously, arise from this cause." Some students were given permission to room and board elsewhere in order to relieve the congestion, and in October, 1865, the faculty asked the board of directors "to provide more ample accommodations for the students already on the ground and others who are likely to come at the beginning of the next seminary year."[16]

The Seminary Building on Franklin Square as it Appeared about 1873

Various makeshifts were proposed, and in some cases, resorted to. Students complained, and the faculty deplored the amount of time it had to spend on "these temporal affairs connected with the house." A 40-room hotel on Chestnut and Twenty-fourth Streets, which was said to be "well adapted to the wants of the seminary," was offered for sale, but the faculty objected to its location, presumably because it was too far west from what was then the center of the city. Also proposed was a "suitable lot" on the northwest corner of Spring Garden and Nineteenth Streets, but the faculty was reluctant to move from the existing site. At last it was decided to secure two vacant lots directly to the north of the seminary's building on Franklin Street and on these to erect, as an enlargement of the old, a five-story building of pressed brick with brownstone trimming to accommodate sixty students. The vestry of St. Michael's-Zion Church was persuaded to donate the ground, and late in the spring of 1872 construction was begun according to a plan "originated" by the president of the board and "elaborated and sketched by Mr. Rush, architect and builder."[17]

The first floor of the new building included three lecture rooms, a chapel, and a dining room. In addition to a library, reading room, and parlor, the second floor contained six "chambers." The remaining three floors were given to larger numbers of similar dormitory rooms. The cost of construction was $17,500, and the heating arrangement and kitchen ranges (in the basement) cost about $1,000 more. Some of the furniture was provided by the ladies of congregations in Philadelphia, Lancaster, Reading, Easton, Allentown, and New York, and Sunday schools were asked to furnish more. Since the condition of the rooms had formerly been described as "filthy and the furniture and carpets in bad order," consideration was now given to "the propriety and expediency of appointing a committee of ladies" from local congregations to oversee the domestic management of the seminary. For many years such committees made periodical inspections and contributed to the physical comfort, although also to the embarrassment, of students. When the building was in readiness it was thrown open to the general public "with appropriate exercises" on Feb. 10, 1873. Upwards of 3,000 persons inspected the building between 10 a.m. and 9 p.m., it was reported, and at least 1,200 "partook of collation," which consisted of "a remarkable variety of substantial food and of rare dainties" prepared by women of local congregations.[18]

The cost of purchasing the original seminary property, of constructing the enlarged building, and of maintaining it year after year was borne by the Ministerium of Pennsylvania alone. During the first few years agents were appointed to visit ministers and congregations of the synod and to collect contributions on commission.[19] In 1867 an "extraordinary and united effort" was made during the Reformation season to commemorate the 350th anniversary of Luther's posting of the Ninety-five Theses, and a total of more than $22,000 was raised for the seminary.[20] To construct the new building in 1872 and 1873 money was borrowed from endowments, and a new appeal was made to repay this; on the floor of the synodical convention in 1874 a total of $8,684 was subscribed, and more was added afterwards.[21] The financial burden resting on the Ministerium of Pennsylvania was increased by the failure of the Ministerium of New York to gather the promised $2,000 a year for its professorship; on the average it paid less than a third of this amount, and so the salary had to be supplemented in Pennsylvania.[22] There was even reluctance to contribute toward the cost, for its own students, of heat, light, and service, although the value of the seminary was evident in the flow of graduates into parishes in New York and northern New Jersey.[23] However, the Ministerium of New York as well as the Ministerium of Pennsylvania gave subsidies to students for the ministry, and this was of indirect assistance to the seminary. Of similar character was the supplementary aid for students provided from time to time by congregations.[24]

The seminary was also the recipient of a few bequests; the largest in this period amounted to $3,000 and was received from the estate of Mr. Christian Klinger, of New York City, in 1880.[25]

The enlarged seminary building failed to meet all expectations. The heating system proved inadequate. "Some of the rooms," it was reported, "could not be heated at all; others were greatly influenced by a change of the weather; only a few of the rooms could be made comfortable." In severe weather as much as a ton of coal was consumed daily, but heat did not reach the top floor. A new heating system was installed but hardly improved conditions. In 1882 additional chimneys were built and individual stoves were placed in every room. This was a more satisfactory arrangement, but it was believed that "affections of the throat, serious colds, attacks of fever and dyspepsy" from which students suffered were a result of the poor heating in winter.[26]

Students complained about things other than want of heat. When the seminary acquired its original building in 1865, G. L. Helmbold was employed as a steward, and quarters were provided in the building for him and his family. All students were required to board in the seminary unless they had special permission to eat elsewhere. Helmbold offered to feed students "for $4.50 a week, including washing and mending of an ordinary character." A committee of students appeared before the faculty in the spring of 1866 "and entered formal and earnest complaint against the steward and the manner in which he manages the affairs of the seminary." The principal complaint had to do with the quality of the food. It was proposed by the students that the steward be dismissed and that a "club system" be introduced. Neither the faculty nor the board of directors was willing "to entrust the domestic affairs of the institution" to the students under a club system, but a committee of the board promised to "labor to make their home comfortable and pleasant and have them furnished with good bread and warm rooms." Friction between students and steward continued. Helmbold finally resigned in 1868 and was replaced by Aaron Windt, who was employed "to attend the fires and be allowed to charge $3.25 per week for board and the current rates for washing." The new steward encountered continuing criticism at the hands of the students, about half of whom found excuses to eat in neighboring restaurants or boarding houses. When Windt died "after lingering consumption" in 1876, his widow took his place for a year and was soon succeeded by a Mrs. Plowman. More and more students preferred to eat elsewhere on the ground that they could get cheaper and more wholesome food at other places nearby. In 1880 the boarding system was therefore abolished, the dining hall was closed, the stewardess was given notice, and a janitor was hired. Students complained about the janitor too — for example, "the conditions of the bathrooms" — but henceforth they had to grumble about food elsewhere.[27]

The constitution adopted for the seminary in 1865 provided that graduation from a college would be required of candidates for admission, "and any departure from this rule shall only be made by a unanimous vote of the faculty."[28] During the first quarter of a century about 5% of the students were admitted without college education, a ratio higher than in any comparable period since then. About 70% of those admitted completed their course. For want of detailed records it is not possible to determine the precise reasons for the withdrawal of so many students, but it appears that relatively few were dismissed for academic deficiencies. The enrollment increased to an average of about 40 at the end of the first decade and an average of about 65 toward the end of the first quarter of a century. In 1873, after the construction of the new building, the enrollment was uncommonly high. The attendance, it was reported, "has been the largest (so far as known) yet connected at any one time with this or any other Lutheran theological seminary in this country."[29] In the early years a fair number of students transferred from Gettysburg Seminary, and to a lesser extent from Hartwick Seminary, but this soon became exceptional.

As would be expected, a majority of the students came from Pennsylvania, New York, and New Jersey. Church-related colleges, in which pre-theological students received financial aid, were the principal sources of students. Gettysburg College furnished 19 of the students who were graduated from the seminary during the first quarter of a century. The former Allentown Collegiate Institute became Muhlenberg College in 1867, when it began to be related to the Ministerium of Pennsylvania, and was represented by 116 students in the seminary's graduating classes during the same period. Thiel College was founded in 1866 as a school of the Pittsburgh Synod, and 37 of its students were among the graduates of the seminary up to 1889. The New York Ministerium sponsored St. Matthew's Academy in New York City, from which several students came, and after the founding of Wagner College in 1883 a half-dozen of its alumni were graduated from the seminary before the close of the first quarter-century. Hartwick sent the same number from central New York. Other schools on the territory of the supporting synods were also represented. The University of Pennsylvania supplied 14 of the graduates, Lafayette College counted 4, Ursinus College and Franklin and Marshall each furnished 3, and many other colleges were represented.

A year after the close of the Civil War the president of Roanoke College inquired whether southern students would be welcome in Philadelphia. "There is every disposition on the part of the faculty," he was told, "to give them a friendly reception, provided they come with a firm and sincere determination to avoid everything that would disturb the peace, harmony, and prosperity of the institution."[30] Roanoke College, in Virginia, had 11 students in the seminary's graduating classes before 1889, and almost as many others came from Newberry College in South Carolina, Catawba College in North Carolina, North Carolina College, and the University of Virginia. Canada was represented by two students from McGill University. Among schools in the Middle West, Capital University had 7 alumni in the seminary's graduating classes, Augustana College had 6, and there were others from Northwestern University, Luther College, Wittenberg, and Concordia in Fort Wayne, Ind. As many as 21 graduates received their academic preparation in Europe, most of them in Germany.

Notable, too, were the students of Swedish, Norwegian, and Icelandic background. C. M. Esbjörn, son of the Swedish-American pioneer Lars P. Esbjörn, was a student in the Philadelphia Seminary, and so was Conrad E. Lindberg, who later became professor of Systematic Theology in Augustana Theological Seminary. Without attempting an exhaustive list, it may be appropriate here to mention some other graduates whose names are especially remembered for one reason or another. Charles S. Albert was for many years book editor of the Lutheran Publication Society, George H. Trabert was a pioneer missionary and historian of English Lutheranism in the old Northwest, Revere F. Weidner was the first president of Chicago Lutheran Seminary, Jeremiah F. Ohl was a leader in the Inner Mission movement in America, George H. Gerberding was professor of Practical Theology in Northwestern Theological Seminary, John Nicum and William J. Finck were parish ministers who were productive historians in addition, John Heischmann was recognized as one of the most eloquent preachers of his time, George Washington Sandt was editor of The Lutheran for a generation, Andrew George Voigt was dean and professor of Systematic Theology in the Lutheran Southern Seminary, John A. W. Haas was president of Muhlenberg College, Joseph Stump was professor of Systematic Theology in Northwestern Theological Seminary, Henry W. Elson was a popular writer and teacher of history, C. Armand Miller was a faithful pastor and author of devotional literature.

Attempts were made to enforce a strict regulation of the lives of all students while they were in the seminary. Rules governing conduct were printed and posted in all rooms, and some of them required a degree of conformity which would have excited rebellion in later times. At first the steward was asked to see to the enforcement of the regulations, but when this quite naturally led to additional friction between the steward and the students, certain members of the Senior class were made overseers. Ultimately, however, the faculty became involved when there were breaches of discipline. One of the rules that was found most burdensome required all students to be in their rooms by 11 p.m., and the outer doors of the seminary building were locked at this time. Strictly forbidden was "all attendance at public places of sinful amusement or of dubious character, such as theaters, the circus, etc." What was not covered in this prohibition could conceivably be included in the more general regulation which made students "accountable for any conduct which may reflect discredit upon themselves or the institution itself." It appears that the members of the faculty were not of one mind about the need for such rigid rules, and among themselves, at least, they conceded that the rules simply accorded with "the sentiments prevailing in the community," that is, with the current mores of American Protestantism.[31]

The location of the seminary in the center of the city was of course an invitation to students to inspect nearby "public places of sinful amusement or of dubious character." Two students were admonished on one occasion for returning to the seminary ten minutes late. On another occasion a student was reported to have been "out of the building to a very late hour of the night, even until 1 o'clock, during the last two weeks." On still another occasion the minutes of the faculty read: "The faculty have heard, not without solicitude, of the frequent absence from the building after 11 p.m." Fifteen to twenty students were reprimanded for going to a theater one evening "to witness the play of Hamlet and the acting of Edwin Booth." As a rule not so many were involved at one time. There is no wonder, at all events, that one student began to have scruples about reading the dramas of Schiller and Shakespeare, although they were recommended by one of his instructors. There was censure, too, for "visiting lager beer saloons." Some students, it was reported, occasionally went "to taverns to take a glass of beer." "In doing this they thought that they made a legitimate use of Christian freedom, whilst they could not deny that they acted against the rules of the seminary." A gentle reprimand was the customary penalty. It must be observed that there was some relation between these regulations and the deteriorating neighborhood in which the seminary was located. A student later recalled "the midnight glitter along Eighth, Ninth, Race, and Vine Streets," "the alluring haunts of the kings and queens of the demimonde," and the unemployed "men of leisure who take their perennial vacation in Franklin Square," opposite the seminary.[32]

It seemed desirable both to the faculty and to the board of directors to have an older person live in the seminary building to watch over and counsel students. For this purpose the venerable C. F. Heyer, who had behind him a long and distinguished career as frontier preacher and missionary in India, was appointed "housefather" in January, 1872. In this position Father Heyer (the designation "father" was then common for older ministers) died less than two years later. According to Professor Mann, "he proved in various ways a real and great blessing to the seminary, enjoyed universal respect and love, and left a most enviable remembrance." When, in 1880, the students organized a missionary society "to awaken and promote a missionary spirit in the minds and hearts of the young candidates for future pastoral duties," they named it the Father Heyer Missionary Society.[33] In 1874 Professor Mann was requested to assume the duties of chaplain or housefather since he lived "only a few steps from the seminary." He was strict but kind and understanding in his relations with students. "There is

John Christian Frederick Heyer, Veteran Missionary and Seminary Housefather

occasion every day for exercising some authority," he wrote. "One student wants to go home after four long weeks in the seminary: he wants to see his father and mother once more or he must prepare for winter clothing. Another one wishes to be absent a few days to preach for a pastor who perhaps suddenly fell sick. Another student again complains of the excessive smoking propensities of his roommate. Again another one finds that his room is too cold or that the victuals are not well prepared or that another student does not behave as he ought at the table."[34]

Dr. Theodore Demme, son of the Rev. C. R. Demme, and Dr. G. Gilbert attended students who were sick. When necessary, students were given free rooms and treatment in the German Hospital, later called Lankenau Hospital. From time to time the board of directors sent formal thanks to the physicians and the hospital for their generosity. In early December, 1875, there was an epidemic of smallpox in the city, and Dr. Demme vaccinated all the students. When symptoms of the disease appeared among some of them, he ordered the school closed, and most students departed for their homes. Before Christmas Richard Aslaxson, a student of Norwegian descent from Wisconsin, and Joel Schaeffer, a student of German background from Missouri, died. Professor Mann visited the sick young men every day, and they were nursed by a fellow student Jacob Q. Upp. "He has by his willingness and faithfulness gained my highest admiration," wrote Mann, "and deserves the thanks of the authorities of the seminary and his fellow students." The seminary was not reopened until Jan. 26, 1876. From that time until 1953 the alumni annually placed flowers on the graves of the two victims of smallpox who died far from home.[35]

When "Father" Heyer was housefather, he participated in the daily worship of the students since he was a resident in the seminary building. Otherwise such public devotional exercises were left to the students, although the faculty had a hand in their arrangement and occasionally attended. They were referred to as "family worship" and were intended as a substitute for the domestic devotions to which students were presumably accustomed when they were at home. A rising bell was rung at 6 a.m., and shortly thereafter the students assembled for morning prayers, which consisted of Scripture reading, hymns, prayer, and the recitation of the Apostles' Creed. Since the seminary was bilingual, it was decided "that both languages be used on each and every occasion, the students determining what part of the exercises, whether the reading of the Scripture, prayer, or singing, shall be assigned to each language from day to day." Later on student leaders, who took turns, were given the option of conducting the worship entirely in English or entirely in German. Evening prayers, conducted in similar fashion, were held at 10 p.m. Students were not under obligation to attend these, for they were encouraged to engage in private devotions. On the other hand, they were required to attend the "family worship" in the morning, although the records indicate that students overslept on occasion or found other excuses for their absence. For use in connection with public worship, a cabinet organ was secured as a gift of two interested ladies in 1867, and thirteen years later the students raised $87.50 to purchase a new organ. The principal provision for the students' public worship was the Sunday services in nearby churches. Every student, the regulations stated, "is expected to become a regular attendant and, if circumstances admit, a full member . . . of some one of the Evangelical Lutheran congregations of Philadelphia . . . . Every student is required to attend public worship with punctuality in the church with which, after having stated his intention to the faculty, he has united."[36]

The academic year extended at first from the first Monday in September to Whitsuntide, with two weeks' recess for Christmas and one week's recess for Easter. Later the academic year began in the middle of September "in view of the oppressive and exhaustive heat that is always apt to visit Philadelphia in the early part of September."[37] No matter how early or late the school year began, students were slow in assembling. In 1881 "not a single Senior and only several Middlemen" were present when the seminary opened. Even applicants for admission sometimes appeared several months late. Because so many students asked for permission to leave early for the Christmas recess in order to assist their pastors at home, the recess was occasionally extended to three weeks. At other times students wrote from home during the Christmas recess, "asking to be excused from returning for periods varying from a week to a month, and delicately stretching out even to 'a month or so.'" The faculty was reluctant to insist on prompt return because many of the absences were believed to be "caused by failure of means of support, family cares, urgent calls for help from pastors." Synods were requested not to allow students to be called away from their studies before the close of the school year. It was the rule of the seminary, in fact, that no students were to preach during their Junior and Middle years, and in their Senior year not oftener than once a month. "Beginning to preach too early and to play the pastor before one is a successful student" was especially deplored but not always effectively prevented.[38]

There were other occasions for the interruption of studies. The assassination of President Abraham Lincoln in 1865 led to an extension of the Easter recess. "The regular working of the institution," wrote Professor Mann, "was not fully resumed until the following Monday in consequence of the great excitement pervading the entire city." Classes were omitted on Oct. 16, 1855 (in response to a request of the students) "owing to the great excitement caused by the grand triennial parade of the Philadelphia Fire Department." Classes were suspended on May 15, 1871, to celebrate "the wonderful triumph of German arms in the late Franco-Prussian War," and also in December, 1879 (in response to a student petition), "to witness the procession and reception of General Ulysses S. Grant."[39] The fact that the seminary was in the heart of the city caused it to be involved, more than it otherwise might have been, in the great as well as the small events of the time. Students also had the opportunity, which some took advantage of, to visit museums and libraries, attend various churches and conventions, hear concerts and lectures, and even enter "public places of sinful amusement or of dubious character."

The academic preparation of many of the students left something to be desired. The faculty was reluctant to be more selective in admitting students on account of the great demand in the church for ministers. Professor Mann observed: "The majority of those who are college graduates are very weak. There is so little of solid knowledge in the ancient languages and of a certain mental independence. The mind not wide awake." In comparison with theological students in Europe, where he had studied, Mann found something wanting in the American students he dealt with. Perhaps he was more than usually discouraged when he wrote of students who "in a frivolous manner prove that they do not realize their responsibility but have a sort of contempt for real learning and theological acquirements." He noted that by 1889 most of the students were coming from church-related colleges, especially Muhlenberg, Thiel, and Wagner. "The ignorance of the students is shocking," he added, "not only in the ancient languages, in which they lack in the most elementary parts of grammar, but generally in all things . . . . They are not at all used to systematic thinking." This was also true of German students who came to Philadelphia from the Mission Institute of St. Chrischona, near Basel. The poorest students were sometimes required to study an additional year in the seminary before being admitted to graduation, but this was exceptional. "Naturally," wrote Professor Spaeth in 1874, "what we accomplish is very unpretentious, and we are well aware that our students do not carry away any remarkable provision of theological erudition."[40]

The seminary's constitution, adopted in 1865, made provisions for a curriculum which had, in fact, been envisaged from the very outset: "The professors shall arrange the classes and the departments of study, as nearly as may be practicable, with reference to a three-year course, and shall teach in German and English, and in any other languages which may be provided for, the chief parts of Exegetical, Systematic, Historical, and Practical Theology."[41] During the first twenty-five years of the seminary's life all the courses of study were prescribed. They were so arranged that by far the greatest weight in the first year was given to biblical study (including consideration of biblical inspiration, the canons, archaeology, introduction, hermeneutics, and exegesis). It was assumed that students had a knowledge of Greek at entrance, and the study of Hebrew was required in all three years, together with exegesis of the Old and New Testaments. In the second and third years the greatest weight was given to Systematic Theology (including Dogmatics, Symbolics, Ethics, and Ecclesiastical Polity). Church History was accorded only a small portion of time in the second and third years. Although the study of Homiletics was begun in the second year, practical courses were reserved for the last year (Pastoral Care, Catechetics, Liturgics, and homiletical exercises), where they were given the major block of time. Some of the courses had to be offered twice — in German for those who understood no English and in English for those who understood no German — and in other courses the instructor employed first one and then the other language.[42]

A meaningful picture of the academic work of the seminary during the first quarter-century of its existence cannot be gained from an examination of the announcement of courses. More decisive are the persons who taught and the theological position and interests they represented.

Charles F. Schaeffer [43] taught from 1864 to the close of 1878, when his "feeble condition" compelled him to give up his work.[44] He died the following year, having entered upon the seventy-third year of his life. Born in 1807, a native of Germantown, Pa., he was a graduate of the University of Pennsylvania and studied theology under the tutorship of his father and of Carl R. Demme. Parishes in Carlisle, Pa., Hagerstown, Md., Lancaster, Ohio, Red Hook, N. Y., and Easton, Pa., were served by him. For three years (1840-1843) he taught in the theological seminary of the Ohio Synod in Columbus, Ohio, and for nine years (1855-1864) he taught in the college and seminary in Gettysburg before accepting the call to the new seminary in Philadelphia. In terms both of age and of academic experience he was the senior of the faculty. On this account as well as because he was at first the only full-time instructor, he was made chairman of the faculty by the choice of his colleagues and afterwards also of the board of

Original Faculty. Top, left to right: William J. Mann and Charles Porterfield Krauth. Center: Charles F. Schaeffer. Bottom: Charles W. Schaeffer and G. F. Krotel.

directors.[45] As such he presided at meetings of the faculty and was its spokesman in relations with the students. The code of regulations, intended to govern student life, was drafted by him, modeled after similar rules with which he had become acquainted in Gettysburg. In 1850 he had received the degree of D.D. from Gettysburg College.

The chairman of the faculty had long been of delicate health. Since he was also hard of hearing, he had to use an ear trumpet. It was said that this was an advantage in a teacher of future ministers, for it compelled them to speak loudly and distinctly.[46] However, the affliction caused Schaeffer to withdraw into himself. "He lived apart. His world was in his study, where he labored industriously and smoked."[47] He painstakingly translated, from the German, J. H. Kurtz's *Manual of Sacred History* (1855), the *Commentary on the Acts of the Apostles* (1866) in Philip Schaff's edition of the Lange Commentary, and John Arndt's *True Christianity* (1868). His *Annotations on the Gospel according to St. Matthew* was published posthumously (1895). In addition, he wrote a score of articles on sundry subjects from the doctrine of election to the division of the decalogue.

As a teacher Schaeffer was more conscientious than inspiring. It was his method, as it was that of most of his contemporaries, to dictate a series of thetical statements or propositions, present supporting evidence from the Scriptures and elsewhere, and then devote such time as remained in an hour to a further discussion or elaboration of the topic at hand. Since the slow dictation from a carefully prepared manuscript consumed much of the time in the class-room, some students unsuccessfully proposed that the dictated material be distributed in printed form and that the time thus saved be utilized for more constructive purposes.[48] It was in this fashion that Schaeffer lectured in German on Dogmatics, his chief assignment, and also on Biblical Exegesis and Hermeneutics (in English) and on some practical subjects (English and German). The manuscripts he prepared for dictation are still extant and reveal not only his minute care but also the character of his theology.

With the initial help of his theological tutor Carl R. Demme and the later assistance he found in books imported from Germany, Schaeffer had gradually been led to a position which was critical of the American Lutheranism of S. S. Schmucker. He was confident that in a limited number of books he had discovered what genuine Lutheranism was. He read the Lutheran Confessions in the light of the orthodoxist theology of the seventeenth century, which he knew through Leonard Hutter's *Compendium* (1610) and the anthology of Heinrich Schmid. It seemed not to occur to him that the writers of the Confessions and the orthodoxist theologians might not be in agreement. He also relied upon reading in the anti-rationalist F. V. Reinhard (d. 1812) and the pietist G. C. Knapp (d. 1825), and he had some acquaintance with his German contemporaries F. A. Philippi and F. Tholuk. These men were Schaeffer's authorities. He digested them with great diligence and care, and he presented the fruit of his studies to his students in an earnest, if pedantic, fashion.

Charles Porterfield Krauth[49] was a man of different mold. He taught in the seminary from 1864 to the fall of 1882 and died the following January, a few months short of his sixtieth birthday. Graduated from both the college and the seminary in Gettysburg, where his father was a colleague of S. S. Schmucker, he served parishes in Canton and Baltimore, Md., Shepherdstown, Martinsburg, and Winchester, Va., and Pittsburgh and Philadelphia, Pa. In 1861 he became editor of *The Lutheran and Missionary* in Philadelphia, in which post he continued until 1867, three years after he became professor in the Philadelphia Seminary. He also served as pastor of a mission congregation in Philadelphia during 1866 and 1867. The following year he was appointed professor of Intellectual and Moral Philosophy in the University of Pennsylvania, to which he also added the position of vice-provost, and served in these offices simultaneously with his seminary professorship to the close of his life. Krauth's restless energy also found other outlets. He was one of the founders of the General Council, the federation of conservative Lutheran synods formed in 1867, and not only served as its president for nine years but also drafted most of its important early declarations. He received the degrees of D.D. in 1857 and of LL.D. in 1874 from Gettysburg College.

In addition to his editorial work, Professor Krauth wrote extensively. His philosophical interest was reflected in his edition of *Fleming's Vocabulary of Philosophy* (1860; revised edition, 1878) and in *Berkeley's Principles* (1874). He translated, from the German, F. Tholuk's *Commentary on the Gospel of St. John* (1859) and served as a member of the American Committee for Bible Revision. He contributed many articles to various encyclopedias and wrote often for learned journals. Many of these articles were gathered in the large volume for which Krauth came to be best known, *The Conservative Reformation and its Theology* (1872). As his biographer has pointed out, it is possible to trace page after page in this work to articles which Krauth had written earlier and which represented various stages in his development. Contradictory and incompatible elements were allowed to stand alongside one another, and this furnished critics with ammunition.[50] For its time, however, it represented the best exposition and defense of Lutheranism available in English.

Like Charles F. Schaeffer, Krauth gradually moved beyond the practices and teaching characteristic of his environment in his youth. Before 1850 he had abandoned the practice of new measures and had embraced many of the traditional Lutheran teachings which S. S. Schmucker was attacking. In private correspondence he ascribed his development largely to the influence and encouragement of his father, a pupil of Carl R. Demme. The son was urged by his father to study the Scriptures in the original languages and to make the German language a tool of theological study because, as he put it, "so much of the best theological literature is contained in it, so much of the literature of our own church." Young Krauth soon developed an excellent reading knowledge of German to supplement his knowledge of Latin, Greek, and Hebrew, and, thus equipped, he read widely and deeply. He had an enormous appetite for books and amassed a private library of great value. It included editions of the works of Luther, Melanchthon, and Calvin, the works of post-Reformation writers from Matthias Flacius and Martin Chemnitz to Calovius, Hutter, and Quenstedt, and more recent authors like Kahnis and Tholuk. What he gleaned from such books he stored in his memory, and he was able to recall it almost at will.

Krauth's chief assignment was to teach Dogmatics, and in addition he taught brief courses in Encyclopedia (introduction to the study of theology) and Church Polity. All of his teaching was done in English, for his knowledge of German was limited to reading. His procedure was "to follow some German author — Luthardt in Dogmatics, Hagenbach in Encyclopedia, Richter in Church Polity — as a general guide, and then, in lectures, to develop, modify, or apply according to the needs of our church here in America."[51] Like Schaeffer, he dictated much of the material which he expected his students to master. When some students complained that Krauth spent nearly two years on the topic of original sin without getting to other parts of Systematic Theology, he explained that he planned to complete the course in nine years, that each class could expect to get a third of the course from him, and that they might obtain the rest from the notes taken by former students.[52] Krauth changed his plan, but the incident suggests that his primary interest was not in the needs of his students at the seminary. He was so preoccupied with his many other duties that the seminary had to be content with his spare time, and in his last years this meant "what attention he could give it after five o'clock in the evening."[53] Physical exhaustion often compelled him to intermit lectures. Once he fell asleep while dictating to a class, and during the last two years he was barely able, as he himself put it, "to creep to the seminary occasionally."[54]

Krauth was more sophisticated theologically than Schaeffer. He was brilliant when he was challenged by a situation, and he could be devastating to antagonists. Professor Charles Hodge, of Princeton Theological Seminary, generously congratulated Krauth on an article concerning infant salvation in *The Mercersburg Review* by declaring, "Your paper proves that you are far better read in Calvinistic theology than I am."[55] As a theologian Krauth was more imitative than creative,[56] but he was able to marshal with great skill and reproduce with rhetorical power what he absorbed in his voracious reading. Like other contemporaries in a time before the influence of biblical criticism had made itself felt, he saw no problem in a simple identification of Scriptures and Word of God. He asserted that the original text of the Bible, "just as the sacred penman left it, is absolutely in every jot and tittle God's Word."[57] Then he proceeded to show an identity between the teachings of the Lutheran Confessions and those of the Scriptures, concluding that the Confessions "must be accepted in every statement of doctrine in their own true, native, original, and only sense."[58] It was on this basis that Krauth meant to erect a theological structure. He was distracted from his systematic work by ecclesiastico-political activity and made some of his most lasting contributions in the field of church polity — significantly it was he who was asked to draft the original constitution of the seminary.[59] However, he was recognized both inside and outside of the Lutheran Church as his age's leading interpreter of Lutheranism in the English language.

The third of the original professors was William Julius Mann, who taught from 1864 to 1891. He resigned on account of his declining health and died the following summer in the seventy-third year of his life. Born in Stuttgart, Württemberg, and educated in the University of Tübingen, he came to America in 1845 at the urging of his life-long friend Philip Schaff, who had himself just crossed the Atlantic to become professor in the Mercersburg Theological Seminary of the German Reformed Church. Mann served a few years in a Reformed congregation, but in 1850 he returned to the Lutheran Church and became assistant to the Rev. Carl R. Demme in the large St. Michael's and Zion Church in Philadelphia. "It is the desire of my heart," he declared, "to serve the church in which I was born and to which I owe my training and education."[60] In 1854 Mann succeeded Demme as pastor of the church and continued in this position to 1883, for nineteen years combining with his parish duties the work of a seminary professor. When in 1870 the imposing "Old Zion Church" was built on Franklin Square, the seminary and the church were separated by only a few houses, and the relation between the two was intimate.

Although Mann was not slow in learning English after his arrival in America, he remained conscious of his accent to the end of his life and was consequently timid about speaking publicly in English. However, when in later years he wrote in English he hardly betrayed that it was an adopted language. It was alleged, in fact, that he spoke English in his sleep.[61] Mann's literary production was extensive. For twelve years (1848-1859) he collaborated with Philip Schaff in editing *Der deutsche Kirchenfreund,* a monthly journal addressed to readers of culture, and Mann himself contributed about 110 articles on a great variety of subjects. Here as well as in articles which he wrote for learned journals he revealed his involvement in the civil as well as the ecclesiastical issues of his day. His small books, *A Plea for the Augsburg Confession* (1856) and *Lutheranism in America* (1857), which were informed replies to S. S. Schmucker and his Definite Synodical Platform, brought Mann to the attention of wider circles among his English-speaking brethren. After he had begun his teaching at the seminary he published *General Principles of Christian Ethics* (1872), an English rendering of part of a work by Mann's favorite teacher in Tübingen, C. J. Schmidt. His literary activity, however, turned more and more to American history. He wrote popular biographies in German of William Penn (1882) and Christopher Columbus (1891), published a volume of essays entitled *Die gute alte Zeit in Pennsylvania* (1884), edited a new edition of the *Hallesche Nachrichten* (2 vols., 1886, 1895), an invaluable collection of sources for the history of the Lutheran Church in colonial America, and wrote the definitive *Life and Times of Henry Melchior Muhlenberg* (1887). He received the degree of D.D. in 1857 from Gettysburg College and of LL.D. in 1888 from Muhlenberg College.

The history of the church provided Mann with more than an absorbing hobby, but he gave no course in this field. The subjects he regularly taught were Symbolics, Ethics, German Homiletics, Exegesis, and Hebrew. In the case of Hebrew he uniformly taught through the medium of English. These classes were not popular, and many students asked to be excused from the study of the language on account of "defective hearing," "infirmities of memory," "ill health and defective eyesight," and similar excuses.[62] Since Mann was a merciless critic of student sermons, there were also mixed feelings about his course in Homiletics. On the other hand, the response to his courses in Ethics and Symbolics was generally favorable, and even enthusiastic. On these subjects he lectured at first only in German, and in the last years, in response to a request of students who did not understand German, his classes became bilingual. In the case of Symbolics (a comparative study of the Eastern Orthodox, Roman Catholic, and Protestant churches) he lectured from a carefully prepared manuscript, but he frequently digressed to illustrate his points from history, life, and experience. In Ethics he lectured extemporaneously and used to full advantage his interest in and knowledge of the contemporary world. "Dr. Mann was the personal magnet of the seminary," wrote one of his students, Theodore E. Schmauk. "He was more alive than any teacher I have ever had, and he shed abroad his living spirit, force, and personal vitality into the minds and hearts of his pupils."[63] Another student, George H. Gerberding, later bore similar testimony: "He got a peculiar grip on me. He made and left an impress as no other teacher ever did."[64]

In his early years Mann was an active participant in the Confessional awakening in America. As he saw it, there were three groups of Lutherans in America in his time. On the left were those, mostly in the General Synod, who sacrificed their Lutheran heritage and transformed the gospel into law. On the right were members of the Missouri and Buffalo Synods, and some outside of these synods, who adhered to the Lutheran heritage but repristinated it uncharitably and pharisaically. In the center were the people of the General Council, a minority in the General Synod, and some, like the Norwegian synods, outside both these bodies who were sincere in their Lutheran profession without denying that non-Lutherans may be Christians too.[65] The fact that he shared with others the spirit of the Confessional awakening did not rob Mann of his independence of thinking. He was equally critical of congregational and episcopal polities, for he believed that presbyteral and synodical organization was best adapted to American churches. Because he was a Protestant by theological conviction he had little patience for those in his day (in the Oxford Movement, in the Mercersburg Movement, and elsewhere) who were attracted by "the grandiose," the theology of glory, in Catholicism. He criticized the liturgical and hymnological standards employed in the preparation of the *Church Book* (1868) and the *Kirchenbuch* (1877) on the ground that their archaic forms could not really edify congregations in the nineteenth century. "Such repristinations of the old," he wrote, "are artificial, forced, contrived, and inconsistent. Instead of making us more conscious of our oneness with the past, they make us doubly aware of the differences."[66] Mann's younger colleague Henry E. Jacobs testified to the versatility and fecundity of the man when he appraised his senior's "wide culture, brilliant gifts, and mental processes, which in their rapidity were a constant astonishment even to those who knew him longest."[67]

When the seminary was founded, two assistant professors were elected to work with the three professors. One of these was G. F. Krotel (1826-1907), at the time pastor of St. Mark's Church in Philadelphia. In the spring of 1868 he became pastor of Trinity Church in New York City, and thus he taught on a limited schedule for only three and a half years. After his removal to New York he remained a friend and supporter of the seminary until his death.[68]

The other original assistant professor was Charles William Schaeffer,[69] a nephew of the first chairman of the faculty. Born in Hagerstown, Md., as the son of a minister, he was graduated from the University of Pennsylvania and the Gettysburg Seminary. He served parishes in Barren Hill, Harrisburg, and Germantown, Pa., devoting twenty-six years of his life (1849-1875) to St. Michael's Church in Germantown. He was the author of the brief *Early History of the Lutheran Church in America* (1857, 2nd ed. 1868) and translated from the German a portion of Mann's edition of the *Halle Reports* (1882). Schaeffer's natural qualities of leadership were recognized in his election to the office of president of the General Synod and of the General Council, and for a third of his career in the ministry he was either president or treasurer of the Ministerium of Pennsylvania. He received the degree of D.D. in 1852 from Gettysburg College and in 1879 from the University of Pennsylvania, and in 1887 he received the degree of LL.D. from Thiel College.

During the first decade of the seminary's history Schaeffer taught only one hour a week, but when the Burkhalter professorship was established, he was elected professor in 1873. From 1875 to 1894 he devoted his full time to the seminary, dying in his eighty-third year in 1896. In view of his practical gifts and the fact that he was then the only full-time professor, his colleagues chose him chairman of the faculty on the death of his uncle in 1879, and he remained in this office until his retirement.[70] Schaeffer made no pretensions to be a scholar, and since he was already in his sixty-first year when he was elected professor, it would not have been reasonable to expect him to achieve academic excellence in his declining years. He was assigned to teach Church History, New Testament, and Practical Theology in the English language, and since he was a hearty, good-natured man who was always accessible, both the students and his colleagues were fond of him.[71]

In 1873, the same year that C. W. Schaeffer was made professor, Adolph Spaeth, pastor of St. John's German Church in Philadelphia, was installed as the first incumbent of the German professorship of the New York Ministerium. He continued as pastor of St. John's throughout the period now under consideration and consequently gave only part of his time to teaching. Since his contribution to the seminary falls more especially in the next period, further consideration of him will be deferred. The same is true of Henry Eyster Jacobs, who was elected

Faculty in 1885. Left to right: Henry E. Jacobs, William J. Mann, Charles W. Schaeffer, Adolph Spaeth

in 1883 to fill the place of the deceased Professor Krauth. In his case the constitutional requirement that to be eligible for election to a professorship a man
"must have spent at least five years in the pastoral office" (that is, in a parish)
was waived and later removed.[72] From 1865 to 1869 Mr. J. C. Haas, organist
and schoolmaster in St. Michael's-Zion Church, offered supplementary instruction in vocal and instrumental music, but he complained about "non-attendance
of the majority of the students."[73] From 1868 to 1872 Mr. Alexander Loos gave
instruction in German to students who were not acquainted with the language,
and he also complained that many did not attend his classes.[74] In 1867 and again
in 1886 some students organized societies "for cultivation of facility in the use
of the German language." It was reported in 1867 that most of the seminary
graduates were "prepared to preach in both the German and the English language."
In 1880 fifteen of sixteen in the graduating class could preach in German, and
this was said to be true of two-thirds of the students in 1885.[75]

Although the seminary was reputed, according to an article in the *Encyclopedia Britannica,* to have "maintained the ablest faculty and the highest character
of any English Lutheran institution,"[76] the shortcomings of the school must not
be glossed over. The faculty included some men of eminent ability who continued
their scholarly growth and literary production, but for the most part their teaching suffered from preoccupation with other duties. To their credit it must be
said that they taught at great personal sacrifice. With reference to his double
burden in professorship and pastorate Mann once remarked, "Usually one wagon
has two horses, but in this case one horse — and a poor one at that — is pulling
two wagons." The assistant professors received no compensation at all, and all
but the full-time professors received "a mere nominal return for their services,"
usually receiving only a fraction of what they were promised.[77]

The chief deficiency in the early years was the want of an adequate library,
and the students were as a consequence limited to a few textbooks and the dictated materials offered by their instructors. Steps were taken, however, to
remedy this situation. The private library of the Rev. C. R. Demme was purchased from his widow for $1,000, provided by a gift for this purpose by the
Muhlenberg family in Reading, Pa., and included with the library was the alleged
wedding ring of Martin Luther.[78] Several years later the private library of the
Rev. C. F. E. Stohlmann, of New York City, was given to the seminary. Mr. G. A.
Dobler, a Baltimore merchant, made annual gifts of new books over a period of
many years. On the death of Professor C. F. Schaeffer, his family donated his
library to the seminary.[79] Still more important was the acquisition of between
10,000 and 15,000 volumes from the private library of Professor Charles
Porterfield Krauth when he died in 1883. In the estimation of the Rev. Beale M.
Schmucker, "No collection of the theological literature of the Evangelical
Lutheran Church, so large, so carefully chosen, assembled at so great cost, has
ever yet been made in this country." In consideration of Krauth's "eminent
services" to the church and his widow's gift of his library to the seminary, the
Ministerium of Pennsylvania promised to pay Mrs. Krauth $500 a year for the
rest of her life.[80] Five years later the private library of B. M. Schmucker himself, supplemented by the liturgical books purchased for his use by the Ministerium of Pennsylvania, found their way to the seminary. The Alumni Association
(organized in 1869) and many individuals also contributed funds for the purchase
of books. By 1889 it was estimated that the seminary had 20,000 books.[81]

In the early years the rules governing the use of the seminary library were
very loose, and many books were lost because they were "at length gradually and
unconsciously merged into the growing library of the student." A room was
originally set aside for a library and reading room, by 1880 another room was
added, and in 1884 the library was further enlarged by addition of the former

dining room. In 1880 a student librarian was appointed to introduce control of the growing collection, and a card catalog was begun in 1883.[82] Thus a measure of order was introduced into the library, and the books were made ready for future academic use.

During the first quarter-century the seminary itself became involved in publication. The *Indicator* was published monthly during the academic year from 1881 to 1891. This was a venture of students, originally led by Theodore E. Schmauk, whose inoculation with printer's ink proved to be permanent. From time to time the faculty suggested that the periodical "has not given satisfaction," and this probably contributed to its demise.[83] Meanwhile, in 1880, a more ambitious publication was proposed to the Alumni Association by its president: "The want of a magazine or quarterly, in which subjects relating to the doctrines of the church can be freely discussed, has often been felt . . . . It has been suggested to me that such a magazine or quarterly might be begun and carried on under the auspices of our association, together with the assistance of the faculty of the seminary." The proposal was approved, and Professor Krauth was asked to serve as editor. Because of his health he declined. A committee of the Alumni Association edited the first numbers of the quarterly *Lutheran Church Review* in 1882. When Professor H. E. Jacobs joined the faculty in 1883, he was requested to edit the theological journal. He did so for almost three years, and then relinquished his office as editor in order to work on literary projects of his own. The editorial burden was thereupon shifted to the entire faculty.[84] It was in this way that the Philadelphia Seminary inaugurated a theological journal that was destined to have a long, influential, and financially precarious career.

Chapter IV

Transplantation to Suburban Mount Airy

1889-1910

IN 1870 THE UNIVERSITY OF PENNSYLVANIA moved its campus from Fourth and Arch Streets in the center of Philadelphia to a new location west of the Schuylkill River. Downtown Philadelphia, where the university had been, was described as "a vile neighborhood, growing viler every day," and it seemed to the university authorities that relocation could not prudently be delayed.[1] A similar move faced the Philadelphia Seminary. "The part of the city in which the present seminary stands," it was reported, "has for a number of years terribly deteriorated socially and morally. Race and Vine Streets, especially west of Seventh Street, belong now to the most depraved parts of the city. Here are two theaters, erected a few years since, and the lowest sorts of taverns abound."[2] Although it was conceded that students benefited from the seminary's "easy access to all advantages of book stores, libraries, lectures, collections of art, and divers churches and preachers of the city," such benefits were more than balanced, in the eyes of at least one student, by the purgatorial conditions of seminary life — "burning heat, bitter, frosty chills, foul air, dingy rooms, clouds of dust, intolerable clatter of coal wagons, horses' hoofs, rumbling cars drowning the voice, distracting the thoughts, and working up the nervous system."[3]

In 1882, when the Rev. Joseph A. Seiss, president of the seminary's board of directors, was also president of the Ministerium of Pennsylvania, he asked the synod to give serious consideration to a relocation of the seminary. "The seminary has just completed the eighteenth year of its sessions . . . . The year has developed more than usual sickness among the students, in one case resulting in death. The costly expenditures for the bodily comfort of the students have not proved satisfactory. The repeated failures in this regard, with other embarrassments and unmet needs resulting, are naturally giving rise to the inquiry, deserving of consideration, whether it would not be of advantage to change the location of the institution to some less confined place, away from the distractions of the city, where it could be better accommodated, where the professors would be in closer living connection with it, where their undivided time and interest could be given to it, and where the costs and the interferences with diligence and quietness in study would be diminished." The synod agreed that further enlargement of the seminary building on the existing site was not feasible. Three alternatives appeared to be open: (1) "A new location within the built-up parts of the city where more ground, freer circulation of pure air, and greater quiet could be found," and yet where the seminary could "enjoy the services of pastors and professors in other institutions as heretofore." (2) "A second location might be found in the outer parts of the limits of the city with still larger grounds and more perfect healthfulness and quiet," but this would make access to the advantages of the city more difficult. (3) "The removal of the seminary to some other place than Philadelphia."[4]

The seminary's board of directors and the faculty favored a location within ten or fifteen minutes from the center of the city by rail. There was some sentiment in the synod for moving the seminary to Lancaster (where the seminary of the German Reformed Church was located) or Allentown (where Muhlenberg College was located), and free land was promised if such a move were contemplated. Meanwhile, in 1883 the Ministerium of Pennsylvania approved "the erection of new and more extensive buildings for our theological seminary at Philadelphia, . . . the estimated cost of which will be $100,000." The faculty and the board of directors continued to explore sites for the seminary, and in 1884 a parcel of about six acres of ground on St. George's Hill, beyond Fifty-second Street in West Philadelphia, was purchased for $15,198. On second thought the property proved to be undesirable. It was learned that the Pennsylvania Railroad was about to extend its freight yard in the neighborhood and that the property would be almost completely surrounded by "a veritable Chinese wall of empty freight cars" and there would be almost constant noise and smoke. As Judge William H. Staake, a member of the board of directors, reported later, Mr. Wesley W. Kurtz, "who had been a most generous contributor to the seminary fund," concluded after visiting the site five times "that we had better give the lot away rather than build on that location."[5] The fact that it was not until 1896, a dozen years later, that the land was finally disposed of by the board of directors[6] seems to confirm the judgment that the location was an undesirable one, whether for a seminary or for some other purpose.

Another property, also about six acres in size, was called to the attention of the board of directors. This was located within the limits of the city (since 1854), about nine miles north of its center. Some members of the faculty and the board were opposed to the site; they preferred a location in West Philadelphia, where it would be possible for the seminary to keep in touch with the University of Pennsylvania. However, they were in time overruled or persuaded otherwise, and in 1887 the board of directors purchased the property for $35,000.[7] It had been owned before the Revolution by William Allen, chief justice of Pennsylvania, after whom Allen's Lane, the street opposite the grounds, was later named. Here he had had his summer home, called Mount Airy, from which the district in which it was located derived its name. Here, near the conjunction of Germantown Avenue and Allen's Lane, the Battle of Germantown had been begun on Oct. 4, 1777. Here in 1807 the Jesuit Francis X. Brosius had opened a school, called Mount Airy Seminary, for the training of children in French. The school seems not to have prospered, for in 1826 it was replaced by the American Classical and Military Lyceum, a school in which several Civil War generals had their preparatory training. This military school was in time followed by the Mount Airy Agricultural Institute, in which, its catalog states, "students are required to devote a portion of each day to the practical operations of the farm, in which sufficient time is spent to insure a familiarity with every branch of husbandry." In 1846 the property was bought by James Gowen, the old Allen house was torn down, and a new residence was built shortly after.[8]

For some years before the seminary purchased it, the estate was unused and neglected. "The trees and bushes," Professor H. E. Jacobs later recalled, "had not been trimmed for years and formed a regular wilderness." A stone

54

The Gowen Mansion as it Appeared about 1889

wall, surmounted by a wooden fence, extended along the length of the Germantown Avenue boundary, and the wooden fence was not removed until 1897. Just inside the fence at the northwestern end of the property was a dilapidated gate house, a small building "evidently occupied in former years," Professor Jacob Fry surmised, "by the gardener." One of the seminary students, Hugo Meyer, was interested in herpetology and at one time kept 400 specimens of snakes there, but the building was torn down about the same time that the fence was removed. The Gowen mansion, which stood back from Germantown Avenue, was more than forty years old when the seminary moved; it was solidly constructed and was surrounded by spacious verandas, as befitted a summer house. There was also a barn on the property, a large and substantial structure.[9] The availability of these buildings for seminary use was a consideration when the property was purchased. Another consideration was the accessibility of the location, within two blocks of stations on the suburban branches of both the Reading and the Pennsylvania Railroads and less than a half-hour in travel time from the center of Philadelphia.[10] Meanwhile, the six acres of ground seemed ample for all conceivable future expansion.[11]

The purchase of the new property, the renovation of the buildings on it, and the necessity of erecting an additional building once again required funds. An appeal was made to the Ministerium of New York for financial assistance. In reply it was said that the New Yorkers were still occupied with collecting money on the endowment of their professorship; "under the circumstances," the synod declared, "it is unfortunately not now possible to gather funds in a systematic way for the seminary building, but it is desired to lay the matter on the hearts of our congregations." This sort of synodical action was of course unproductive. The Ministerium of New York contributed a total of $615.56 in the course of the next ten years.[12] This left the burden of raising $100,000 on the

Ministerium of Pennsylvania. In 1885 the Rev. Reuben Hill, a son-in-law of Charles F. Schaeffer, was appointed financial agent of the seminary. For ten years, until his death in 1895, he was responsible not only for the gathering of funds for the seminary but also for the business management of the school.[13]

When $30,000 was in hand the building of a dormitory on the new site in Mount Airy was undertaken. Built of stone native to its location, the dormitory was constructed in a U-shape, with two wings united by a central structure at the head of a court 37 feet wide by 80 feet deep. The whole building was divided into seven equal compartments, separated by fire-proof walls extending to the roof, and was intended to accommodate 80 students. The overall dimensions

A View of the Dormitory as it Appeared about 1889

were 110 by 108 feet. Chimneys were erected to allow for heating by means of individual stoves in every suite of rooms, but just before completion of the building it was decided to install a furnace for steam heat. In its day the dormitory was a commodious and impressive building, especially in comparison with the accommodations formerly available on Franklin Square. "Like the staid and solid church it represents," wrote Professor H. E. Jacobs, "it makes no effort to attract notice, but stands firm and massive and, with all its plainness, constrains admiration . . . . Every part of the entire structure, from cellar to garret, is a credit to the designer, the Rev. R. Hill, the building committee, the architect, and the builder . . . . As long as the seminary and its fruits shall live, Brother Hill should be held in honor."[14]

With the dormitory completed and the Gowen mansion converted, with a minimum of renovations, for classroom use, the new home of the seminary was dedicated on Oct. 4, 1889,[15] the twenty-fifth anniversary of the founding of the school and the one hundred twelfth anniversary (not then recognized) of the Battle of Germantown. The Rev. George H. Gerberding, an alumnus of the class of 1876, composed a "greeting to the new seminary" on this occasion. Of its thirteen stanzas the first reads:

> School of the prophets, hail!
> Removed to regions fair,
> We greet thee in thy bright, new home,
> Engirt with beauty rare.
> We greet thy buildings all!
> How beautiful they stand!
> Their turrets, walls, foundation stones
> So nobly wrought and planned![16]

When the seminary was moved to Mount Airy in 1889 there were four men on the faculty. During the two remaining years of his active life Professor Mann commuted to the seminary from his home in West Philadelphia. Professor C. W. Schaeffer traveled back and forth from his home in Germantown during the five years of teaching left to him. Professor Spaeth continued to serve as pastor of St. John's Church in Philadelphia, near which he had his residence, for six more years. Professor H. E. Jacobs commuted at first from West Philadelphia, but in 1891 the seminary bought a house for him adjacent to the campus at 7304 Boyer Street.[17] As the only resident professor in the early years at Mount Airy, Jacobs shared with Reuben Hill, who lived nearby on Mount Airy Avenue and was now named superintendent of grounds and buildings, the duties which had formerly been performed by the housefather. However, other members of the faculty soon moved to the campus. In 1895 Professor Spaeth, having turned over most of his pastoral duties to an assistant, moved into a new house next to Professor Jacobs at 7300 Boyer Street; the building was designed by Mrs. Spaeth, who also held a mortgage on it for $9,500.[18] The following year two identical houses were built on the campus opposite the dormitory. A gift of $30,000 from Miss Elizabeth Schaeffer, member of the Church of the Holy Communion in Philadelphia, made it possible to erect these buildings and cancel the debt on the Spaeth house. Professor Jacobs was moved into one of the "Schaeffer memorial houses," and Professor Jacob Fry, who had been elected to fill the vacancy created by Mann's retirement, occupied the other. Professor George F. Spieker, who succeeded C. W. Schaeffer, lived in the house on Boyer Street vacated by H. E. Jacobs.[19] The removal of the seminary to Mount Airy therefore led gradually to a resident faculty of full-time professors.

The removal required other changes. As in the last years on Franklin Square, so during the first decades in Mount Airy, the seminary made no provision for the boarding of students. Since there were no restaurants, as there had been in the city, students were compelled to get their meals in boarding houses. An attempt in 1894 to form a boarding club and take over the Mount Pleasant House, a few blocks away, proved to be impracticable, and so students continued to scatter at mealtime among more or less hospitable homes in the neighborhood, where they paid for their meals by the week. The "White Swan," on Germantown Avenue, near Mount Airy Avenue, sometimes dispensed alcoholic beverages, but the disciplinary records of the seminary suggest that indiscreet drinking was left behind on Franklin Square. Only once did the faculty find it necessary to call attention to "the impropriety of and evil results from students' visiting saloons," although even in this case it was expressly mentioned that there had been no misconduct.[20] It deserves to be remarked that there was a change not only in the environment but also in the attitude of most members of the faculty.

The removal of the seminary from the center of the city also made it more difficult for students, to say nothing of the families of faculty members, to participate in the life and worship of a congregation. The nearest Lutheran church was St. Michael's in Germantown, almost a mile away. In those days the existing horse cars on Germantown Avenue did not travel so far north as the seminary, and it was consequently necessary to go to St. Michael's on foot in all kinds of weather. Such conditions led in 1893 to the formation of the Mount Airy Lutheran Mission Society, the introduction of regular Sunday services, and the organization of a Sunday school. In addition to faculty families and students, Lutheran families of the neighborhood participated. Services were conducted in the seminary's chapel on the first floor of the Gowen mansion. Professor H. E. Jacobs and the Rev. Reuben Hill at first shared pastoral responsibilities. In 1895 the people who were worshiping together formally organized a congregation and chose the name Lutheran Church of the Ascension. The following year the Rev. Jacob Fry,

The Chapel in a Room on the Main Floor of the Gowen Mansion

who had for five years been dividing his time between his pastorate in Trinity Church in Reading, Pa., and his teaching in the Philadelphia Seminary, was called as "provisional pastor" and continued in this position until his death twenty-four years later.[21]

By 1898 the small chapel in the Gowen mansion had been outgrown. The only larger space then available was in the old barn, just east of the dormitory, where the library and tennis courts were afterwards located. This was described as "a very substantial building with massive stone walls." The students used it as a gymnasium. A glee club had been organized among the students to sing for church societies, and the $700 raised in this way had been used to throw a floor across the second story of the barn, build interior stairways, and provide window openings. The hall or auditorium on the second floor was large enough to seat 250 persons, and it was used occasionally for special lectures. This hall in the barn was converted into a chapel in 1898, and Professor H. E. Jacobs nicknamed it "St. Barnabas." With some assistance from the Alumni Association, heat and gas light were introduced into the building. Other renovations were made to convert the first floor into reading rooms as well as a recreation room equipped with gymnasium apparatus. Here, according to the Catalog of 1894-95, students had "ample facilities for exercise in inclement weather and a large hall for social purposes at annual reunions." For five years the second floor of the old barn served as a chapel for the seminary and for the Church of the Ascension. Meanwhile the room in the Gowen mansion which had before served as a chapel was converted into a much needed additional classroom and furnished as such by the widow of the Rev. Reuben Hill in memory of her husband,[22] and more than a generation of students knew it as the "Hill Memorial Room."

The Barn when Converted into a Chapel and Assembly Hall

The seminary did not long use the converted barn for its chapel. In 1903, after years of planning and negotiating, the Rev. William Ashmead Schaeffer, missionary superintendent of the Ministerium of Pennsylvania, and his sister Miss Kate Schaeffer made a gift to the seminary of a fully furnished church edifice with an attached parish house. Since the building was intended to be a memorial to the parents of the donors, the late Professor Charles W. Schaeffer and his wife Elizabeth Ashmead Schaeffer, it was stipulated that it be called the Schaeffer-Ashmead Memorial Church. It was erected on the southwest corner of the campus, facing Germantown Avenue. The donor provided: "The congregation known as the Church of the Ascension . . . is to have the free use of the said memorial church on Sundays for English services and for Sunday school, on festival days whenever it may so desire, and also at such other times as the church may not be needed for service in connection with the seminary and its students."

The Schaeffer-Ashmead Memorial Chapel

This privilege was granted for fifteen years, subject to renewal, on condition that the congregation would pay "at least two-thirds of the cost of janitor's services, light, and heat and an equitable portion of the expense of necessary repairs or alteration to the building." After his death the congregation erected a bronze tablet in memory of William Ashmead Schaeffer in gratitude for "his noble gift to the seminary."[23]

Since the removal of the seminary to Mount Airy, students continued to assemble for morning prayers five days a week. Instead of conducting the exercises "half in English and half in German," as was before customary, the exercises were now required to be all in English or all in German. Moreover, in place of the informal "family prayers" which had been observed on Franklin Square, in 1889 Professor H. E. Jacobs, as the housefather, introduced Matins according to the new Common Service. He asserted that there were two purposes for morning worship in the seminary: "(1) Our private edification as Christians. (2) The liturgical cultivation of the students as those who are in future to conduct the public worship of the church." There was a great deal of experimenting as to the time of common worship. Matins were held at 8:30 a.m., then 10 a.m., then 9:30 a.m., then 8:30 a.m. On some days Vespers were substituted for Matins. In some years Vespers were conducted daily at 4 p.m., 6 p.m., or 7 p.m. It is clear that difficulty was experienced in arranging a chapel program that was satisfactory to all with respect to content and convenience. The bylaws adopted by the board of directors in 1894 not only provided that the faculty "may make provisions for public services in the seminary chapel, so far as deemed desirable, in English and German," but added, "The Holy Communion may also, at proper times, be administered in connection with these services." Actually the first recorded Communion service was on Ash Wednesday, 1890, when no other Lutheran service was readily accessible to those on the campus. The following year flagon, paten, and chalice were presented to the seminary by St. Mark's Church in Philadelphia, and it was decided by the faculty to have one Communion a year, alternately in English and German. This remained the practice for about twenty years.[24] The Rev. Gomer C. Rees was appointed "musical director for all seminary services" in 1900 and continued to give some time to this until 1909.[25]

The construction of the Ashmead-Schaeffer Chapel was soon followed by the building of a library. When the seminary was relocated in Mount Airy the existing collection of about 20,000 volumes was placed in the rooms on the top floor of the Gowen mansion. It required several years for students, who were employed under the direction of Professor H. E. Jacobs, to arrange the books in some kind of order. Modest funds were provided by the board of directors and by the Ministerium of Pennsylvania to employ a student librarian, repair old books, and buy some new ones. The private library of Professor Mann was given to the seminary on his death, and the archives of the Ministerium of Pennsylvania, of which he had long been curator, were moved to the seminary two years before, in 1890. Not only was the increasingly valuable collection of books located in inconvenient and cramped quarters, however, but it was subject to the hazards of fire and the deteriorating effects of intense heat in summer. Accordingly there were frequent suggestions from the faculty that a more suitable building be provided.[26]

The board of directors finally agreed to attempt to raise $30,000 for a library building and engaged an architect to make plans for it. About this time the attention of Professor H. E. Jacobs was called to an item in a newspaper which reported that Mr. B. Frank Weyman (1842-1919), a manufacturer of tobacco products in Pittsburgh and holder of the patent for "Copenhagen" snuff, had sold his business for a reputed $3,000,000. Personally acquainted with Mr.

The Krauth Memorial Library

Weyman and knowing him to be an active and benevolently disposed member of First Lutheran Church in Pittsburgh, Professor Jacobs wrote to him in the hope of enlisting his financial support for the proposed library building. Mr. Weyman's initial response was negative. Later he decided to give $10,000. After further urging he offered $50,000. In January, 1906, Jacobs reported that he had received "a communication from a friend of the seminary (who does not desire his name to be known), offering $50,000 for the erection of a library building on the seminary grounds to be known as the Krauth Memorial Library." Three conditions were attached to the gift: that the donor's name should not be revealed, that the library should be a memorial to a former pastor of his, the late Charles Porterfield Krauth, and that the Rev. Luther D. Reed should serve as his representative in the planning of the building. When the scope of the project was enlarged, an additional gift of $50,000 was made by the "generous donor," as Mr. Weyman was uniformly referred to in board and faculty minutes in order to shield his identity.[27]

The Krauth Memorial Library was completed in 1908, twenty-five years after the death of the man it honored. It was located at the southeastern end of the existing campus (the barn was razed to make room for it) and was described as "a handsome specimen of collegiate Gothic architecture, built of local stone with Indiana limestone tracery and trimmings, in the form of a great cross 132 feet in length and 92 feet in width, with a massive central tower." It was believed that with its space for an estimated 90,000 volumes it would "amply provide for the present and the remote future requirements of the seminary and the church." Two spacious vault rooms were provided to contain rare books and archives. But more was obviously needed than a building and its furnishings. In 1906 the Rev. Luther D. Reed had been appointed director of the library, and for a half-dozen years the "generous donor" paid his salary and contributed several thousand dollars to library maintenance. Before 1912 the director raised an additional $30,000 by solicitation in person or by mail among alumni and interested laymen. Miss Mary E. Kaighn, who had been working in the Library of Congress, was employed in 1907 "to take charge of the technical work of cataloging" and collaborated with the director in making a new classification scheme. On this basis the work of cataloging about 30,000 books was begun; it took at least three years to complete the task with the assistance of three temporarily employed catalogers.[28] The library was thus made ready for more fruitful use in the succeeding period of the seminary's history.

For many years it had seemed desirable to have a central heating plant. The building of the library offered an opportune time to realize this hope. In 1907 the board of directors accordingly authorized the erection of a "steam heating plant" and the installation of the necessary connections with the dormitory, lecture hall, chapel, library, and four professors' residences. A loan was secured for $9,000 of the total cost of $14,000. The Rev. John J. Heischmann, of Brooklyn, N. Y., who vividly recalled how he suffered in the poorly heated seminary building on Franklin Square when he was a student, promptly raised $1,200 for this worthy purpose.[29] In 1893 Mr. George Pehlman succeeded Adam Klinger as janitor, became the licensed engineer of the heating plant, and served the seminary almost until his death in 1961.[30] Shortly after the seminary was located in Mount Airy it was found desirable to place several lights on posts for illumination of roads and walks at night. These were originally gasoline lamps. In 1912 they were changed to oil lamps, although the introduction of electricity soon followed.[31] In 1890 a bell was presented to the seminary by the Rev. C. N. Conrad, of Rochester, N. Y., and it was rung in early years at 6 a.m. and 11 p.m. Neighbors found this disturbing. For example, Mr. Warren G. Griffith, a lawyer, wrote to Professor Jacobs: "I am compelled on behalf of myself and neighbors living on Mt. Airy Avenue, to ask you to give us some relief from the annoyance caused by the ringing of the seminary bell. It may be well for the young men of the seminary to be aroused at 6 a.m. and earlier, but we who are not accustomed to rise so early find it very disagreeable to be disturbed at that hour." The ringing of the bell was discontinued.[32] It may be added that there was mention of a tennis court as early as 1904.[33]

During these years in which additions and improvements were being made in the seminary's physical plant, its relations with the Ministerium of New York were deteriorating. That synod had undertaken in 1872 to establish a German professorship in the Philadelphia Seminary and to raise $30,000 in order to endow it. Until this sum might be raised it was decided to pay $2,000 a year to the incumbent as salary, and in return for this the Ministerium of New York was granted representation on the seminary's board of directors. The Rev. Adolph Spaeth, of Philadelphia, was nominated by the synod in New York as its professor and was duly elected in 1873 by the Ministerium of Pennsylvania. Again and again in subsequent years the Ministerium of New York resolved to raise money to complete its endowment, but it managed to raise only $7,000 by 1889. It also defaulted on its payments of Professor Spaeth's salary, for between 1889 and 1895 he received an average of $956 a year.[34] This was no financial hardship for Professor Spaeth as long as he remained in his parish and received the salary of a pastor in addition. But when he determined to devote his full time and strength to his teaching, he resigned the New York professorship in 1894 after serving for twenty-one years and was elected instead to a professorship of the Ministerium of Pennsylvania. The failure of the New York Ministerium to raise the money it pledged may be accounted for in part by a want of unanimity in sentiment. Already in 1883 its commitment to the Philadelphia Seminary was hedged about with a reservation: "It is hereby expressly declared that, although our professorship is at present located in the theological seminary at Philadelphia, the synod nevertheless reserves the right, if important reasons make such a change appear advisable, to remove the professorship to another institution and use the interest, from the money gathered, in the same way as before."[35] Representatives of the synod declared that they were embarrassed to serve on the board of directors when their synod's obligations were so flagrantly neglected.[36]

When Professor Spaeth presented his resignation to the Ministerium of New York, that body proceeded to nominate as his successor the Rev. John A. Dewald, of New Brunswick, N. J., with the understanding that he should teach only two days a week by commuting to Philadelphia.[37] It was suspected by some that Dewald was chosen because he would not expect to receive the full salary, and accordingly the financial pressure on the synod would be relieved. However this may be, the seminary faculty opposed his election on the ground that he was more a pedant than a scholar and because, as a native German, he had little acquaintance with American church conditions.[38] In an attempt to forestall his election by testing his ability as a teacher, the faculty invited Dewald to deliver a series of lectures at the seminary on the Old Testament. The lectures proved to be unsatisfactory even to the most favorably disposed students, and the faculty declared that, "in view of the practical requirements of the seminary, we are not prepared to recommend the endorsement of the nomination" to the Ministerium of Pennsylvania.[39] This synod, according to the by-laws, had to elect the professor upon nomination by the Ministerium of New York. The board of directors endorsed Dewald's nomination by a close vote in order to throw the onus of his rejection on the Ministerium of Pennsylvania rather than on the seminary, and the synod complied by defeating the candidate by a vote of 125 to 110. The New York delegate, the Rev. A. Richter, who attended the meeting of the Ministerium of Pennsylvania in 1897, described what happened in this way: "The synod demanded information concerning the reason for the strong opposition [to Dewald in the board]. It emerged from the discussion that even those who had voted for Pastor Dewald in order to prevent a break with New York as a result of a rejection of its nominee did not regard him as suitable for the seminary professorship. Although it was acknowledged that he is a man of unimpeachable character and unquestionable knowledge, the chief objection to him that was mentioned was his inadequate mastery of the English language. Besides, it was deemed dubious whether he had sufficient skill to teach in the seminary in Mount Airy, however adequate his skill may have been in his home in New Brunswick, where in former years he prepared a number of students for the ministry."[40]

The members of the Ministerium of New York were offended by the rejection of their candidate. They expressed their confidence in Dewald, and action on a motion to dissolve the synod's relation with the Philadelphia Seminary was narrowly averted. It was decided not to nominate another candidate "for the present," and for twelve years the professorship remained unoccupied. During the first six of these years the Ministerium of New York was not represented on the seminary's board of directors. Additions were made to the endowment of the professorship, but when it was discovered that the synod's treasurer in 1876 and 1877 had misappropriated some money due to Professor Spaeth, this amount was paid with interest. Spaeth returned the $2,300 to the synod for liquidation of a debt resting on Wagner College, and this was calculated to appease ruffled feelings. An abortive attempt was made to divert the endowment of the theological professorship to Wagner College, but during all these trials the Philadelphia Seminary had a uniformly warm friend and influential supporter in the Ministerium of New York in the person of the Rev. George C. F. Haas, son of the instructor in music in the early years of the seminary on Franklin Square.[41]

Part of the friction between the Ministerium of New York and the Philadelphia Seminary involved displeasure with what was regarded as neglect of the German language in the seminary. Unlike the Ministerium of Pennsylvania, which was bilingual and became increasingly English-speaking between 1889 and 1910, the Ministerium of New York preserved its German character because English-speaking ministers and congregations were constantly being siphoned off into other synods on its territory. As a consequence this synod was especially concerned about the education of ministers who would be able to preach in German. It was reported in 1882 that twelve of the thirteen members of the graduating class in the Philadelphia Seminary had a knowledge of German. However, some of these, it was said, "do not have such mastery of German as is required of a minister in a German congregation. For this shortcoming the seminary is less responsible than the preparatory schools. The seminary cannot concern itself with grammar and elementary exercises. These are the tasks of preparatory schools."[42] With this conviction Wagner College was founded in Rochester, N. Y., the next year as a "Lutheran Pro-seminary."[43] It was not until 1917, when it was removed to Staten Island, N. Y., that Wagner became a four-year college.

The demand for German-speaking ministers was not limited to the territory of the Ministerium of New York. The influx of immigrants from Germany and from other lands in which German was spoken preserved the lives of many German congregations on the entire eastern seaboard and led to the founding of new ones in the middle and far West of the United States and Canada. Since 1881 *Der Siloah* was published regularly to promote the interests of the General Council's board of German home missions. Within a period of five years fifty German-speaking ministers were placed in mission congregations. Those who were acquainted with the situation were "profoundly impressed with the vastness of the work" and also with "the inadequacy of the men and means at present at our command" to supply German-speaking as well as English-speaking people with the bread of life.[44] The Philadelphia Seminary made a contribution toward meeting the need, for 17 out of 161 graduates in the eight years from 1889 to 1897 were able to preach in German and 58 more were equipped in some measure to preach in German or "Pennsylvania Dutch" as well as in English. In 1910, it was reported, 50 out of 52 students would be able to preach in English, 22 would be able to preach in German "with various degrees of excellence," and 1 each would have the linguistic ability to preach in Slovak, Swedish, Danish, and Norwegian.[45]

Since the demand for German-speaking ministers could not be met in this way, the General Council instructed its board of German home missions in 1881 "to consider whether any connection with educational institutions in Europe" might be helpful. In 1883 the board entered into an informal relation with Ebenezer Lutheran Seminary in Kropp, Schleswig, which had been founded the previous year by the Rev. Johannes Paulsen (1847-1916) with the express purpose of educating German ministers for service in America. Modest financial contributions were sent to Germany, but it was largely with its own funds that Kropp trained and sent candidates for ordination to America. In 1887 the faculty of the Philadelphia Seminary reached an agreement with Pastor Paulsen that his graduates should spend an additional year in Philadelphia in order to become better acquainted with American conditions before entering upon their parish duties in a strange land.[46] Unfortunately this agreement was misinterpreted or misunderstood. Some Kroppers took it to imply that their training was inferior, which was not intended. On the other hand, they were enrolled as hospitants (defined as students who "fail to pursue all the branches studied by their class")[47] and were often made to feel unwelcome. When German ministers (some of them Kropp graduates and others not) championed the cause of Johannes Paulsen and the Kropp Seminary, a bitter controversy ensued. The Rev. Frederick Wischan, of Philadelphia, and the Rev. J. J. Kuendig, of Reading, Pa., wrote critically of the Philadelphia Seminary in the *Lutherisches Kirchenblatt,* and the Rev. G. A. Hinterleitner, of Pottsville, Pa., put out a polemical sheet called *Kelle und Schwert.* Professor H. E. Jacobs responded in a series of articles in *The Lutheran.* In 1898 the faculty ordered the *Kirchenblatt* excluded from the seminary reading room "because of its frequent attacks on the seminary." In

Johannes Paulsen, Founder and
Director of the Kropp Seminary

1903 Wischan was formally rebuked by the Alumni Association "because he has often publicly cast dishonor upon our alma mater and has unfairly and unjustly attacked its professors." In 1905 the Ministerium of New York protested in German against Professor H. E. Jacobs' slurring remarks about Kropp graduates, and he did not help matters when he refused to reply to the complaint "unless the correspondence be entirely in English."[48]

The "Kropp Controversy" extended over more than twenty years, and neither side was blameless. By 1930, when the seminary in Kropp ended its career, more than two hundred ministers had been sent to America, and they contributed to the growth and prosperity of the Lutheran Church in the United States and Canada.[49] However, the insistence with which some of these men promoted the German language was more romantic than realistic in the changing conditions. As late as 1909 a complaint was received from St. Paul's German Church in Philadelphia that the seminary had departed from its original charter by not according equal emphasis to German and English. The faculty replied that "if there was less German instruction, it was because so few students came from German congregations or understood that language."[50] Meanwhile there was a small minority in the Ministerium of New York that proposed the establishment of a German seminary in connection with Wagner College.[51]

Difference in language played the major role in the formation of still another synod on the territory of the Ministerium of New York. English-speaking congregations had withdrawn from that body in 1867 to form the New York Synod.

Since that time additional congregations became English-speaking or, in some instances, were organized by English-speaking people. In 1895 fifteen of these congregations formed an English conference within the Ministerium of New York, and in 1902 this conference withdrew amicably from its parent body to form the Synod of New York and New England.[52] In view of this the board of directors of the Philadelphia Seminary requested the Ministerium of Pennsylvania "to invite certain synods, from whose members important contributions have been made to the endowment and support of this seminary, to elect such persons as they may choose to serve as their representatives in this board of directors, namely, one clergyman and one layman from the Ministerium of New York, one clergyman and one layman from the Pittsburgh Synod, and one clergyman and one layman from the recently organized Synod of New York and New England, on condition of the continuance of their interest in and support of this institution . . . . This would . . . give to this seminary more of the general and representative character originally intended in its organization." The Ministerium of New York accepted the "friendly invitation" in 1903 and thus resumed a relationship which had been interrupted for six years. The Pittsburgh Synod, which had long been sending its students to Philadelphia but which had never had a formal relation to the seminary, "availed itself of the privilege." The new Synod of New York and New England "unanimously accepted" the invitation.[53]

Although the Ministerium of Pennsylvania, which had been bearing most of the burden of maintaining the seminary, reserved for itself thirty of the thirty-six seats on the board of directors, the way was now opened for a more fruitful cooperation of the synods in the future. The Rev. Joseph A. Seiss, who had served as president of the board for almost forty years, died in 1904. He was succeeded by the Rev. G. F. Krotel and by the Rev. Mahlon C. Horine. Together these men served for four years and were succeeded in 1908 by the Rev. Theodore E. Schmauk.[54] Other leading members of the board during these years were the Rev. Samuel Laird, of Philadelphia, the Rev. Philip Pfatteicher, of Easton, Pa., and the Rev. Oliver P. Smith, of Pottstown, Pa., each of whom served more than a quarter of a century. Among the laymen were Dr. Samuel P. Sadtler, professor of Chemistry in the University of Pennsylvania, who served for forty years; Judge William H. Staake, of Philadelphia, who served a total of thirty years; Mr. E. Augustus Miller, Philadelphia lawyer, who served for twenty-five years; Mr. W. Frederick Monroe, Philadelphia shoe manufacturer, and the Hon. Jacob A. Geissenhainer, of New York, both of whom served about the same length of time.

Several noteworthy gifts and bequests were received by the seminary in the first two decades in Mount Airy. In 1891 a scholarship fund was established by the deceased wife of Professor L. M. Haupt, of the University of Pennsylvania, in memory of her father, the Rev. Benjamin Keller. The endowment was expected to produce $200 interest a year, and this was to be applied to the assistance of worthy students who would be able to preach in English, with preference given to "worthy sons of needy ministers." The conditions of the scholarship also stipulated: "Anyone addicted to the use of tobacco or intoxicants shall be denied or deprived of the benefits."[55] In 1895 the will of Mr. Samuel Lentz, of St. John's German Church in Philadelphia, left the seminary about $5,000 for the support of needy students planning to preach in German.[56] In 1896 the seminary received just short of $54,000 from the estate of Mr. Henry Singmaster and his wife Rosanna, of Stroudsburg, Pa., an equal amount being received by the Gettysburg Seminary.[57] The same year the seminary benefited from a legacy of Mr. Isaac Fegley, a member of the board of directors for a dozen years, to the extent of $10,000.[58] In connection with the 150th anniversary in 1898 of the founding of the Ministerium of Pennsylvania, a jubilee appeal for $150,000 was made, a sixth of the proceeds to go into the synod's treasury and the remaining five-

66

sixths to be divided between the Philadelphia Seminary and Muhlenberg College. For reasons which are not now apparent, less than half of the goal was realized, and the benefit to the seminary was limited.[59]

The enrollment of students in the seminary always fluctuated to some extent. On the whole, however, the gradual increase in the number of students on Franklin Square continued in the new location in Mount Airy during the first decade, at the end of which attendance reached a high of 92 students. From 1900 to 1910 enrollment declined to a low of 43 students in 1907 and 55 in 1910. Some reasons for this decline might be suggested. The strengthening of the Southern Seminary in Columbia, S. C., and the gradual growth of the Chicago Seminary (founded in 1891) caused students who might before have gone to Philadelphia to turn to schools nearer home. However, the decline was too large to account for in this way. The rule adopted by the Augustana Synod in 1899, requiring students of the synod to attend its own seminary in Rock Island, Ill.,[60] also affected too few to be of significance. The fact of the matter is that the decline in enrollment was common to all Protestant seminaries in America. The explanations attempted at the time — the growth of materialism in American life, the neglect of the humanities, the greater attraction of other professions, etc.,[61] — proved to be inadequate in the light of the later upsurge in enrollment. It is doubtful whether a full and satisfactory explanation can be given for the decline in the number of students in the first decade of the twentieth century.

As before, the largest numbers of students received their preparatory education in church-related colleges: Muhlenberg (161), Wagner (80), Thiel (36), Roanoke (25), Gettysburg (4), Lenoir-Rhyne (3), Wittenberg (2), Wartburg (2), and such additional Lutheran colleges as Augsburg, Augustana, Bethany, Capital, Luther, St. Olaf, and Susquehanna. Other eastern schools from which students came were Lafayette College (8), University of Pennsylvania (6), Columbia University (2), and Johns Hopkins University (1). Most students came from Pennsylvania, New York, New England, and New Jersey, but there were others from Maryland, Virginia, North and South Carolina, Tennessee, Ohio, Illinois, Iowa, Wisconsin, California, and Ontario.

For a while entering students were required to write a brief spiritual autobiography, and an experiment was made with a sort of qualifying examination. The following six questions had to be answered in writing by students who entered the seminary in September, 1897: "(1) Translate the original Greek of I Cor. 13:13, Gal. 6:18, and the Lord's Prayer as given in Matthew and Luke, showing their differences especially in the fourth petition. (2) Translate a [designated] paragraph of Latin from St. Augustine. (3) State briefly the principal events in the history of Israel from the Exodus to the destruction of Jerusalem, 588 B.C. (4) Give the chief cities and countries in which the Gospel was preached and churches founded by St. Paul. (5) In what sense can it be said that the Roman Empire aided the cause of Christianity. (6) Write out from memory Luther's explanation of the second article of the Creed as given in his Catechism." Of interest in these questions is the assumption that students would come with a knowledge of Latin and Greek as well as of Bible history. To be sure, the faculty found the answers "in many instances very unsatisfactory," and this was probably the major reason for discontinuing the examination after 1903.[62]

That some students had special linguistic equipment is attested by the fact that in 1893 Professor C. W. Schaeffer was congratulated on his eightieth birthday in English, German, Norwegian, Icelandic, Russian, and Polish.[63] While most of the students were preparing to be clergymen, the charter of the seminary was not interpreted so literally as to exclude other qualified individuals who, by way of exception, attended selected classes as auditors.[64] Now, as earlier, regular students who had been admitted to the seminary were, in accordance with wide-spread academic practice at the time, "matriculated" in the presence of the faculty "at the end of four months' probation."[65]

In order to protect students from being distracted unduly from their studies, strict regulations were adopted concerning their participation in what later came to be called field work. Juniors and Middlers were forbidden to preach during the academic year, except in very extraordinary circumstances, and then only with permission of the faculty. Seniors were permitted to preach, but never oftener than once in four weeks, and then only if this did not require the preparation of a new sermon each time. Students were permitted to assist occasionally in the administration of the Lord's Supper, "the number of communicants being large." Such regulations as these were repeatedly brought to the attention of students, ministers, and synods. There were also repeated complaints by the faculty that pressure was put on students by pastors and congregations to violate the rules, that students received too many requests to preach, that too many students were drawn away from their studies by calls from mission boards, etc. The extent of actual student participation in church work by the close of this period is indicated in a report in 1909 that during the preceding academic year students had preached 1,012 sermons, made 145 addresses, made 108 hospital and 21 prison visits, engaged in settlement work 67 evenings, devoted 45 hours to catechetical instruction, taught 254 hours in Sunday schools, and made 15 private sick calls.[66]

The rigid regulations which had governed student life on Franklin Square were relaxed in Mount Airy. On the one hand the environment was altered, and on the other hand it was now felt that the former rules were too restrictive for adult students. Although a bell was at first rung at 6 a.m. and 11 p.m. to indicate the time to rise and retire, this practice, as has already been noted, was soon abandoned when neighbors complained. The earlier practice of locking doors of the dormitory at 11 p.m. was also given up, and students were no longer subject to inquisition if they returned to the seminary after that hour. Since the removal to Mount Airy, students were required to pay what was called a "contingent fee" of $10, and then $20, "for a suite of rooms." A committee of ladies inspected dormitory rooms at least once a year, and in 1898, on its recommendation, the seminary began to furnish bed linens "so as to secure regular changes in their use." A student who married during the academic year without permission was subject to dismissal, and one student who broke his engagement to marry was cited to appear before the faculty "to show cause why he should be continued as a student." As a matter of fact, marriage before graduation was exceptional; only a half-dozen students were married while in the seminary between 1889 and 1910. The faculty also looked askance at some kinds of summer employment in which students engaged. For example, a student was advised not to work as a street car conductor on the ground that "the requirement to serve in that capacity on Sunday would be inconsistent with his position as a theological student and future minister." There were restrictions on recreation insofar as it interfered with the study of others. Mention has been made of a gymnasium in the old barn. In good weather students played on the "lawns," and they competed in baseball and tennis with students of the Philadelphia Divinity School (Episcopal).[67]

Before the removal of the seminary to Mount Airy the students were examined orally at the close of the year by members of the faculty in the presence of the entire board of directors. This practice was modified in 1889 to the extent that only a committee of the board sat in on the annual oral examinations. From 1904 to 1914 theses required of Seniors for graduation were read by the board's committee as a substitute for the oral examinations, and in 1914 the board of directors gladly relinquished all responsibility in this area. When the seminary was located on Franklin Square, commencement exercises were held in one or another of the city churches with a minister as speaker. After the removal to Mount Airy, commencement exercises were held in St. Michael's Church in Germantown, and in order to give the exercises an academic character it was decided in 1892 to substitute short speeches by a half-dozen Seniors for what had before turned out to be a sermon by the invited minister. This was not popular with the graduating classes, and in 1905 the faculty returned to the practice of inviting a prominent clergyman to deliver a commencement address. These exercises were always held in the evening until 1912. Public exercises were also held annually on a Thursday in October (called Seminary Day) from 1894 until their discontinuance in 1941 to commemorate the founding of the seminary on Oct. 4, 1864.[68]

The names of some of the alumni in this period came to be prominently associated in one way or another with the later history of the church. Only a few can here be singled out. I. Chantry Hoffman came to be identified for a generation with the domestic mission enterprise. John A. Morehead distinguished himself as executive secretary of the National Lutheran Council. Walton H. Greever founded the *American Lutheran Survey* and became the second secretary of the United Lutheran Church in America. Frederic Sutter was pastor of a congregation in New York City for almost sixty years and president of the board of trustees of Wagner College for fifty years. Paul Zeller Strodach achieved recognition as a liturgiologist, and Ernst W. Neudoerffer was one member of a noted family of foreign missionaries. John W. Horine, L. Franklin Gruber, and John C. Mattes taught theology in Columbia, S. C., Chicago, Ill., and Dubuque, Iowa, respectively. Frank N. D. Buchman became the leader of the Oxford Group Movement, later called Moral Re-Armament.

Now, as before, members of the faculty attended the meetings of the board of directors and submitted oral, and later written, reports of their work. The faculty also continued to elect its own officers. When Professor C. W. Schaeffer died in 1896, therefore, his colleagues chose Professor Spaeth to be chairman of the faculty, and he was re-elected annually until his death in 1910. The routine administration of the seminary, however, fell increasingly into the hands of Professor H. E. Jacobs. As the only resident professor when the seminary first moved to Mount Airy, he was asked to serve as housefather, and for his additional services he demanded and received a salary which was 10% higher than that of his colleagues. In 1894 the board of directors appointed him as the first dean, and thus he was made the executive officer of the seminary. As symbols of his office the board of directors installed a telephone in his home in 1903 and authorized him in 1904 to purchase a mimeograph or similar apparatus, but did not provide him with a secretary.[69]

From 1889 to 1910 the faculty consisted of only four men. Professors Mann and C. W. Schaeffer did not long survive the removal to Mount Airy. Including the men who replaced them, the faculty during these two decades included, in the order of their seniority, Professors Adolph Spaeth, Henry E. Jacobs, Jacob Fry, and George F. Spieker. A review of the careers of these men will enable us to catch a glimpse of the theology of the Philadelphia Seminary in this period.

Adolph Spaeth,[70] the oldest child of a surgeon, was born in 1839 in Esslingen, Württemberg, and studied in Tübingen University, where Professor Mann had studied before him. He served as vicar in a village church near his home and then became tutor in a noble family in Scotland, where he first learned to speak English. In 1864 he received a call to Philadelphia to be assistant pastor, under Professor Mann, in St. Michael's and Zion Church. After three years in this position he was called as pastor of St. John's German Church and served the

Faculty in 1895. Seated, left to right: Adolph Spaeth, Charles W. Schaeffer, Henry E. Jacobs. Standing: George F. Spieker and Jacob Fry

congregation until his death forty-three years later (1867-1910). He was an active participant in the life of the church at large, for he was president of the General Council for eight years, assumed leadership in its foreign mission work for decades, was an ardent supporter of the female diaconate, and had his hand in all liturgical and hymnological developments of his time. He contributed extensively to various German and English church papers and wrote many articles for encyclopedias in Germany and America. An impression of his power as a preacher can be gained from his *Saatkörner* (1893), a collection of homiletical sketches on lessons of the church year which primed the pump for many a later preacher. His consuming interest in the history of the church is reflected in his German biography of his colleague, *Wilhelm Julius Mann* (1895), the definitive English biography of his father-in-law, *Charles Porterfield Krauth* (2 vols., 1898, 1909), and the *Documentary History of the Lutheran Ministerium of Pennsylvania, 1748-1821* (1898), of which he was co-editor. In the major field of his teaching he published, apart from many articles, only the *Annotations on the Gospel according to John* (1896). In 1875 he received the degree of D.D. from the University of Pennsylvania, and in 1896 the degree of LL.D. was awarded to him by Muhlenberg College.

Spaeth was a professor in the seminary from 1873 to his death in 1910, and so the whole span of his teaching covered thirty-seven years. Throughout this period he divided his time between his parish and the seminary. He scheduled his classes from 8 o'clock to 10 o'clock in the morning so as to be free the rest of the day for his parish duties and his studies. After 1893, when he secured an assistant in his parish, and especially after 1895, when he moved to Mount Airy, he had more time for the seminary, although he still did not give his whole time and energy to teaching. His major assignment was the New Testament, and he gave courses in Introduction, Hermeneutics, and Exegesis of the New Testament as well as a course which was an exegetical and homiletical treatment of the appointed lessons of the church year. Spaeth's interpretation of the New Testament tended to be traditional, and for the most part he did not acquaint his students with the ferment which was then going on in biblical studies. By temperament he was a romanticist, and this was evident not only in his adherence to older biblical views but also in his predilection for the archaic in hymnody, music, and liturgy. He invited German-speaking students to his home for occasional liturgical exercises and for readings in Luther's works, and those who participated in these classes became acquainted with the breadth of their professor's culture and the force of his personality. Most of his students were kept at a distance by his aristocratic bearing. In his regular classes he dictated in formal fashion, first in German and then in English. Those who understood German found no help in the repetition in another language, and those who understood only English were bored during the first half of the hour.

In addition to Adolph Spaeth, a second man who taught in the seminary throughout this period was Henry Eyster Jacobs.[71] He was born in 1844 in Gettysburg, Pa., when his father was professor of Mathematics and Natural Science in Gettysburg (then called Pennsylvania) College. The son was graduated from both the college and the seminary in Gettysburg. After tutoring in the college, serving as home missionary for a year in Pittsburgh, and spending two years as principal of Thiel Hall in Monaco, Pa., he returned to Gettysburg College and taught Latin, Greek, and History for thirteen years. During these years he continued his interest in theology. Like others of his contemporaries he believed that he might discover what Lutheranism really is by studying the writings of the dogmaticians of the seventeenth century, and he entered upon a systematic reading of their thick Latin tomes. This interest led quite naturally to his translation of Leonard Hutter's *Compend of Lutheran Theology* (1868, with G. F. Spieker), H. F. Schmid's *Doctrinal Theology of the Evangelical Lutheran Church* (1876, with C. A. Hay), and *The Book of Concord, with Historical Appendixes* (2 vols., 1882, 1883). These translations gave him a reputation which led to his call to the Philadelphia Seminary as the successor of Charles Porterfield Krauth. While he was professor in Philadelphia, he wrote several hundred articles for church journals and encyclopedias. Many of his books showed the historical cast of his mind: *The Lutheran Movement in England* (1890), which pursued an inquiry begun years before by Krauth; *History of the Evangelical Lutheran Church in the United States* (1893), in the "American Church History" series; *Martin Luther* (1898), a biography which also made use of materials gathered by Krauth; *The German Emigration to America, 1709-1740* (1899); and *The Lutheran Cyclopedia* (1899), edited with J. A. W. Haas. In the biblical field he translated Meyer's *Commentary on Ephesians and Galatians* (1884) and *Revelation* (1887) and prepared *Annotations on the Epistle of Paul to the Romans* (1895). In the field of systematic theology he published *Elements of Religion* (1894) and *A Summary of the Christian Faith* (1907). Most of his literary production was concentrated in the last decade of the nineteenth century. Thiel College conferred on him the degree of D.D. in 1877 and of LL.D. in 1892, and he received the degree of S.T.D. from Muhlenberg College in 1907.

Jacobs took a quiet but active part in the life of the church. When in his early years the General Council had considered the establishment of a seminary in Chicago, he had been proposed as professor.[72] Later he served on the General Council's liturgical committee and board of foreign missions. Typical of his irenical spirit was his participation in the series of "diets" and "general conferences" held from 1877 to 1904 for the purpose of reconciling the various Lutheran bodies in America. He lived to see their culmination in the formation of the United Lutheran Church in America in 1918.

During most of his academic career Professor H. E. Jacobs taught Dogmatics, Apologetics, and Introduction to the Study of Theology. After Professor Mann's death he also taught Symbolics and, occasionally, the History of Doctrine. He suffered a serious illness in the fall of 1910[73] and never completely recovered his strength thereafter. He continued to teach until 1930, although long since overtaken by the infirmities of age, and died in 1932 in his eighty-eighth year.[74] The span of no other teacher's career in the history of the seminary equals or approaches his forty-seven years. Before 1910, when he was at the height of his physical and mental power, it was his practice to employ textbooks, call upon his students to recite on the basis of their assigned reading, and discuss in detail such problems as his students raised. In the case of Dogmatics he began by using his own translation of Schmid's selections from the orthodoxist theologians of the seventeenth century. Before the close of the nineteenth century he felt hampered by the "scholastic rigidity" of this work[75] and substituted his own *Elements* and then his *Summary*. Even these books, it must be said, adhered to the scholastic method of the seventeenth century, not only in their rather uncritical use of biblical proof texts but also in their Aristotelian cast. Jacobs was influenced very little by the theology of the nineteenth century; he rejected Schleiermacher and Ritschl and found little to commend in either Martensen or the Erlangen school.[76] He was, however, a man of vast learning who devoted the whole of his time and energy to study and teaching, and so he gave an example of scholarly application unequaled among his predecessors and contemporaries.

The third of the four professors who dominated the faculty in the early decades in Mount Airy was Jacob Fry. The son of a congressman, he was born in 1834 in Trappe, Pa. He was a graduate of Union College and the Gettysburg Seminary and was pastor of First Church in Carlisle, Pa., and Trinity Church in Reading, Pa. At the convention of the Ministerium of Pennsylvania in 1891 he was nominated by the president of the board of directors and his personal friend, Joseph A. Seiss, to fill the vacant St. John's professorship. Since the income from the endowment was insufficient, it was proposed that Fry remain in his parish in Reading and commute to Philadelphia for two days of teaching a week. With this understanding he was elected by acclamation. He continued under this arrangement for five years, and in 1896, when he was called to be the stated preacher of the Church of the Ascension (on the seminary campus) at a salary of $200 a year, he moved to Mount Airy and devoted the major part of his time to teaching. Thus in 1896, for the first time in the history of the seminary, all the professors resided on the campus. Professor Fry continued to teach and preach until his death in 1920, when he was eighty-six years of age.[77] His alma mater, Union College, conferred on him the degrees of D.D. in 1873 and of L.H.D. in 1911, and he received the degree of LL.D. from Muhlenberg College in the latter year.

In addition to a history of his congregation in Reading, Professor Fry wrote short textbooks which were used in his own classes: *Elementary Homiletics* (1893), which went through several revisions, and *The Pastor's Guide, or Rules and Notes in Pastoral Theology* (1915). Homiletics and Pastoral Theology were the disciplines for which Fry was responsible in the seminary. It was his practice to dictate, and later to read with his students, a few of his "rules and notes" and then to "enlarge, explain, apply, and illustrate" them extemporaneously.[78] Since at that time most students attended Sunday services in the chapel where Fry preached, he had an opportunity to illustrate and enforce in his own pulpit what he taught in the classroom about preaching.[79] It was reported that during World War I he preached critically about submarine warfare on the basis of the text, "Every one of you should know how to possess his vessel in sanctification and honor" (I Thess. 4:4). In his instruction he guardedly defended such use of a text. "Is not this as reprehensible as to use an unfinished statement in Scripture as a text, or to wrest it entirely from its connection? If we put a meaning into a passage which evidently was not in the writer's mind, are we really expounding God's Word or are we making it suit our own fancy? . . . These are serious questions, not to be lightly dismissed or overruled. But at the same time we should consider that these objections can be urged against the spiritualizing of the miracles and other acts of our Lord . . . . Where texts are chosen by way of accommodation and used cautiously and wisely, there is force in the argument in its favor . . . . It is employing the art and power of illustration drawn from the Word of God itself and attracts attention from the start through the story or narrative on which the sermon is based."[80] Fry had strong opinions of his own about other matters too. "The zeal of some intemperate temperance persons who seek to abolish wine from the communion table and substitute some other drink in its stead should be quietly but firmly resisted." "The custom in some places for the minister to hurry to the door to shake hands with every person present is not to be commended." "Y.M.C.A.'s, W.C.T.U.'s, Christian Endeavor, etc. are rarely to be commended to our people, as they are generally conducted on 'new measure' lines."[81]

The last of the professors during the early decades in Mount Airy was George Frederick Spieker.[82] Born in 1844 in Elk Ridge Landing, Md., his parents later were members of a German-speaking Missouri Synod congregation in Baltimore. He was graduated from Baltimore City College, attended the Gettysburg Seminary for two years, and was graduated from the Philadelphia Seminary. He was pastor in Kutztown and Allentown, Pa., taught German for two years in Gettysburg College after C. F. Schaeffer's departure in 1864, and taught Hebrew in Muhlenberg College from 1887 to 1894. At a convention of the Ministerium of Pennsylvania in the latter year he was nominated from the floor for a professorship in the Philadelphia Seminary. The nomination was made by by the Rev. Charles J. Cooper in behalf, he said, of 70,000 Pennsylvania Germans who were not properly represented in the seminary. Although opposed by members of the board of directors and the faculty, Spieker was elected. He had been a classmate of H. E. Jacobs in Gettysburg Seminary and had collaborated with him in the translation of Leonard Hutter's Compend of Lutheran Theology (1868). Later he wrote Annotations on the Second Epistle of St. Paul to the Corinthians (1897). Roanoke College conferred on him the degree of D. D. in 1887, and he received the degree of LL. D. from Thiel College in 1911.

As the successor of Charles W. Schaeffer, Spieker was assigned responsibility for courses in Church History and also in Hebrew and the Old Testament. Although he had linguistic gifts and was always conscientious, he had limited success as a teacher. This may have been due in part to impaired health, but it was also a consequence (as the few articles he wrote illustrate) of a constitutional inability to organize his thoughts and communicate coherently. It is clear, however, that he had no sympathy with current biblical criticism, which he dismissed summarily as an attack on the Bible.[83] Popular among his fellow ministers, his modesty "prevented him, except on rare occasions, from participation in public discussions."[84] He was cheerful in his suffering and died in his sixty-ninth year, after teaching in the seminary for nineteen years.

In addition to these four professors — Spaeth, Jacobs, Fry, and Spieker — there were several instructors. Professor Mann had long found the teaching of Hebrew to be a chore and requested relief from it. In 1891 the faculty reiterated its position that no student should be excused from the study of this language "except in cases of illness or other unavoidable necessity." Occasionally a student was excused on the testimony of an oculist "that his eyes would not endure the strain."[85] In 1891 the board of directors appointed, as part-time instructor "in Old Testament language and theology," Herman V. Hilprecht, later professor of Assyrian and Comparative Semitic Philology in the University of Pennsylvania.[86] After a year he was succeeded by Carl Elofson, pastor of a congregation of the Augustana Synod in Philadelphia, who soon had to relinquish his duties on account of ill health. From 1893 to 1898 Theodore W. Kretschman, pastor of Christ Church in nearby Chestnut Hill and later professor in Susquehanna University, taught Hebrew. He was succeeded from 1898 to 1905 by Carl A. Blomgren, pastor in Philadelphia who resigned to become professor of Old Testament Languages and Literature in Augustana Theological Seminary in Rock Island, Ill. Finally, from 1905 to 1910 Albert T. Clay, an alumnus of the Philadelphia Seminary who later became professor of Semitic Philology and Archaeology in the University of Pennsylvania, gave the courses in Hebrew.[87]

An appraisal of the faculty as a whole and of the theological position which it took during the first two decades in Mount Airy reveals an orientation which is at first sight somewhat astonishing. As Professors C. F. Schaeffer, Mann, and Krauth in the preceding quarter of a century, so Professors Spaeth, H. E. Jacobs, Fry, and Spieker in this period were intent on restoring a theology and a practice of the past. No matter in what discipline of theology they were teaching, their attention was concentrated on a tradition. Most of their literary work was historical, and it was calculated, broadly speaking, to demonstrate the superiority of the orthodoxism of the seventeenth century to the pietism and rationalism of the eighteenth century or the revivalism of the nineteenth century. Since there was a tendency to be content with the discovery of historical precedents and to be rather uncritical in the adoption of them, there was actually more of a spirit of romantic repristination at work than there was of disciplined historical inquiry. This is especially evident in the refusal to employ the historical method in biblical study and the reluctance to depart from an exegesis which was imbedded in the doctrinal and liturgical tradition which was embraced. To be sure, there were differences of degree within the faculty; as Professor Mann had been theologically more open and flexible than Professor C. F. Schaeffer, so Professor H. E. Jacobs was more irenic than Professor Spaeth. It must also be remembered, of course, that the theological climate of the Lutheran Church at the time was such as to encourage denominational traditionalism.

The Philadelphia Seminary was regarded by some as the theological center of the General Council of the Evangelical Lutheran Church in North America.[88] Certain it is that its faculty was often appealed to for theological opinions. For example, during the controversy over predestination, which agitated the Lutheran Church especially in the Middle West, the faculty in 1884 expressed its judgment in a statement drafted by Professor Mann in response to a request of the Ministerium of New York. When individual communion cups began to replace the common cup, the faculty in 1903 declared its opinion in a statement drafted by Professor H. E. Jacobs in response to a request of the Ministerium of Pennsylvania. Individual congregations and ministers also sought the counsel of the faculty. For example, questions were raised about divorce and remarriage, the significance of ordination (reply: it is "nothing more than the formal ratification and approval of the call"), the propriety of a man's marrying his deceased wife's sister (reply: there is no absolute impediment), and the like.[89]

The opinions of individual members of the faculty were expressed most frequently in the pages of *The Lutheran Church Review,* the theological quarterly edited by the faculty and published by the Alumni Association. Professor H. E. Jacobs shared editorial labors with his colleagues but remained editor-in-chief until 1895, when he felt "constrained by the pressure of other and onerous duties" to resign, whereupon the Rev. Theodore E. Schmauk, of Lebanon, Pa., took his place. The Alumni Association annually gave $50 to Jacobs, and then to Schmauk, "as evidence of appreciation of his work as editor." The faculty was not always pleased with Schmauk's editorial policies but continued to contribute articles to its burgeoning pages.[90]

Chapter V

Physical Expansion and Frustrations
1910-1938

THE YEAR 1910 may be said to have marked the beginning of a new era in the history of the Philadelphia Seminary. Bold new programs were launched, and although in many cases they failed to achieve the intended results, they at least represented earnest endeavors in this direction. As in the past, so now, most of these programs were initially conceived in the faculty, but only the board of directors had the power and authority to bring them to fruition.

The president of the board from 1908 to the time of his death in 1920 was an imaginative and skillful leader, the Rev. Theodore E. Schmauk, who commanded respect as the president of the General Council. He was succeeded by Mr. E. Clarence Miller, who continued as president of the board until his death in 1944. A broker in Philadelphia and the first treasurer of the United Lutheran Church in America (1918-1944), Mr. Miller was the only layman to serve as president of the seminary board during its first century, and he did so with marked devotion. These two presidents were supported in the development of a forward-looking program by such board members as the Rev. George Washington Sandt, editor of *The Lutheran* to 1930; the Rev. Nathan R. Melhorn, editor of *The*

Theodore E. Schmauk and E. Clarence Miller, Presidents of the Board of Directors

Lutheran after 1930; the Rev. Ernst P. Pfatteicher, president of the Ministerium of Pennsylvania; the Rev. F. A. Kaehler, of Buffalo, N. Y.; Mr. W. Frederick Monroe, shoe manufacturer in Philadelphia; Mr. Frederick C. Hassold, Philadelphia restauranteur; Mr. William H. Hager, owner of a department store in Lancaster, Pa.; Mr. Gloss K. Mohr, merchant in Philadelphia; and Mr. Windsor F. Cousins, Philadelphia attorney. During these years the board of directors met semiannually, and its executive committee met five times a year. As before, a large majority of the board members was elected by the Ministerium of Pennsylvania. Others were elected by the Ministerium of New York and the Synod of New York and New England, merged in 1929 into the United Synod of New York and New England. Still others were elected by the Pittsburgh Synod. Reunited with its General Synod counterpart in 1919 after a separate existence since 1867, the Pittsburgh Synod divided its support of the Philadelphia Seminary with the Gettysburg Seminary and the seminary of Susquehanna University, and after the latter was closed in 1933 the synod gave some financial support to the Chicago Seminary and to Hamma Divinity School in Springfield, Ohio.

In order to help finance a new program in the Philadelphia Seminary an appeal for funds in the congregations of the Ministerium of Pennsylvania was proposed in 1911. It was not until 1914 that the appeal got under way, and then it was tied to an appeal for Muhlenberg College and fell far short of the goal, realizing a total of $118,000 for the seminary by 1920.[1] The Synod of New York and New England raised about $20,000 and the Pittsburgh Synod almost as much in parallel efforts.[2] Meanwhile, in 1917, the Ministerium of New York made a final effort to complete the endowment of its professorship in the Philadelphia Seminary which it had been working on in a desultory way since 1872. A Reformation jubilee appeal was made for Wagner College as well as the seminary. It was the first large and successful campaign ever launched in the synod and brought the total amount in the endowment of the professorship to $55,000.[3] During this period, unlike the former one, the professor of the Ministerium of New York received his full salary after 1914. The supporting synods also began to make annual appropriations to the seminary — an average of about $400 a year from the Pittsburgh Synod, an average of about $3,000 a year from the New York synods, and an average of about $16,000 a year from the Ministerium of Pennsylvania.[4]

In 1910 the board of directors proposed, under the leadership of its president, the Rev. Theodore E. Schmauk, to use available funds for an expansion program. This was a heroic decision in view of the declining student enrollment during the preceding decade. It was apparently believed that the enrollment would increase again, especially if there were an improvement in physical facilities and academic offerings. In any case, something had to be done. A start had to be made to rebuild the faculty. Professor Spaeth died in 1910 and left a vacancy to fill. The health of Professor Spieker was impaired, and he lived only three years more, until 1913. Professor Fry was seventy-six years old in 1910, and it was hardly to be expected that he would live to be eighty-six before his death. Professor H. E. Jacobs was comparatively young, for he was only sixty-six years old in 1910, but this was the year in which he suffered from a severe illness, and there was no way in which to foresee that he would live twenty-two years more, even with greatly reduced strength.

Under these circumstances the board of directors had no choice but to act, and it is to its credit that it decided to do more than merely fill existing and anticipated vacancies. Moreover, it resolved to avoid the potential embarrassment or disaster of leaving the choice of faculty personnel to the whim of synodical conventions. The experience with Dewald's nomination on the floor of the Ministerium of New York and with Spieker's nomination on the floor of the

Ministerium of Pennsylvania gave the board of directors reason to proceed with expedition but also with care. Meanwhile, the faculty insisted on the observance of the bylaw which required that the board "consult" with the faculty before making a nomination. The provision that "the board, having consulted with the faculty, shall nominate" somebody for a professorship means, the faculty asserted, that "(a) this consultation should be official, and not an informal consultation with individuals, . . . and (b) this act of consultation with the faculty should precede the act of nomination by the board."[5] The validity of this interpretation was acknowledged by the board and its propriety as an academic procedure was respected, with but few exceptions, in the subsequent history of the seminary.

In accordance with the suggestion of the board and the faculty of the seminary, the Ministerium of New York nominated the Rev. Henry Offermann, pastor of Immanuel Church in Philadelphia, to occupy its professorship, which had been vacant since 1894. His choice was especially acceptable because he was a graduate of the Kropp Seminary in Germany. As a gesture of reconciliation, the Rev. John A. Dewald made the motion which resulted in his synod's nomination. When Offermann was subsequently elected by the Ministerium of Pennsylvania in 1910, it was decided that he should teach the introduction, exegesis, and theology of the New Testament and that he should lecture in English rather than in German. Thus bilingual instruction in the seminary came to an end, not because of Germanophobia, least of all on Offermann's part, but on the ground that demand for German-speaking ministers was declining and that such students as might still come from Germany were especially in need of acquaintance with the English language.[6]

In the same year, 1910, the board of directors, with the concurrence of the faculty, took steps to make the teaching of the seminary more relevant to the twentieth century. It seemed desirable to provide instruction, the board resolved, in "the great practical questions of missions, education, and the Confessional and philosophical problems before the church today." In an unprecedented action the board of directors then nominated its own president, the Rev. Theodore E. Schmauk, and its own vice-president, the Rev. Edward T. Horn, as professors. After reflection the former "deemed it inadvisable that he should be called to any chair at the present time" but offered to lecture without compensation on a part-time basis, and did so for nine years. The latter accepted the nomination, was elected by the Ministerium of Pennsylvania in 1911, and taught in the seminary until his death only three years later. In addition, the board of directors nominated and the synod elected the Rev. Luther D. Reed to a part-time professorship, with the understanding that he should receive no additional stipend for this inasmuch as he was already receiving a salary as director of the library. Schmauk's field was designated as "the chair of the Confession and Defense of the Christian Faith," Horn's as "the chair of Ethics and the practice and theory of Missions," and Reed's as "the chair of Liturgics, including Church Music and Hymnology."[7] All this was achieved with the outlay of only one additional salary, which commended itself to an economy-minded constituency.

In 1911 the way was opened for another professorship. The Rev. S. G. Weiskotten, pastor of the Church of the Redeemer in Brooklyn, N. Y., had interested a parishioner of his in the seminary. This was the Hon. Charles A. Schieren, merchant, banker, philanthropist, and former mayor of Brooklyn. He gave $40,000 for the endowment of a professorship and $10,000 for the erection of a house on the campus for the incumbent. In 1913 the Rev. Charles M. Jacobs, son of the seminary's dean, was nominated by the Synod of New York and New England, after consultation with the board of directors and the faculty, and was elected by the Ministerium of Pennsylvania. Although it was originally planned

Charles A. Schieren, of Brooklyn, who
Endowed a New Professorship

that the new professor should teach the History of Christian Thought, the death
of Professor Spieker in 1913 made it necessary for him to assume responsibility
for the whole field of Church History.[8]

Still another professorship was endowed by a bequest of Major Enos R.
Artman, member of the Church of the Holy Communion in Philadelphia, and the
full amount of $40,000 was received by the seminary in 1915. In the same year
the Rev. C. Theodore Benze, at the time teaching students in the Kropp Seminary
in Germany about church life in America, was elected as the first incumbent. He
was assigned the field of the Old Testament and, since Professor Horn died that
year, also some responsibility for Missions.[9]

Enos R. Artman, of Philadelphia, who
also Endowed a Professorship

During the decade from 1910 to 1920 the faculty was therefore markedly increased in size. While during previous decades there had been only four men on the faculty, during most of this decade there were seven. When Dr. Schmauk died in 1920, his place was taken by the Rev. Emil E. Fischer, pastor of Christ Church in Allentown, Pa. Professor Fry died just a month earlier and was succeeded in 1921 by the Rev. John C. Seegers, at the time pastor in Wilmington, N. C. These replacements kept the number of professors at seven throughout the decade from 1920 to 1930, too, and in addition there were several instructors and assistant professors: Paul E. Scherer (1917-1918, 1919-20), Charles P. Wiles (1919-24), Carl H. Kraeling (1924-29), and O. Frederick Nolde (1925-31). Between 1930 and 1938 three professors died — H. E. Jacobs in 1932 and C. T. Benze and J. C. Seegers in 1936 — and their places were taken (in a numerical sense) by O. Frederick Nolde in 1931, Russell D. Snyder in 1931, and Paul J. Hoh in 1937, and new instructors and assistant professors were appointed: Theodore G. Tappert (1931-1938), Charles M. Cooper (1936-1944), and George R. Seltzer (1937-1946). Special courses of lectures were also given from time to time between 1910 and 1938. Among others, the Rev. Jeremiah F. Ohl was lecturer on Inner Missions, the Rev. John Henry Harms on the English Bible, Professor Abdel Ross Wentz, of the Gettysburg Seminary, on the History of American Christianity, the Rev. Otto Kleine on German Homiletics, and the Rev. J. M. Bellan on Slovak Homiletics. There were also part-time instructors in Hebrew — Emil E. Fischer (1910-13) and Emil G. H. Kraeling (1914-16) — and Mr. Robert Schurig gave instruction in voice culture (1914-38).

Changes were made in the seminary's administration when the faculty proposed in 1920 that the office of dean be replaced by the office of president and that it be the function of the latter "to represent the seminary, outline its policy, and coordinate the work." The proposal, made at the time of the death of Theodore E. Schmauk, who was simultaneously lecturer and president of the board of directors, was intended in part to clarify the relations and functions of the board and faculty. It was symbolic of this clarification that after 1920 diplomas were conferred by the president of the seminary rather than by the president of the board. The purpose of the change was also the hope of introducing more efficiency into the administration of seminary affairs. This was not accomplished at once, for the venerable H. E. Jacobs, dean since 1894, was chosen as the first president in a gesture of respect despite his "failing strength." Only when his son, Professor Charles M. Jacobs, was made president in 1927 did the seminary establish administrative offices, appoint the Rev. Frederic W. Friday as registrar (to keep students' financial accounts, to develop a system of academic records, and to supervise employees), and secure stenographic help.10

Seal of the Seminary Engraved in 1894

Incidental to the inauguration of a new president in 1927 was the choice of dark blue and old gold as the colors of the seminary, as the choice of a dean in 1894 had led to the engraving of the seminary's seal.[11]

One of the reasons for the expansion of the faculty and also for the increase in administrative burdens during this period was the formal inauguration of graduate studies. Ever since 1884 there had been agitation among the alumni of the seminary for graduate courses, and when a request was addressed to the faculty, the faculty replied in 1886 that the seminary was not legally competent to offer degrees. Nevertheless, graduate courses were authorized by the board of directors in 1870, and in 1894 the bylaws were revised to read, "With the consent of the board of directors, the faculty may also arrange for a post-graduate course of special study for two or more years." The faculty itself proposed the introduction of formal graduate courses in 1902 and annually after 1908. During all these years graduates of other seminaries, especially from the Middle West, united with the "hospitants" from Kropp Seminary to take selected courses which were offered for undergraduates or to "pursue such studies as the dean may approve."[12] Among these so-called graduate students were Constantin M. Esbjörn (1883), alumnus of Augustana Seminary in Illinois, Niels P. Gravengaard (1892), alumnus of the Danish Lutheran Seminary in Wisconsin, and Emil W. Matzner (1910), alumnus of Wartburg Seminary in Iowa.

The endowment of the Schieren professorship in 1913 offered an opportunity to realize the hope for a graduate school. In his negotiations with the board of directors and the faculty the suggestion was made to Mr. Schieren, and adopted by him, that the incumbent of the new professorship should be a man "whose time, attention, and energy shall be given particularly, though not exclusively, to organizing . . . and teaching in a postgraduate course." The board of directors assigned to Professor Charles M. Jacobs, who was elected to the new chair, the teaching of the History of Christian Thought and the administration of a "graduate department." It was made clear that the graduate school should be a part of the seminary and that the members of the seminary's faculty should not only determine what graduate courses were to be offered but also offer them as a rule. Provision was made from the outset for two kinds of graduate student: (1) Those who gave their whole time to study and therefore resided on the campus and (2) those who were parish ministers and commuted to the campus for one or two days a week.[13] "One of the purposes of our graduate school," Charles M. Jacobs asserted when he was inaugurated, "will be to emphasize the necessity in these days of a scholarly and studious ministry; to impress upon the rising generation of pastors the importance, to them and to the church, of an education which does not stop when they have mastered those rudimentary and elementary truths without some knowledge of which they cannot be ordained; to make them feel that as witnesses for Christ they need to know to whom to speak as well as whereof they speak and to be in touch with and abreast of the thought currents of modern life. . . . We aim not only to proclaim to the men of the church the necessity of this kind of knowledge, but to help them to attain it, so far as we may; to show them the way to things new and old which they need in order to make their ministry thoroughly effective . . . . The time has come when the church itself must open to the widest the door of opportunity to those whose inclinations lead them toward the scholar's life. We trust that the graduate department of our seminary may be the beginning of a systematic training of scholars by the church."[14]

The graduate school, the first in any Lutheran seminary in America, was opened promptly in the fall of 1913. Six students were enrolled the first year. Enrollment gradually increased to 18 in 1920, and then more quickly to 46 in

1930 and to 87 by 1938. From the beginning, various Lutheran bodies were represented, and non-Lutherans enrolled as well as Lutherans. The proportion of part-time students, as compared with full-time students, grew more and more as the enrollment increased, but there were always some who devoted all of their time to study. During these years the heaviest teaching loads were carried by Professors C. M. Jacobs and H. Offermann, although other members of the faculty participated too. The pattern quickly developed of concentrating classes on Tuesdays and Thursdays, although classes for resident students were sometimes held on other days as well. As in the case of undergraduates, so in the case of graduate students, costs were modest. There was no charge for tuition. There was a registration fee of only $5.00, plus an additional fee of $5.00 a course, but after 1920 even these small charges ceased for a time. Resident graduate students naturally paid the same for their board and room as undergraduates.

Even before the opening of the graduate school in 1913 the proposal had been made that graduate fellows be appointed. In 1916 the board of directors established such a fellowship by providing an annual stipend of $400. The board decided that "the faculty, subject to the approval of the executive committee" of the board, should appoint a fellow every year from the recent alumni of the Philadelphia Seminary or any other Lutheran seminary and that the fellow should pursue studies in the graduate school and do such other work (normally tutoring) as may be assigned by the faculty. The following year a second fellowship was established by the board of directors with similar provisions. In 1924 the first of these fellowships was endowed by a bequest of $10,000 from Dr. Benjamin Sadtler, who has already been mentioned as a member of the board of directors for almost forty years.[15] Synods were asked to ordain the fellows on the ground that they were "engaged in instructing students in the Word of God," and they were uniformly ordained except in the few instances when they performed no tutorial function. In the early years fellows were required to affirm publicly that they would teach in accordance with the Scriptures and the Confessions, but in later years the Confessional subscription associated with their ordination was deemed sufficient.[16] The two fellowships were appraised as having great value. On the one hand, the fellows were said to "bridge the chasm which ordinarily exists between professors and students." On the other hand, the fellowships were declared to be "the best and the widest and the cheapest means of providing the church with future theological professors."[17] Of the following men who were fellows between 1916 and 1938, nine later became professors of theology and four became college presidents or professors: Paul E. Scherer, Carl H. Kraeling, Joseph S. Kleckner, Russell D. Snyder, O. Frederick Nolde, J. Raymond Houser, Russell W. Stine, Benjamin Lotz, Henry C. Cornehlsen, Jr., William E. Eisenberg, F. Eppling Reinartz, Theodore G. Tappert, John W. Doberstein, Gustave W. Weber, William C. Berkemeyer, Edmund A. Steimle, Thomas B. Kline, Richard C. Klick, Henry E. Horn, Joseph W. Inslee.

As early as 1895 inquiry had been made concerning the right of the seminary to confer degrees under the laws of the commonwealth of Pennsylvania. When the graduate school was established in 1913 steps were finally taken to secure the right. The necessary changes were made in the charter, in 1916 the power to grant degrees in theology was received, and the first degrees were conferred at the commencement exercises in 1917. To be eligible for the degree of bachelor of divinity, candidates were required to be college graduates, have "a satisfactory general average in all subjects" while in the seminary, take a specified number of advanced courses (called "degree courses") in addition to Hebrew, pass examinations to demonstrate a reading knowledge of Latin and German, and prepare a thesis after graduation. It was therefore customary for students to receive a diploma at graduation, and only a limited number were later admitted to the degree of bachelor of divinity when they had completed the writing of an acceptable thesis. The degree of master of sacred theology was awarded to candidates who completed twenty-four semester hours in the graduate school and presented "a satisfactory thesis upon some advanced subject in theology."[18] Although the seminary possessed the legal right to grant doctorates in theology, it did not consider itself academically competent to do this before its centennial. Honorary degrees were never awarded. The question was inevitably raised whether a denominational school of theology could grant degrees to non-Lutherans, and this question was answered affirmatively on the ground that the degrees were academic and not confessional.[19]

Mention has been made of the personal connections which members of the faculty had with the University of Pennsylvania in the early decades of the seminary's history. It is not surprising, therefore, to learn that when the seminary was founded in 1864 Professors Charles Porterfield Krauth and Charles W. Schaeffer were asked to ascertain whether arrangements could be made with the trustees of the university "to secure certain privileges in that institution to the students of this seminary and also to offer corresponding advantages to any students of the university who may wish to avail themselves of the instruction imparted in this seminary."[20] There is nothing in the records to indicate that anything came of this. The removal of the seminary to Mount Airy made the contemplated arrangements more difficult. It was not until 1906 that a similar proposal was made by the dean of the Philadelphia Divinity School (Episcopal) in behalf of all theological seminaries in and near Philadelphia. At the time the faculty of the Philadelphia Seminary was "not ready to enter into such an arrangement."[21] However, in 1921 the University of Pennsylvania offered scholarships to ten seminary students approved by the seminary faculty. These scholarships permitted students of theology to study in the university's graduate school of arts and sciences without payment of tuition. The number of scholarships was reduced in 1939 from ten to five for reasons of economy, but through all the years since 1921 some seminary students took advantage of the opportunity to broaden their education.[22]

Building Erected after the American Revolution is Converted into a Refectory

The year 1910, which marked the rebuilding of the faculty and the shaping of plans for a graduate school, also introduced a period of physical expansion. "The day will come," the president of the board of directors reported to the Ministerium of Pennsylvania in 1910, "when it will be difficult to secure additional grounds and buildings and when the church will probably regret that she has not taken the advantage of opportunities still existing." The need of a common dining hall to take the place of boarding houses in the neighborhood was especially mentioned. "A refectory would become a proper center of the social life of the students." Steps were taken in the same year to purchase the adjoining property to the north of the campus along Germantown Avenue. A large stone homestead, built in 1792, and a barn which had been used two generations before by the Mount Airy Agricultural Institute were on the property. In 1911 the board of directors ordered the purchase of this property for $35,000 and authorized a loan to make the transaction possible. The barn was torn down to make room for the residence of the Schieren professor in 1913. Meanwhile, about $1,000 was spent to make the homestead usable as a dining hall and, with a Mrs. Johnston as matron, the refectory was opened in the fall of 1912. The building was enlarged in 1914 and again in 1925 at a cost of about $7,500. From 1920 to 1956 Mrs. Agnes Vansant was matron.

At first the charge for board in the refectory was $3.50 a week. Although the cost of the building, the utilities, and equipment were not taken into account, it was soon found impossible to feed students for the announced price. By 1915 the charge for board was $4.00 a week, and the rise in costs during and following World War I caused further increases to $5.00 in 1919 and $5.75 in 1920. It was in the latter year that the girls from the neighborhood who had been employed as waitresses were replaced by student waiters. After this the increasing enrollment in the student body made it possible to keep the charge for board from rising higher; in fact, in some years students received rebates at the close of the year. This ended in 1930, when a fixed charge of $200 a year, and later $210 a year, was levied on students who ate in the refectory. Students who had pre-

Graduate Hall as it Appeared when Acquired in 1923

84

viously eaten in boarding houses were generally pleased with the refectory and testified that it contributed to health and fostered community of interest.[23] The dean wrote in the Catalog in 1918: "It provides a place for the informal discussion of all subjects that are of any possible interest in student life, and the possession of this common meeting place has done more than any other one thing to keep the seminary free from cliques and group jealousies."

The campus was extended farther by the acquisition in 1919 of a small grove north of the library for $6,000. Even before this, negotiations had been begun for the purchase of a property beyond the grove and extending to Gowen Avenue. This Hammer property, including a large stone house, was purchased in 1923 for $39,000. Without making alterations in the building, the house was "reserved entirely for the work of the graduate school, thus providing that department of the seminary with a physical center." Living quarters were here provided for eight or ten resident graduate students, and the first floor was converted to classroom use.[24] Meanwhile additional houses were secured for the expanding faculty. As early as 1905 a house on Boyer Street, behind the library, had been purchased for $14,000 to protect the seminary property. This house was rented to a tenant until 1914, when the Ministerium of New York paid $10,000 to make it the home for the incumbent of its professorship, and it was accordingly occupied by Professor Offermann. In 1922 another house at 7314 Boyer Street was purchased and temporarily rented, and a house at 7204 Boyer Street was bought for occupancy by Professor Reed. These two houses cost about $20,000, and in 1930 still another house was purchased at 7322 Boyer Street.[25] Thus a total of about $135,000 was expended to secure new land and buildings. The use of gas for illumination was replaced by electricity in the public buildings and then in the professors' homes between 1917 and 1923.[26] In 1917, on the 175th

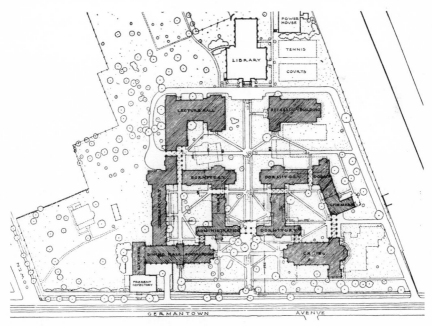

Architects' Projection (1923) of Proposed New Buildings on the Existing Campus

anniversary of the arrival in America of Henry Melchior Muhlenberg, a bronze monument, representing the patriarch preaching to an attentive congregation, was erected on the campus as a gift of the Sunday schools of the Ministerium of Pennsylvania. In 1937, at a cost of $10,000, most of it supplied by special gifts, the chapel chancel was enlarged and renovated.[27]

A more ambitious plan for physical development was set in motion before this, after World War I. Some of the seminary buildings, like the lecture hall, the refectory, and the graduate hall, were converted residences which were poorly adapted to the use to which they were put, and they were, in addition, old buildings which were not economical to maintain. In 1927 President Charles M. Jacobs said of the Gowen mansion, later called Hagan Hall, that "renovation would not remedy the defects of the building," and three years later he declared: "The classrooms in the administration building are almost shamefully inadequate . . . . I do not know of another institution of the church in which the facilities for work are so poor."[28] Such a realization, and the expectation that "the day of small undertakings and temporary structures is past," led the board of directors to adopt a "development plan" which would ultimately replace all the public buildings of the seminary except the library and power house. The Philadelphia architects Day and Klauder were engaged to prepare plans for a school with a potential of two hundred students. Included in the plans which were drawn were a new lecture hall, administration building, dormitories, recreation building, dining hall, and chapel, all to be connected with vaulted archways and done in the Collegiate Gothic which was then popular. "A fundamental idea," it was explained, "has been to provide a group of buildings which, when entirely completed, shall be harmonious and beautiful but which may be progressively realized without the necessity of disturbing existing structures, at least for some time to come."[29]

The cost for the entire complex of buildings was estimated to run to at least $615,000. In the spring of 1923 the board of directors approved plans for the construction of the lecture hall, which was to include ten classrooms of various sizes to accommodate from thirty-five to two hundred students, besides offices for members of the faculty. The estimated cost of this unit was $180,000. An appeal for $1,500,000 in the supporting synods was postponed, however, in view of the announcement by Muhlenberg College that it planned an appeal for $1,000,000 in 1924. Conscious of the "growing inadequacy of the seminary's physical plant," the board of directors decided to appeal for funds in 1927. When it was made known that the Board of Pensions of the United Lutheran Church would launch a church-wide campaign for $4,000,000 in 1928, the seminary's appeal was again postponed until 1930. By that time the country was in the trough of the great economic depression. The dream of new seminary buildings collapsed.[30] The old buildings continued to be used for more than forty years after they had been declared obsolete and inadequate.

The failure of the "development plan" was related to another failure. Since the close of the nineteenth century the relations of the seminaries in Philadelphia and Gettysburg had become more cordial and cooperative. For example, Professor H. E. Jacobs, of Philadelphia, and Professor Edmund J. Wolf of Gettysburg, had long been personal friends and had shared many convictions and hopes. The same may be said to have been true in the next generation of Professor C. M. Jacobs, of Philadelphia, and Professor Abdel Ross Wentz, of Gettysburg. These personal ties were part of a larger drawing together of the General Synod and the General Council which culminated in 1918 in the merger that brought into being the United Lutheran Church in America. It was perhaps inevitable that the suggestion should be made that the theological seminaries which had long been neighbors geographically and were now related ecclesiastically ought to unite as their church bodies had done. The Gettysburg and Philadelphia faculties met in "joint conference" in 1919 to discuss "common interests." In 1921 the faculty of the Philadelphia Seminary proposed a meeting with the Gettysburg faculty to discuss, among other things, the possibility of merging the two seminaries. The board of directors took up the proposal and appointed a joint board-faculty committee to consult with representatives of other seminaries "for the purpose of discussing the advisability of a closer relationship." Gettysburg declined the invitation, stating that "the present relations are entirely satisfactory to us" and that "any agitation at this time would be prejudicial to the best interests of all concerned."[31] The overture to merge which the Philadelphia Seminary made at the very time when it was drafting plans for physical development is significant, for it indicates its willingness to give up its own separate existence for what it believed to be in the best interest of the church's theological education in the East. Only when the suggestion of merger was frustrated did the board of directors proceed with its development plan, and this was in turn frustrated, as we have seen, by other circumstances.

Another attempt was made to merge seminaries. In 1926 the United Lutheran Church adopted a resolution which declared "that seminaries located in contiguous territory be urged to consider whether the needs of the church may not be best served by consolidation or by such affiliation as may unify and correlate their work." At the invitation of a special commission on theological education of the United Lutheran Church, representatives of four seminaries in the Middle Atlantic States (Gettysburg, Philadelphia, Hartwick in central New York, and Susquehanna in Selinsgrove, Pa.) met in Harrisburg, Pa., in November, 1927. Consolidation was there approved in principle, "provided plans can be worked out so that nothing essential for which the various institutions have stood need be sacrificed." For authority to act, however, the matter was referred to the several boards of directors. The board of Hartwick Seminary promptly withdrew from further consideration of merger by declaring, "We cannot favor any merging of seminaries which would deprive this territory [that is, the state of New York] of a Lutheran theological seminary." In June, 1928, representatives of the three Pennsylvania schools met again in Harrisburg, Pa., and reaffirmed the position taken before. The following April they decided to recommend merger at a location "within a radius of twenty miles, more or less, of City Hall in Philadelphia." By the summer of 1929 the boards of the three seminaries had given general approval to four agreements: (1) that the charter of the merged school be that held by Gettysburg, (2) that members of the faculty be obligated to the doctrinal position of the United Lutheran Church, (3) that members of the board of directors be elected by supporting synods in ratio to their size, and (4) that the merged school be located within twenty miles of the center of Philadelphia. Several conditions were added: The Philadelphia Seminary asked that elections of all professors be confirmed by the synods in which professorships originated. The Gettysburg Seminary asked that no site then occupied by an existing participant in merger be chosen as the site for the new school. The Susquehanna Seminary asked that participation in the merger be understood to be subject to the approval of a majority of the supporting synods.[32]

The decision concerning merger was thus shifted to the supporting synods of the three seminaries. All the synods in the Philadelphia Seminary's constituency approved of merger (Pennsylvania Ministerium, New York Ministerium, New York and New England Synod, and Pittsburgh Synod). Three of the six supporting synods of the Gettysburg Seminary approved of merger (Maryland, West Virginia, and Pittsburgh) while two (Alleghany and West Pennsylvania) disapproved and one (East Pennsylvania) postponed action. Both of the supporting synods of the Susquehanna Seminary (Alleghany and Susquehanna) disapproved. The attempt at consolidation consequently failed to gain the necessary support.[33] The tradition of rivalry between Gettysburg and Philadelphia, and between the General Synod and the General Council, undoubtedly played some part in the defeat of the proposed merger. Differences in piety, if not in theology, had also survived the union of general church bodies to form the United Lutheran Church. However, sentiments of loyalty on the part of alumni and on the part of people in general toward institutions with which they had long been familiar and over which they exercised some control probably played a larger role. Certainly the promise of greater accomplishments for theological education with consolidated resources was not sufficiently persuasive to overcome institutional inertia.

After the merger proposals had been defeated, the United Lutheran Church adopted a recommendation in 1932 that the number of theological seminaries be reduced by consolidation and that the four seminaries in Pennsylvania and New York be merged. However, the recommendation was adopted "with full and clear recognition of the fact that according to the constitution of the United Lutheran Church, as interpreted . . . in advance of the merger of the three general bodies, the control of theological seminaries is the function of the synods."[34] In other words, the fate of the proposed merger was in the hands of synods which had already defeated it. However, the United Synod of New York and New England (formed in 1929 by a merger of the Ministerium of New York, the New York and New England Synod, and the New York Synod) found the burden of supporting two seminaries (Philadelphia and Hartwick) and two colleges (Wagner and Hartwick) too great to bear during the deepening economic depression of the 1930's. The synod's board of education recommended seminary merger, and even suggested that continuing contributions should be made contingent on evidence of concrete steps toward merger. "The seminary situation," the New York Synod's board of education reported in 1934, "shows signs of bringing about an entirely different spirit in synod — a more enthusiastic support of theological education — if a merger can be effected. Synod is giving shamefully little for the supremely important cause of theological education at the present time. Your board is convinced that a larger appreciation is nevertheless unjustified until a merger of Mt. Airy and Hartwick seminaries takes place. We cannot afford to support two seminaries. When that merger takes place, synod can rightfully be challenged to increase substantially its present contribution." The Philadelphia Seminary declared itself ready to merge with Hartwick, but the latter refused.[35]

In 1930 Hartwick had transferred its school of theology to Brooklyn, N. Y., where it conducted classes in a parish house in the hope of demonstrating that it had a mission. It continued a precarious existence until 1940. When the school finally closed, the United Synod of New York and New England had only one seminary to support. Before this, in 1934, the seminary connected with Susquehanna University in Selinsgrove, Pa., closed as a victim of academic attrition and of the economic depression. It was ironical that the two weakest seminaries should resist merger most stubbornly and that neither of them should survive despite their will to live. There was an element of truth in the suggestion of an alumnus of the Philadelphia Seminary that the uncertainties and postponements resulting from merger negotiations "have caused a delay in gathering funds that has lost us a golden opportunity which cannot soon be regained."[36] However, not to have worked for merger would have been more irresponsible, and in the last analysis the proposed campaign for funds was postponed for other reasons.

During the whole period from 1910 to 1938 the seminary was living beyond its means or, to put it differently, the church was not supporting it to the extent of its needs. The annual operating costs increased from $25,000 to about $75,000 as a result of the increase in property and its maintenance, the doubled faculty, the expanded enrollment, and the rising cost of living. The average annual deficit was $15,000. From time to time Mr. E. Clarence Miller, president of the board of directors after 1920, quietly contributed large sums to reduce the accumulated deficit, and by the time of his death in 1944 these personal gifts exceeded $150,000.[37] Even at that, the total accumulated deficit in 1938 was $112,000. This might well have been greater than it was if it had not been for the receipt of gifts and legacies, interest from which was in most cases applied to current expenses. Among the larger bequests was $5,500 in 1917 from the estate of the Rev. John Nicum, of Rochester, N. Y.; $6,000 in 1917 from the estate of Julia M. Kitzmiller; $14,000 in 1919 from the estate of Dr. Henry Grim, of Allentown, Pa.; $5,000 in 1920 from Miss Emma Schmauk in memory of her brother, Theodore E. Schmauk; $5,000 in 1921 from the estate of Mr. James N. Mohr and the same amount from the estate of Mr. W. Fred Monroe; $5,000 for scholarship aid in 1922 from Mr. Charles Freihofer, of Philadelphia, in memory of his son William Albert, who died in World War I; $17,000 in 1922 from the estate of the Rev. William Ashmead Schaeffer, of Philadelphia; $16,000 in 1927 from the estate of Mr. Charles W. Wattles, of Pittsburgh; $5,000 in 1929 from the estate of Miss Emma A. Endlich, of Reading, Pa.; $24,000 in 1929 from the estate of Mr. Frank E. Ritter, of Philadelphia; $15,000 in 1929 from the estate of Samuel N. Potteiger, Esq., of Reading, Pa.; $5,000 in 1929 from the estate of Mr. Theodore C. Birnbaum; $27,000 in 1931 from the estate of Amelia A. McCreary, formerly of Erie, Pa.; $10,000 in 1931 from the estate of Dr. D. D. Fritsch; $10,000 in 1935 from the estate of Miss Cornelia Schiedt, of Philadelphia; $10,000 in 1935 from the estate of Mrs. Anna D. T. FonDersmith, of Lancaster, Pa.; and $20,000 in 1936 from the estate of Ada Norton Jamison.[38]

During the economic depression of the 1930's expenditures were reduced to a minimum in the seminary, as they were generally throughout the church.[39] Needed repairs in buildings were postponed, paint was not applied although it might have prevented wood from rotting, grass was left uncut, and the salaries of professors were reduced from $3,600 to $3,240.[40] Reduction in expenditures was accompanied by efforts to devise new ways of raising money. When synodical appropriations declined sharply, special annual congregational offerings were requested on Reformation Sundays in the Ministerium of Pennsylvania and on Jubilate or Cantate Sundays in the United Synod of New York and New England. The former offerings averaged $6,000 a year between 1932 and 1941, and the latter averaged $200 a year between 1936 and 1941. In 1932 the first direct appeal was made to the seminary's alumni, and the Alumni Gift Fund produced an average of about $1,500 a year. In 1935 the Rev. Milton J. Bieber was employed to solicit private gifts and contributions for the seminary, but after two years he had scarcely raised enough money (and much of this was from the faculty) to pay expenses.[41] It was said afterwards that the seminary depended too much on individual donors.[42] The truth of the matter seems rather to have been that there were not enough of them, but in any case the seminary leaned heavily during the depression years on the liberality of such friends.

Student enrollment fluctuated, as it always had. On the whole, however, there was a fairly steady increase from 55 undergraduate students in 1910 to 73 in 1920 and to 116 in 1930. Thereafter the effects of the economic depression made themselves felt, and enrollment receded to 76 undergraduates by 1938. In 1924, when enrollment was rising, it was reported that the dormitory "was crowded to its utmost capacity." Provision was therefore made to house additional students on the top floor of the lecture hall, where the library had been years before. In 1928 it was reported again, "The accommodations of our dormitories are taxed to the uttermost." To relieve the situation one of the Schaeffer residences, then occupied by Professor Seegers, was converted in 1930 into a dormitory, called North Hall, to accommodate 22 students.[43]

Most of the students continued to come from the territory of the supporting synods in Pennsylvania, New York, New Jersey, and New England. Most of them also continued to receive their academic preparation in church-related colleges, the largest numbers in Muhlenberg, Wagner, Thiel, and Roanoke in this order. Fewer and fewer students came from the Kropp Seminary, in Germany, which finally closed in 1931. Yet the student body was becoming increasingly cosmopolitan as more and more states and provinces were represented and as the changing character of immigration into the United States began to be reflected among the students. To provide a ministry to scattered Lutherans who had come from eastern Europe — notably Hungarian, Slovak, and Wendish people — the General Council established what it called a Slav Mission Board in 1905. This board sent the Rev. A. L. Ramer, graduate of the seminary in 1895, to the Austro-Hungarian Empire to become familiar with the languages and cultures of the new immigrants. On his return in 1908 he became superintendent of "Slav missions" and soon began to send to the seminary young men of Hungarian, Slovak, and Wendish background in order to prepare them for work among their own people.[44] As German-speaking students became less numerous, they were sometimes replaced by these others. In 1928, for example, seven congregations were being supplied by seminary students who preached in Hungarian, Slovak, Danish, Norwegian, Swedish, and German.[45] Besides, from the close of World War I to the beginning of the economic depression in 1929 there were exchange students and refugees from France, Russia, Japan, Yugoslavia, Czechoslovakia, Romania, Italy, India, and Germany. Such students were warmly received, but the attitude toward women students was rather ambiguous. In 1924 a woman was admitted to classes as an auditor, in 1928 a woman applicant was denied admission on the ground that the seminary was chartered as a school to train men for the ministry, and in 1933 women who were majors in Religious Education in the University of Pennsylvania were permitted to attend classes for credit.[46]

The health of students was generally good, but occasionally a student required hospitalization. The faculty repeatedly expressed the seminary's thanks to Lankenau Hospital and its staff "for the many favors shown to students of this seminary, free of charge, in times of illness," and on occasion the board of directors made a modest gift to the hospital in appreciation for free medical and surgical care of students.[47] In the fall of 1918 an epidemic of influenza, which swept through the world, struck Philadelphia, and 12,790 persons died in the city before the sickness waned. Dozens of bodies lay unburied in Ivy Hill Cemetery, near the seminary, for want of labor, and some students volunteered to dig graves. In response to a request of city authorities, churches as well as schools, theaters, and other places of public assemblage were closed for several weeks. Seminary classes were not interrupted, although the fall opening of the graduate school was postponed "on account of the prevailing influenza."[48]

When the United States entered World War I in 1917, eighteen students left their studies in the seminary to serve in the armed forces. One of these, William S. Wright, died while in uniform, being stricken with influenza in Camp Hancock, Georgia. Students who remained on the campus were often restless, a professor observed. "When men are torn between the desire to enlist in the army and the conviction that the country needs preachers as well as soldiers, it is hard to interest them in academic subjects." Students were reminded of the war in the refectory, where the regimen of one meatless, one wheatless, and one eggless day was observed every week for the duration. Moreover, heat was reduced or shut off in parts of some buildings "on account of the scarcity of coal and the appeal to avoid unnecessary heating of rooms."[49] Further evidence of the war was the appearance on the campus of so-called sub-juniors. With the reorganization of some colleges, notably Muhlenberg, for the purposes of the Student Army Training Corps, provision was made at the seminary for pre-theological students who were ineligible for military service and whose college work was interrupted. Courses in English, Latin, Greek, French, Logic, Philosophy, Sociology, and History were offered by some members of the faculty and by several seminary upper classmen to five college students for one year.[50]

As World War I affected seminary students, so did the great economic depression which began in the fall of 1929. Missionary expansion at home and abroad ground to a halt. The demand for ministers quickly fell off. Circumstances offered an opportunity to be more selective in admitting students to the seminary. "A larger number of applications has been rejected than in any previous year," reported President C. M. Jacobs in the fall of 1931. Even then there were more graduates than there were places to fill. In the spring of 1935 it was reported that several graduates of the previous year were still without regular work and only three of the thirty-five students about to be graduated had received calls. As late as April, 1938, half of the graduating class was without prospect of calls. Under these circumstances the seminary offered five modest scholarships annually from 1933 to 1938, and three annually from 1938 to 1941, to provide a fourth year of study in the graduate school to selected unemployed alumni.[51] A more radical proposal, which received no support, was that the seminary be closed for a year and that the members of the faculty be given a sabbatical for study.[52]

In 1909 the Student Association was organized for the first time to supplant an earlier Reading Room Association. The Father Heyer Society continued its existence, raised money annually for mission projects, and in 1916 organized voluntary mission study classes among the students which continued in a desultory fashion for a dozen years. Short-lived, too, was a German Literary Society, formed in 1911 to cultivate interest and facility in the use of the German language. This society introduced an annual family Christmas observance before the holidays which continued until 1940. Other social events were faculty receptions for entering classes in September and for departing Seniors in May.[53]

The faculty continued its attempts to curb student preaching. Too many students, it was said, were being drawn away from their studies by requests which came to them from congregations and mission boards. Not only students but also congregations needed protection, and it was therefore proposed that only those upper classmen who were authorized by their synods should be permitted to preach, and then only after promising to preach in accordance with the teaching of the church.[54] However, there was mounting pressure from outside the seminary to give students more opportunity for practical experience. By 1927 about half of the students were consequently assigned to parishes or welfare institutions for field work, and regular visitation in the wards of Lankenau Hospital began in 1932. When, partly as a depression measure, a year of internship was introduced by some Lutheran seminaries (Augustana and Concordia), the faculty expressed its preference for an option of a year's parish assistantship or a year of graduate study.[55]

Chapel services were held every morning, on Mondays through Fridays, as before. Students took turns in reading Matins, except on Wednesdays, or sometimes on Thursdays, when the Service was often used with a sermon by a visiting preacher or by a member of the faculty. There was some ambivalence in the response of students toward the preaching of their teachers, whom they heard regularly in the classroom, especially since there was a temptation to use the sermon for an extension of remarks made in lectures. Perhaps it was on this account that for some years President Charles M. Jacobs delivered several series of meditations on Tuesday mornings. Whatever the circumstances of their origin may have been, testimony to the helpfulness of the meditations was reflected in student attendance; while the average chapel attendance involved 52% of the student body on other days, the attendance hovered around 96% on these Tuesday mornings. In 1918 members of the Senior class preached once a week, but the experiment was soon dropped. When proposed again in 1923, the Seniors vetoed the plan. In 1932 and again in 1939 a few Seniors suggested the same thing, but in both instances a large majority of the class objected, and the proposal was abandoned. A small group of students requested permission to introduce daily Vespers in 1925, and this was allowed as a voluntary service, which lasted a short time. Holy Communion was celebrated by the seminary community on Ash Wednesday and Ascension Day until 1917, when, with few exceptions, the Lord's Supper was observed four times a year — besides the Communion services, the catalog put it, available in other congregations.[56]

The earlier custom of "matriculating" students some six months after they had entered upon their studies was continued. As a matter of fact, this practice was now elaborated and given an importance which it had not previously had. Before 1912 first-year students had simply appeared before the faculty and confirmed the seriousness of their intention to study for the ministry. In this year, however, matriculation was transformed into an act which had religious rather than academic overtones, and accordingly it was moved from the faculty room to the chapel. In connection with Matins a special order, adapted by Professor Reed from medieval precedents, was used. For almost a half-century this form of matriculation was observed in the Philadelphia Seminary and was even borrowed for use in other schools of theology. It was occasionally interpreted as a rite which conferred on students a kind of ecclesiastical endorsement. More often it was understood as a formal incorporation of students in the seminary community, and it was therefore moved in later years from four or six months to six weeks after the beginning of the school year. The academic ambiguity involved in distinguishing between enrollment and matriculation remained, however. When it appeared that the "matriculation service" had no real function to perform, and in fact suggested what could not be defended, its use was discontinued in 1961, and matriculation was no longer regarded as an act separate from the admission of a student to the seminary.[57]

During the period from 1910 to 1938 the curriculum was subjected to a series of important changes. Bilingual courses, as already noted, came to an end in 1910. The earlier custom of combining classes in some courses — for example, Middlers had sometimes met with Juniors, or Seniors with Middlers — was discontinued as the faculty was enlarged. Moreover, the earlier practice of having three unequal terms in the academic year, separated from one another by the Christmas and Easter recesses, was now supplanted by an arrangement of two semesters of equal length. In 1919 another important change was made in the external structure of the curriculum by the introduction of elective courses. Three kinds of courses were now offered to undergraduates. (1) Prescribed courses were described as general treatments of "theological subjects with which every minister of the gospel should have an exact acquaintance." (2) Elective courses, chosen by students according to their interests, were said to "give the curriculum its flexibility and adapt it to the gifts and the needs of the individual students." (3) Degree courses were "highly specialized courses," according to the Catalog, and were open only to students who maintained "an average grade of 85% or over" and who were candidates for the degree of bachelor of divinity. The enlarged faculty made this change possible, too, although the teaching load

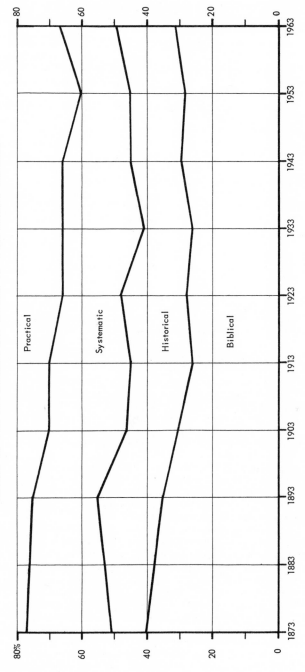

TRENDS IN THE DEPARTMENTAL WEIGHT OF PRESCRIBED COURSES

Practical

Systematic

Historical

Biblical

The computation is based on announcements of courses, which were not always accurate reflections of the courses themselves, and therefore the table is only relatively faithful to the actual weight of departments. For example, courses announced as practical were sometimes largely historical or systematic. Moreover, the introduction of electives after 1919 and the great expansion of field work after 1937 are not reflected in this graph. When changes were made they were not always made on principle but were dictated by the available personnel.

was as high as sixteen hours a week. With the limited number of available class-rooms, this meant that on some days classes were held from 8:30 a.m. to 9 p.m.[58]

In 1925 the faculty considered further revisions in the structure of the curriculum, for it was discovered that the earlier changes had had the undesir-able effect of requiring students to spend too much time in the classroom — an average of eighteen hours a week, or twenty-four hours for candidates for the degree of bachelor of divinity — and that this was not conducive to independent study on their part. Besides, the earlier changes had resulted in the addition of many short courses — students were confronted with an average of seven to ten courses at a time — and it was recognized that the students' interest and atten-tion were dissipated as a consequence. Only modest changes were actually made before 1938 to correct such deficiencies because of the inflexibility of the faculty and its reluctance to depart from what had become customary.[59]

A sharp decline in the linguistic equipment of entering students became evident in this period. Before World War I most students who entered the semi-nary had more or less acquaintance with Latin and Greek. As late as 1921 only two out of twenty-four Juniors had no reading knowledge of New Testament Greek, and provision had to be made for a remedial course. The number of those who entered the seminary without previous exposure to this language increased rapidly, and by 1938 more than half of the entering students were required to take a course in elementary Greek, usually offered by one of the fellows. Elec-tive courses in Ecclesiastical Latin and in "theological" German were also offered from time to time either by a fellow or by an instructor. By 1935 the requirement that candidates for the degree of bachelor of divinity demonstrate a reading knowledge of Latin and German was dropped. Ten years before this the requirement of Hebrew had been discontinued.[60]

It was expressly asserted that the study of theology is essentially his-torical,[61] and a heavy emphasis continued to be placed on the past. In the case of courses in Church History, the ancient church and the Reformation received the major attention, and it was only exceptionally that the history of the church since the sixteenth century was treated. The Dogmatics of the seventeenth century was still normative in Systematic Theology, although it was appealed to with less and less assurance than formerly. The historical method was employed with great caution in New Testament studies, but on the whole it was repudiated in the inter-pretation of the Old Testament. Significant, however, was the recognition that since "none of us lives as his grandfather lived," the seminary had to provide an education "that differs widely from that which was given in the third quarter of the nineteenth century." President Charles M. Jacobs, at least, realized that "theology is not static but dynamic, not a science fixed and complete and com-prised in formulas that must be handed down as infallible tradition, but a science ever growing, ever learning from the Word of God, ever seeking new forms in which to express eternal truth."[62] By no means all of his colleagues shared this conviction, and therefore only tentative steps could be taken to put it into effect. More time was devoted since 1910 to Apologetics and Ethics in relation to the changing world. Some attention was given to the world-wide missionary enter-prises of the church. The study of the worship of the church, and of the arts re-lated thereto, was greatly extended. Finally, the new interest in parish education was reflected in the curriculum. Notable, therefore, was the expansion of offer-ings in Practical Theology.[63] It was this, in addition to the introduction of elective courses, that led investigators of the Institute of Social and Religious Research to make the judgment: "The Lutheran Theological Seminary is out-standing among the seminaries of its denomination, and the program of study shows a much greater development than is to be detected in Lutheran institutions generally."[64]

It must be added, however, that the so-called "practical instruction" sometimes had only a tenuous relation to the theology taught elsewhere in the seminary. There was also a hiatus between the announced program of theological education and the actual achievement. For example, it was asserted that the seminary was trying "to teach men to think rather than to recite" and that the faculty was concerned not only to impart conclusions arrived at by theological investigation but also to teach students how to reach them by independent study.[65] Approach to this commendable goal was frustrated not merely by the generally employed lecture method (a common academic scapegoat) but especially by the absence of vital discussion [66] and in many cases by the want of creative example. The heavy teaching loads may be appealed to as an extenuating circumstance, but there were other reasons to account for the situation. In the first place, although the professors observed all the social amenities in their relations with one another, they seldom engaged in serious theological conversation among themselves, and for the most part they were not active participants in the development of academic policies. They cherished their independence, and it even happened that one of them appealed to the circumstance of his election by a synod in support of his claim to freedom from direction by his peers. Typical of the individualism is the fact that before 1925 courses were not listed in the Catalog by departments, which existed only in embryonic form, but by the professors in the order of their seniority. In the second place, most of the professors did not have the benefit of graduate study, and some of them did not succeed in compensating for this by their own efforts. This is hardly surprising in the case of men who were called from parishes in the middle, or even toward the close, of their careers. Many years earlier the Rev. Beale M. Schmucker had protested against regarding professorships as "havens of rest to which faithful and learned men who have borne the burden and heat of pastoral labor may look forward as resting places."[67] In the third place, the controversy between Fundamentalism and Modernism which was shaking American Christianity to its foundations during these years increased the academic timidity of many members of the faculty. Ministers and lay people in the seminary's constituency who had for generations been taught the orthodoxist view of the Scriptures were not prepared to deal with the literary and historical criticism of the Bible. Under the circumstances there was a tendency in the faculty to avoid the problem for the sake of peace, but a few members of the teaching staff took their responsibility more seriously and prepared the way for a joining of the issue with theological integrity.

Under the leadership of Charles M. Jacobs, who became president in 1927, a change was made for the better. The curriculum began to occupy the attention of the faculty as a whole, even if little progress was made beyond the discussion of principles.[68] An effort was made to achieve more balance and better sequence in the curriculum. Even more important in the long run was a new plan for the development of the faculty. "My personal opinion," said President Jacobs in 1927, "is that the seminary should have a relatively small faculty [i.e., professors] composed entirely of heads of departments, to be assisted in their teaching work by a corps of assistant professors and instructors." A pattern was thus established which continued to be followed for some time after C. M. Jacobs' death in 1938. Shortly before this he ventured an appraisal of the faculty he headed: "In scholarship, in teaching ability, in fidelity to the standards of Lutheranism, and in the ability of its individual members to work together, it has never been surpassed at any time in the history of the seminary." Just a few months before his death he added: "For the first time in our history we have, within the faculty itself, replacements for any of the older members who may be incapacitated . . . . I believe that this is the strongest teaching force that has ever been gathered in any seminary of the Lutheran Church in America at any one time." It was in 1938 that the Philadelphia Seminary, along with Gettysburg and Augustana as the only other Lutheran schools, was placed on the first list of seminaries accredited by the American Association of Theological Schools.[69]

We need to look more closely at the "older members" of the faculty between 1910 and 1938, omitting reference here to Dean H. E. Jacobs and Professors Fry and Spieker, who continued to teach for some time, inasmuch as they have already been dealt with at length in the previous chapter.

Professor Henry Offermann [70] was the first in chronological order. Born in Hannover, Germany, in 1866, he was a graduate of the Kropp Seminary and was sent to America in 1889 to minister to his countrymen who had crossed the Atlantic before him. He was pastor of Christ Church and Trinity Church in Camden, N. J., for eleven years and of Immanuel Church in Philadelphia from 1900 to 1912, devoting some time to graduate study in the field of Semitics in the University of Pennsylvania. Having been elected professor in 1910, he divided his time between his parish and his professorship for two years before moving to the campus. As a pastor and preacher he was remembered for his warm sympathy and his simple clarity. He was an interested participant in the life of the church, a member of many of its boards and committees, and a regular contributor to the *Deutscher Lutheraner* and the *Lutherischer Herold*. He wrote some fifty articles for theological journals but only one book, *Introduction to the Epistles and Gospels of the Church Year* (1924), and the book-length treatment of Matthew in the *New Testament Commentary* edited by Herbert C. Alleman (1936). He retired in 1944 and died in 1953, in his eighty-seventh year. Muhlenberg College conferred the degree of D.D. on him in 1908.

Faculty in 1913. Left to right: Jacob Fry, Henry Offermann, Henry E. Jacobs, Luther D. Reed, Edward T. Horn, Charles M. Jacobs, Theodore E. Schmauk

When he was called to the seminary it had been intended that Professor Offermann should teach the Old Testament, but the death of Adolph Spaeth in 1910 caused him to be shifted to the New Testament. This was congenial to him, and by his diligence he soon mastered the literature of and about the New Testament. While he was a competent philologist, his interest was theological and his concern was to acquaint his students with the Gospel. In his carefully prepared lectures he conveyed to them something of what the Gospel meant to him in his personal life and the central place it occupied in the teaching of St. Paul and in the church of the Augsburg Confession. Insofar as he can be classified, he was most deeply influenced by representatives of the Erlangen school of theology from J. C. K. von Hofmann to his contemporary Ludwig Ihmels. With the Erlangen school, Professor Offermann no longer looked upon the Bible as a collection of proof texts but as a witness to God's redemptive acts in history. Most of his students were hardly aware of this theological position, however, for he cautiously concealed from them all but the conclusions which he had reached in his study. Although this was intended to help and protect his students, in the final analysis it proved to be a disservice to them, for it left them without the means to cope with the problems which were bound to confront them later. That he was held in the highest affection is nevertheless suggested in these lines from a brash student parody:

> When Offermann reads from the Greek
> In sentence cha-*ract*-er-is-tic,
> The angels in heaven
> Come down at eleven
> And crowd in to hear him just speak.[71]

In 1911 Theodore E. Schmauk[72] began nine years of service as a lecturer in the seminary. Born in Lancaster, Pa., in 1860 as the son of a minister, he received his education in the University of Pennsylvania and the Philadelphia Seminary, in both of which Charles Porterfield Krauth was one of his teachers. On his graduation from the seminary in 1883 he was called as assistant to his father in Salem Church in Lebanon, Pa., where he in time succeeded his father and remained a total of thirty-seven years. During fifteen of these years, from 1903 to 1918, he also served as president of the General Council. He was on the editorial staff of *The Lutheran* for the last thirty years of his life, was editor of *The Lutheran Church Review* for twenty-five years, and still found time to participate in civic activities and the work of historical societies. So many-sided were his interests that in his Lebanon parsonage (he was never married) he had separate rooms, each with its own desk and filing cabinets, for his parish work, his administrative duties, and his literary work. Dr. Schmauk's interests are reflected in his books. He fancied himself as a defender of the faith of the fathers, and this posture was expressed in *The Negative Criticism of the Old Testament* (1894) and *The Confessional Principle and the Confessions of the Lutheran Church* (1909). He was a pioneer in the field of parish education and wrote many textbooks, including *The Christian Kindergarten* (1906) and *How to Teach in Sunday School* (1920). His interest in Pennsylvania history came to flower in *History of Old Salem in Lebanon* (1898), in *The Early Churches in the Lebanon Valley* (1902), in the *History of the Lutheran Church in Pennsylvania* (1903), and in an annotated edition of Benjamin Rush's *Account of the German Inhabitants of Pennsylvania* (1910). In the almost 200 articles which he contributed to *The Lutheran Church Review* Dr. Schmauk dealt with a wider spectrum of subjects. Unfortunately the quantity of his production was not always matched by its quality. He received the degree of D.D. from Muhlenberg College in 1897 and the degree of LL.D. from Augustana College in 1910.

This was the man who, from 1911 to 1920, commuted to Philadelphia every week in order to lecture for five, and sometimes six, hours a week on Apologetics and, after Professor Horn's death in 1915, on Ethics and Christian Education. One of his students reported that in his lectures Dr. Schmauk usually adhered to a carefully prepared manuscript. "At times he would read word for word what he had written, but his reading was so eloquent that it never became wearisome to the class. At other times he used a very full outline as the basis of his lectures. But whether the lecture was delivered from outline or from manuscript, the style was brilliant, sparkling, scintillating . . . . The student was at liberty to interrupt at any point of the lecture in order to ask a question. Such questions were always answered with a fullness of thought and knowledge that was astounding . . . ."[73] Dr. Schmauk's alert mind, natural eloquence, and wide reading equipped him to be stimulating in the classroom. Although he did not possess the solid scholarship or the theological maturity of Professor Offermann, these two men shared the same hesitation about taking students academically into their confidence. While Professor Offermann skirted problems, Dr. Schmauk demolished them. The latter's theology was so conditioned by his involvement in the ecclesiastical politics of his day that he always tended to support what was "safe."

In the same year in which Dr. Schmauk became a lecturer in the seminary, Edward T. Horn was elected professor.[74] Born in Easton, Pa., in 1850, he was graduated from Gettysburg College and the Philadelphia Seminary. After a brief pastorate in Philadelphia he served St. John's Church in Charleston, S. C., for twenty-one years and Trinity Church in Reading, Pa., for fourteen years. He was active in the work of the United Synod in the South and the General Council, especially as a member of the joint committee on the Common Service. He was the author of several short textbooks, *The Evangelical Pastor* (1887) and *Outline of Liturgics* (1890), and of the *Annotations on Philippians, Colossians, Thessalonians,* etc. (1897). He translated Wilhelm Loehe's *Three Books on the Church* (1908) and published *Summer Sermons* (1908). The field of Professor Horn's teaching was Ethics and Missions. He lived only three and a half years after his election, dying early in the spring of 1915 in his sixty-fifth year. Roanoke College and Newberry College conferred the degree of D.D. on him in 1887, and in 1906 he received the degree of LL.D. from the latter.

Also elected to a professorship in 1911 was Luther D. Reed.[75] The son of a minister, he was born in North Wales, Pa., in 1873 and was graduated from Franklin and Marshall College and the Philadelphia Seminary. He served as pastor in Allegheny (Pittsburgh) and Jeannette, Pa., from 1895 to 1904. His ministry was interrupted several times by extended absences occasioned by physical debility, and in 1902 he spent almost a year traveling in Europe for the cultivation of his interest in church music and art. He was one of the organizers and the president (1898-1906) of the Lutheran Liturgical Association, whose *Memoirs* he edited. In 1906 he was named director of the Krauth Memorial Library, in 1911 he was elected professor, and he continued to occupy both positions until his retirement in 1945. He served as secretary of the joint committee which prepared the *Common Service Book* (1917) and as chairman of the joint commission which produced the *Service Book and Hymnal* (1958). He also served on other committees which were concerned with church music and architecture. For a score of years he was the only member of the faculty who was furnished with secretarial help and he used this effectively to promote his special interests. In his early years he edited, with Mr. H. G. Archer, a number of texts of liturgical music. Most of his literary work was published in later years. In addition to about twenty articles in church journals, he wrote *The Lutheran Liturgy* (1947; revised edition 1959) and *Worship: a Study of Corporate Devotion* (1959). During his teaching career he received the degree of D.D. in 1912 from Thiel College and Muhlenberg College, and the latter conferred on him the degree of A.E.D. in 1936.

The area of Professor Reed's teaching in the seminary was Liturgics and Church Art. For many years he also directed the student choir and was responsible for chapel services. Three times during the period from 1911 to 1938 he secured short leaves for the purpose of travel in Europe and returned with slides to illustrate his lectures on art and architecture. Students responded with a parody:

> Stand up for Pappy Reed, boys,
> He runs three shows a day
> In art and architecture
> In his own virile way.
> The paintings are so life-like,
> The churches grand indeed.
> But who's that in the doorway?
> Why, that is Mrs. Reed!

Essentially romantic and mystical in temperament, Professor Reed was attracted by the old more than by the new. Neither in the classroom nor in his writings was he concerned with the way in which people in the past actually worshiped, however, for he centered his attention on selected monuments of text or form and tended to idealize them. He was more an advocate than a scholar and more an artist than a theologian. He awakened in his students an appreciation of beauty but had scant sympathy with their quest for truth. The influence he had on his students, and through them on the church as a whole, was incalculable, for he was a diligent and persistent advocate of what he considered "good taste."

Next to Professor Reed in chronological order was Charles M. Jacobs,[76] who was elected professor in 1913. Born in Gettysburg, Pa., in 1875 as the son of Henry E. Jacobs, he was graduated from the University of Pennsylvania and the Philadelphia Seminary. He pursued graduate studies in the University of Pennsylvania and in the University of Leipzig, Germany. Alongside of his service for twelve years as pastor of St. Peter's Church in North Wales, Pa., and of Christ· Church in Allentown, Pa., he was instructor of History in the Chestnut Hill Academy (1895-96) and in Muhlenberg College (1905-09). In 1913 he was called to the Philadelphia Seminary, where he was professor of Church History for twenty-five years and also president during the last eleven years of his life. He was prominently associated with many boards and commissions of the church, and his influence was especially felt in the formative period of the National Lutheran Council and in conversations looking toward church union. Under Professors Albert Hauck and Theodor Brieger in Leipzig, Professor Jacobs had come under the influence of the Luther Renaissance in Germany and contributed to its introduction in America. With Preserved Smith he edited and translated *Luther's Correspondence and Other Contemporary Letters* (2 vols., 1913, 1918), and he was the chief collaborator in the *Works of Martin Luther, with Introductions and Notes* (6 vols., 1915-32). His *Story of the Church* (1925) is a survey of the history of Christianity. The basically theological orientation of Professor Jacobs may be seen here and also in *The Way: a Little Book of Christian Truth* (1925) and *What Then Is Christianity?* (1940). Some of his chapel addresses were published in *Helps on the Road* (1933) and *The Faith of the Church* (1938). He was also the author of more than fifty articles in theological journals, symposia, and encyclopedias. He received the degrees of D.D. in 1913 and of L.H.D. in 1929 from Muhlenberg College, and in the latter year Augustana College conferred on him the degree of LL.D.

Faculty in 1927. Front row, left to right: Emil E. Fischer, C. Theodore Benze, Henry E. Jacobs, Charles M. Jacobs, Henry Offermann, Luther D. Reed. Second row, left to right: Henry Cornehlsen (fellow), Carl H. Kraeling, O. Frederick Nolde, Benjamin Lotz (fellow), John Henry Harms, Robert Schurig, John C. Seegers, Frederic W. Friday (registrar)

Professor C. M. Jacobs was to this period of the seminary's history what Mann had been to the first period and H. E. Jacobs to the second: the most stimulating teacher and, even before he was made president, the academic leader of the faculty. His incisive mind and his lucid exposition were seen at their best in his treatment of the history of Christian thought. In the graduate school, especially, he showed the limitations in the scholastic theology of the seventeenth century and the good and bad alternatives which had since been proposed. Like Offermann, Professor Jacobs was deeply influenced by the Erlangen school of theology as well as by the recovery of the theology of the Reformation. "The Word of God," he said, "is the center of the church. It is the church's dearest possession. When it is lost, the church's life is gone . . . . With all the emphasis we lay upon the Scriptures, we do not identify them with the Word of God. We confess that the Word of God is a means of grace; none of us will say that the Bible is a means of grace, save as it preserves in human language and passes down from generation to generation the record of God's Word." As for the Creeds and Confessions, "they deal not with absolutes but with alternatives. Therefore we think of the Confessions not as final utterances in theology and not as laws for religious thought but as their framers intended them to be regarded, as witnesses and guides to truth."[77] In comparing the literary style of Professor Charles M. Jacobs with that of his father it used to be said that a great advance had been made in a generation; the same could be said with respect to their theology. His students caught something of his spirit in their parody:

> Just as Martin Luther in the days of yore,
> Thumbed his nose and chuckled while the devil swore,
> You with pen and pamphlet good ol' Satan goad
> With a well-aimed copy of *Helps along the Road*.
> On, then, Uncle Charlie,
>   History's on your side;
> Join the church together
>   So it can't divide.

In 1915 C. Theodore Benze[78] was added to the faculty. Born in Warren, Pa., as the son of a minister, his college education was received at the hands of private tutors, and he was graduated from the Chicago Lutheran Seminary. For eleven years he was pastor in Beaver Falls and in Erie, Pa., served as president of Thiel College for four years, and in 1913 was sent by the General Council to the Kropp Seminary in Germany to acquaint students there with the conditions of American church life. The outbreak of World War I led to his recall and to his election as professor in Philadelphia. After the war he was given a leave of absence for eighteen months in order to serve abroad as a representative of the National Lutheran Council with the American Relief Administration.[79] He wrote a few articles and assisted Dr. Schmauk in some of his literary work, especially by translating documents. He died in 1936 in his seventy-first year. Muhlenberg College conferred on him the degree of D.D. in 1909.

Professor Benze's teaching assignment was the Old Testament and Missions. He had an uncommon gift for languages, ancient and modern, and among other things read Russian newspapers, French novels, Swedish sermons, German monographs, Latin essays, and the Bible in its original tongues. However, he lacked the gift of organizing his knowledge and communicating it coherently. It can nevertheless be said with confidence that his view of the Scriptures had more kinship with the seventeenth than with the twentieth century.[80] Some of his students irreverently referred to his repudiation of biblical criticism at the same time that they testified to his genuine, if pompous, cordiality:

> Benze walks with me,
> And he talks with me,
> And he tells me I must beware
> Of J, D, and E
> Redacted by P —
> Wellhausen is only a snare!

On the death of Dr. Schmauk in 1920 the Rev. Emil E. Fischer was called as professor to teach Ethics and Apologetics. Also the son of a minister, he was a native of Philadelphia, where he was born in 1882. A graduate of Rutgers University and the Philadelphia Seminary, he was pastor of the Church of the Holy Trinity in Brooklyn, N. Y., and of Christ Church in Allentown, Pa., for a total of thirteen years. From 1910 to 1913 he commuted from Brooklyn to Philadelphia in order to serve as part-time instructor in Hebrew, and he acquitted himself so well that he was proposed for a professorship, although in an entirely different field. He served on various boards and committees of the church, notably the Board of Foreign Missions of the United Lutheran Church for twelve years, wrote a score of articles for theological journals, and was the author of *Social Problems and the Christian Solution* (1927). When, in 1943, he was elected president of the Ministerium of Pennsylvania, he resigned his professorship after teaching for twenty-three years. He died in 1961. During his career as a teacher he received the degree of D.D. from Muhlenberg College in 1920 and from Rutgers University in 1933.

When he entered upon his teaching, Professor Fischer resolved that, in his association with his students, he would "endeavor to be frank and free, sympathetic with those who may have special difficulties, eager to elicit that expression of personal opinion which is indicative of the active mind."[81] This remained his purpose. He was always conscientious in the preparation of his lectures, which

Faculty in 1937. Front row, left to right: O. Frederick Nolde,
Henry Offermann, Charles M. Jacobs, Luther D. Reed, Emil E.
Fischer. Back row, left to right: Richard C. Klick (fellow),
Frederic W. Friday (registrar), Theodore G. Tappert, Russell D.
Snyder, Charles M. Cooper, Robert Schurig (voice culture)

were delivered with freedom and fervor, but the unnatural separation (for which
he was not responsible) of Apologetics and Ethics from Dogmatics compounded
his problems and tempted him to exalt the categories of philosophical ethics
and seek arguments for the defense of doctrines isolated from their context. On
the death of H. E. Jacobs he was assigned the teaching of Dogmatics, too, but by
this time the pattern of his thought was too fixed. He taught at a time when
Systematic Theology was not very popular in America and did not succeed in
reversing the trend. Compared with Dr. Schmauk, Professor Fischer was open
and receptive to the currents of thought in his day, but he lacked the assurance
and boldness of his predecessor in dealing with them.

The last of the "older members" of the faculty during this period was John
C. Seegers, who was born in Columbia, S. C., in 1867. A graduate of Newberry
College and the Philadelphia Seminary, he was pastor successively of churches
in Richmond, Va., Albany, N. Y., Easton and Reading, Pa., and Wilmington, N. C.
For four years, from 1914 to 1918, he was professor of Practical Theology in the
Southern Seminary, and in 1921 he was called to the Philadelphia Seminary to
succeed Jacob Fry in the same position. For many years he was an active leader
in the field of home missions, both in the South and in the North. He wrote little
for publication. In 1936, after teaching for fifteen years, he died in his sixty-
ninth year. Newberry College conferred on him the degree of D.D. in 1909.

Professor Seegers was respected as a man of fine courtesy and of genial
humor. He was fond of puns, and his alliterative expressions were called
"Seegerisms" by his students. He was a skillful manipulator of a limited fund of
ideas. "He held the great truths of the Bible," a colleague wrote, "with a firm
and simple faith. He had accepted in his youth a theology that satisfied his need
for a precise and articulate system of Christian thought. He was little troubled
and not at all disturbed by the questions that so often beset the theologian's
mind."[82]

THE
PHILADELPHIA SEMINARY
BULLETIN

PUBLISHED IN
OCTOBER, DECEMBER, FEBRUARY, APRIL AND JUNE, BY THE
LUTHERAN THEOLOGICAL SEMINARY AT PHILADELPHIA

VOLUME I   OCTOBER, 1916   NUMBER I

THE SEMINARY BULLETIN

A NEW publication should have undeniably good reasons for its appearance. This little paper believes that it has a sphere of real influence in the effort to bring items of information and interest concerning the Philadelphia Seminary and its Alumni to graduates and other friends and thus aid in binding them more closely to the Institution and to each other.

The Seminary, though its student body is never large, has always drawn from a very wide territory. Scarcely a year since its foundation has it been without men from the South, the West, New England, Canada and Europe, as well as from Pennsylvania and adjacent States.

... are scattered from the Atlantic to the
... Texas and Porto

PHILADELPHIA SEMINARY BULLETIN

VOLUME XXIX

OCTOBER, 1944

NUMBER 1

Varied Program Features Seminary Day

A LARGE number of alumni, friends, and members of the Women's Auxiliary gathered at the Seminary on Thursday, September 28, for the annual Seminary Day festivities. Wartime conditions were reflected in the less than usual number of automobiles parked on the campus, as well as in the inability of the Refectory to serve the customary Seminary Day luncheon.

Mr. Werner Speaks

In the morning, the annual Seminary Day service was held in the Chapel following the academic procession of the choir, student body, faculty and officiants from the Library.

The sermon was preached by the Rev. Oscar V. W... of St. John's Church ... Pasto... Wern... for... a...

Auxiliary Meets

Following this service of recognition, the Women's Auxiliary held its semi-annual meeting while the men adjourned to the Library auditorium where the Rev. Otto L. Schreiber, Ph.D., described and presented ... a collection of Luther... be the most co...

Luncheon Planned

Announcement was made of the forthcoming mid-winter luncheon of the Auxiliary to be h... jamin Franklin H... nut Streets, on ... 12:30. A...

The Seminary Bulletin in its Original (1916) and its Altered (1944) Format

103

In this period, as in the previous period, the faculty was sometimes asked for a formal opinion on some currently vexing problem. The Ministerium of Pennsylvania requested and received faculty opinions on the propriety of using lay readers (1925), the advisability of pew communion (1933), and the principles of ecclesiastical polity (1934). More important were several historic statements which members of the faculty drafted: H. E. Jacobs' "Constructive Lutheranism" (1919), C. M. Jacobs' "Declaration of Principles Concerning the Church and its External Relationships" (1920), and C. M. Jacobs' and H. Offermann's "Declaration on the Word of God and the Scriptures" (1938).

During the period from 1910 to 1938 the seminary put out several publications. *The Lutheran Church Review* continued to be published quarterly. Dr. Schmauk edited it until his death in 1920, and then it was returned to the faculty. For six years it was edited by Professor C. M. Jacobs, and the business management was handled by the library staff. In 1926 the Rev. Paul J. Hoh became the editor. Meanwhile negotiations were under way looking toward a merger of the *Review* and *The Lutheran Quarterly,* published in Gettysburg. An agreement was reached whereby the merged journal would be published jointly by the

SONS OF MOUNT AIRY

Paul J. Hoh, '18   F. Eppling Reinartz, '29

Sons of Mount Airy,
  Lift your spirit high;
Let ring the chorus
  Till it rend the sky;
Hail, School of Prophets—
  This the song we raise—
Hail, Alma Mater,
  Glorious be thy praise.

Sons of Mount Airy,
  Sacred are these halls,
Rich in tradition
  Memory recalls.
Honor her story,
  Walk her blessed ways;
Hail, Alma Mater,
  Glorious be thy praise.

Sons of Mount Airy,
  Proudly bear her name,
Show forth her spirit,
  Spread abroad her fame.
To earth's remote bounds
  Throughout length of days:
Hail, Alma Mater,
  Glorious be thy praise.

School Song by Paul J. Hoh and F. Eppling Reinartz

104

Philadelphia and Gettysburg seminaries, and it began to appear under the name *The Lutheran Church Quarterly* in January, 1928. During the first decade the major editorial burden of the journal rested in the hands of Professor Raymond T. Stamm, of Gettysburg.[83] A second publication was undertaken at the suggestion of the Alumni Association, which proposed that a news bulletin be issued every other month, except during the summer. Thus the *Philadelphia Seminary Bulletin* came into being in 1916,[84] and it has served ever since to inform alumni and friends of the progress of the school. The Alumni Association also proposed a third publication. As early as 1895 it suggested that a history of the seminary and a record of the seminary's alumni be prepared. Work on the project was finally authorized in 1908, but it was not until 1923 that *The Philadelphia Seminary Biographical Record* finally appeared.[85] It was compiled, without the history, by the library staff under the direction of Professor Reed. In 1936 the students in the seminary also began to publish *The Seminarian,* a modest sheet devoted to news and opinion.

Miss Mary E. Kaighn, who entered upon her work in the library in 1907, continued as assistant librarian until 1933, when she retired after twenty-six years of quiet, efficient service. She was succeeded by Miss Winifred V. Eisenberg, who headed the staff of three women for sixteen years until her resignation in 1949. Book expenditures averaged less than $600 a year during the period before 1938, but some books continued to be acquired through gifts. There were about 43,000 volumes in the collection by 1938, besides books and manuscripts in the archives. In 1937 the seminary library became a participant, with 150 other libraries in Philadelphia and five neighboring counties, in a union catalog, and this made the extensive resources of the whole area accessible to the research student.[86]

The seminary faculty was involved in what might be called extension courses in addition to the courses offered in the graduate school. Lectures were given on the campus for ministers for one week every summer from 1917 to 1922, the average attendance being about 55. From 1922 to 1924 members of the faculty lectured in New York City at a series of pastoral institutes. Beginning in 1933 a pastors' convocation was also held annually on the campus under the auspices of the Alumni Association, and this was regularly held during the Easter recess, when dormitory space was available.[87]

The commencement exercises which closed the academic year and which were held in the chapel were transferred from the evening to the morning, usually on a Thursday in May, in 1912. By 1931, the classes having grown, the chapel was no longer large enough. The faculty proposed having the exercises in the nearby Sedgwick Theater, but some members of the board of directors feared that this might subject the seminary to criticism, and accordingly the exercises were moved to St. Michael's Church, a mile away. In 1927 members of the graduating class first wore gowns, but not caps. From 1922, until the economic depression ended the practice, graduates were presented with modest gold crosses by lay board members.[88]

Without repeating the names of men who have already been mentioned in other connections, some of those who were graduated between 1910 and 1938 and have had distinguished careers may here be singled out by way of illustration. Among many ecclesiastical administrators Franklin Clark Fry, president of the Lutheran Church in America, and Paul C. Empie, executive secretary of the National Lutheran Council, stand out. Pastors and preachers might choose John Schmieder, of Kitchener, Ont., and John L. Deaton, of Baltimore, Md., as typical of the best tradition in parish ministers. Frederick L. Coleman is representative of the foreign missionaries and H. Grady Davis of the professors of theology in this generation. Welfare work of one kind or other increased since 1910, and Ambrose Hering and Henry J. Whiting exercised leadership in this area. There were editors, too, and among them Theodore K. Finck, who labored in the field of parish education, and G. Elson Ruff, editor of *The Lutheran* and for a long time also a book editor, deserve mention.

Chapter VI

Academic Advances and Prospects of Change

1938-1964

T HE LAST QUARTER of the seminary's first century was not a time of physical expansion. There was little outward change in the appearance of the campus. To be sure, several hurricanes thinned out the old trees, but where it seemed desirable uprooted trees were replaced and the rich variety of foliage was preserved. Among the trees were persimmons, gingkos, magnolias, dogwoods, willows, larches, white birches, poplars, osages, catalpas, American beeches, Dutch elms, balsams, chestnuts, spruces, cedars, pines (Hungarian, Austrian, Scotch, yellow, and white), maples (Japanese, Schwedlerie, Norway,

The Grove, North of the Library, as it Appeared about 1910

107

red, sugar, and soft), and oaks (white, black, red, pin, and scrub). Four houses on the edge of the campus were purchased as residences for professors: one at 7318 Boyer Street was bought in 1944 for $13,650, a second at 7238 Boyer Street was bought in 1952 for $16,000, and two adjoining houses at 42 and 46 East Gowen Avenue were bought in 1957 for $38,000. In addition, a new house was built on the campus in 1959 at a cost of $38,000 to provide a residence for the registrar.[1] The last was the only new construction on the campus since the library was built more than fifty years before.

The other buildings on the campus, which had been neglected during the economic depression, continued to deteriorate during World War II, when materials and labor were scarce. At the close of the war in 1945 it was finally decided to undertake a thorough program of renovation. The chairman of the committee on property of the board of directors, Mr. Peter P. Hagan, inspected all the buildings and reported in 1946, "As I looked over the property I just felt that it was an impossible task, for everything looked so bad that I did not know where to start." On the basis of a detailed estimate of the needs of each building, it was at first supposed that the cost of modest renovation would run to $70,000. Of this amount $11,000 was pledged by members of the board and the faculty, and it was decided to solicit special gifts for the remainder. By the time the first stage of the renovations was completed in 1948, more than $200,000 had been expended. Most of this was raised through the efforts of Mr. Hagan, whose

Gowen Mansion as Renovated and Renamed Hagan Hall in 1947

personal gifts amounted to about $40,000. More than half of the total was spent on the old Gowen mansion; its crumbling verandas were removed and the overhang of the roof reduced, while on the inside the basement was excavated to provide an additional story. The renovated mansion was then named Hagan Hall.[2]

Actually only a part of the necessary renovation was thus completed. During the next five years major attention was given to the library. Here, too, some interior structural changes were made, notably the conversion of the auditorium in the north wing into two stories by throwing a floor across it. This increased the usable space for readers and for the growing collection of books. Meanwhile, not only was the exterior of the building repointed and the windows releaded, but the interior walls and floors were renewed and new furniture and lighting were provided. Besides changes in the library, the central heating plant was converted from coal to oil, and new underground steam pipes leading to various buildings were laid. Together with the routine renovation of other buildings, the repaving of roadways, the repair of the wall along Germantown Avenue, and the laying of new cement walks, it was reported in 1953 that a total of about $525,000 had been spent in the course of the preceding seven years "in an effort to catch up with much needed and long delayed renovations and improvements."[3] To prevent a repetition of such costly neglect of the seminary buildings, provision was made for the annual allocation of funds for maintenance and for the addition of a general maintenance man to the staff.[4] When George Pehlman retired in 1953, Jack Kranich, who had already been on the staff for sixteen years, became the chief of the grounds crew, and since 1955 Nelson Blank was the general maintenance man.

The renovations of the old buildings actually did little more than postpone necessity for new construction. When, in 1959, a committee of the American Association of Theological Schools inspected the seminary, it reported that student housing was "antiquated in appointment," that classrooms were inadequate, and that the campus had "no gymnasium, no auditorium, and no union building." The general impression made on the committee was that the seminary's buildings were "not quite bad enough to inspire in the students a sense of social reform or prophetic rebellion, nor yet proper enough to inspire social graces." In 1961 a committee of the board of directors expressed the judgment that "the total plant of the seminary is basically inadequate and unsatisfactory for meeting present and future needs."[5]

The decisions involved in the improvement program were the responsibility of the board of directors. On his death in 1944 Mr. E. Clarence Miller was suc-

Frank M. Urich and Harold S. Miller, Presidents of the Board of Directors

ceeded as president of the board by the Rev. Frank M. Urich, D.D., of Philadelphia. The latter retired in 1951 after seven years and was in turn succeeded by the Rev. Harold S. Miller, D.D., of Brooklyn, N.Y., who remained president until his retirement in 1962. At that time the board of directors chose the Rev. Gunnar Knudsen, D.D., of Reading, Pa., as its chairman. Laymen on the board who rendered long and distinguished service during this period included Mr. Peter P. Hagan, Philadelphia carpet manufacturer; Carl F. R. Hassold, investment broker in Philadelphia; Mr. Claude B. Wagoner, Philadelphia attorney; Judge James F. Henninger, of Allentown, Pa.; Professor Roy H. Johnson, of Thiel College in Greenville, Pa.; Mr. George M. Gebhardt, banker in Pottsville, Pa.; and Mr. William F. Drehs, professional photographer in Reading, Pa. Among the clerical members of the board who were especially active over a long period of years were the Rev. Emil W. Weber, D.D., of Pottsville, Pa.; the Rev. Arnold F. Keller, D.D., of Utica, N. Y.; the Rev. George T. Miller, D.D., of Egg Harbor City, N. J., and the Rev. Samuel E. Kidd, D.D., who was a member of the board before as well as after his election as president of the Ministerium of Pennsylvania.

In 1943 the charter and the bylaws of the seminary were changed to provide for a more equitable representation on the board by the supporting synods; communicant membership and current appropriations and gifts were made determinative.[6] After 1950, when the Synod of New Jersey was organized by the transfer to it of congregations and ministers from the adjacent synods in Pennsylvania and New York, it elected its own representatives to the board of

The Lutheran Church in America was
Formed by Merger in 1962

directors. When the Lutheran Church in America was formed in 1962, three additional synods were represented on the board: the New England Synod, as a new synod now separate from the New York Synod, and the Slovak Zion and Caribbean Synods.[7]

The seminary's administration shared responsibility with the board of directors for the improvement program. The Rev. Frederic W. Friday, who was registrar from 1927 to 1944, supervised such work as was done on the grounds and in the buildings in his time. Some of this responsibility fell to the lot of the Rev. Edward T. Horn III, who was registrar from 1944 to 1946. In the latter year the Rev. John A. Kaufmann was appointed registrar. Born in 1920 in Wyomissing, Pa., he was graduated from Lehigh University and the Philadelphia Seminary and did graduate work in the latter (S.T.M.) and in the University of Pennsylvania. It was during his term of office as registrar that the extensive renovations which have been described were made. Not only did he supervise the work that was done and often assist in the work itself, but he exercised increasing influence in the decisions that had to be made and the policies that had to be formulated.

The president of the seminary, as the administrative head of the school, of course also had a hand in the shaping of policies pertaining to physical as well as academic matters. When President Charles M. Jacobs died in the spring of 1938, Professor Reed, as "the member of the faculty longest connected with the seminary," was appointed acting president, "pending the election of a successor to Dr. Jacobs." Before accepting the appointment, Professor Reed sought "a re-assuring statement concerning his health" from his physician. A year later, after his sixty-sixth birthday, he was made president and continued in this position for six years — "an interlude," he himself called it — until his retirement in 1945. His connection with the seminary had spanned almost half of its history. He had personally known all but three of its professors, and in his old age he had been called, he declared, "to an office to which I had never aspired and for whose duties I was unprepared and, in my own judgment, unqualified."[8] Many administrative duties were assigned to other members of the faculty during these years, the heaviest of them being borne by his successor.

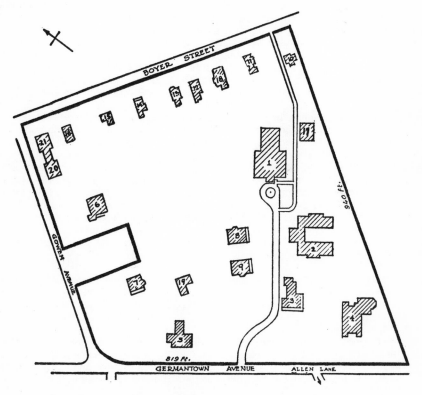

Plan of the Seminary Campus in 1963. 1. Library. 2. Main Dormitory. 3. Hagan Hall. 4. Chapel. 5. Refectory. 6. Graduate Hall. 9. North Dormitory. 17. Power House. Others are Faculty Residences

A professor since 1937, Paul J. Hoh was elected president of the seminary in 1945 and continued in this position until just before his death seven years later. Throughout his administration he carried three-fourths of a full teaching load; yet, unlike his predecessors, he spent most of his time in his office and devoted much of his energy to planning, promotion, and the counseling of students. Under his direction the administrative offices were enlarged and brought to a high degree of efficiency. Besides the registrar and a secretary, a bookkeeper-office manager (Miss Margaret Ost served for almost nineteen years, until 1961) and two additional stenographers were in time employed to care for the increasing work load. President Hoh was frequently summoned to speak in behalf of the seminary, and it was under his leadership that most of the physical improvements were planned and carried out. During his last years he was overtaken by ill health and died of leukemia in 1952.9

In President Hoh's last illness Professor Russell D. Snyder was named acting president "until such time as a president shall be elected." Six months later, in 1952, the Rev. Henry H. Bagger was elected president. Born in 1893 in Brooklyn, N. Y., he was a graduate of Muhlenberg College and the Philadelphia Seminary and did graduate work in English Literature in the University of Pennsylvania (A.M.). He was pastor of St. Paul's Church, Morgantown, W. Va., and First Church in Butler, Pa., before serving as president of the Pittsburgh Synod from 1930 to 1940. For twelve years thereafter he was pastor of Trinity Church in Lancaster, Pa. He was a member of the executive board of the United Lutheran Church for sixteen years and a member of its board of education for ten years. He was also a member of commissions on Lutheran unity for a total of twenty-eight years. The author of *Forty Thousand Strong* (1939), he received the degrees of D.D. from Gettysburg College in 1933 and of LL.D. from Muhlenberg College in 1953. Dr. Bagger was the first president of the seminary to be chosen from outside of the faculty and the first to serve in this office without previous experience in theological education. As a matter of fact, he was elected with the understanding that teaching (in Church Administration and practice preaching) should occupy only a minimum of his time and that he should concentrate on the internal and external administration of a corporation whose operating budget rose from $200,000 to $365,000 during the ten years of his incumbency. These were years of little change and quiet growth, undisturbed by either war or economic depression, during which President Bagger made it his modest goal, as he once put it, "to maintain the greatness of the past and continue it into the future." On his retirement at the close of the year 1962 an interim administration committee, consisting of the chairman of the board, another member of the board, and Professor Snyder, was appointed to serve until the election of a new president.10

It was under such leadership in the board and administration that the program of physical renovation and improvement was undertaken after World War II. The way was prepared for this in 1941 and 1942 by a "united appeal" conducted in the Ministerium of Pennsylvania to raise a total of $500,000 for the Philadelphia Seminary and Muhlenberg College. Professor Hoh rather than President Reed assumed leadership in behalf of the seminary during this effort, and members of the faculty were drafted to meet more than 400 speaking engagements. Like previous financial appeals for both college and seminary, this one barely reached half of the goal, but the $150,000 received by the seminary was applied to wiping out the operating deficits accumulated over many decades. In 1943 the deficits which remained were written off by the board of directors — that is, undesignated endowment funds were used to pay the deficits — and an attempt was made thereafter to balance the current budgets. Of a little help in this direction was the Reformation day appeal for higher education in the United Synod of New York and New England — somewhat parallel, although on a much

more modest scale, to the united appeal in the Ministerium of Pennsylvania —
from which the seminary received $5,382 between 1944 and 1947.[11]

More significant in the long run was the increase in annual appropriations
from the supporting synods, an almost tenfold increase (in inflated dollars, to
be sure) between 1938 and 1963. The Ministerium of Pennsylvania advanced its
annual appropriation of $18,000 in 1938 to $102,000 in the seminary's fiscal year
1962. The United Synod of New York and New England raised its annual appropriation from $1,795 in 1938 to $75,000 in 1962, an especially noteworthy advance. During the same period the Pittsburgh Synod increased its appropriation
from $770 to $9,778, and the Synod of New Jersey, organized in 1950, brought
its appropriation to $11,250 by the seminary's fiscal year 1962. Even at that, the
per capita giving for theological education in the supporting synods of the
Philadelphia Seminary remained less than half of that of the Illinois, Indiana,
Northwest, Pacific Southwest, and Canada Synods and remained lower than almost
any other synod. There was a concurrent increase in student fees, and the seminary benefited from this especially during the war-time acceleration, it was
pointed out, when students were paying for an additional term while the faculty

COME, YE SONS OF OLD MOUNT AIRY

Henry B. Luffberry '42   Luther F. Schlenker '38

1. Come, ye sons of old Mount Ai-ry,   Swell her hymn of praise;
2. Go , ye sons of old Mount Ai-ry,   From her hal-lowed halls,

God-ward in a might-y cho-rus,   Now your voi-ces raise.
In - to fields of val-iant ser-vice   Christ, the Sav-iour calls.

Let the strains de-clare her glo-ry,   And her praise pro-claim;
On-ward, then, ye fear-less proph-ets,   Count-ing gain but loss,

Till the earth and sky re-ech-o   Her un - dy - ing fame.
Till the sons of ev-'ry na-tion   Gath-er 'neath the cross.

was doing extra teaching at the same salary. The consequence of all this was that the seminary's fiscal year 1945 ended without a deficit for the first time in thirty-eight years, [12] and the seminary continued thereafter to operate with a balanced budget, with the exception of fiscal years 1947 and 1948.

The improvement program itself was made possible by additional income. The gathering of about $200,000 in gifts through the personal solicitations of Mr. Hagan has been mentioned. A similar amount was raised by the church-wide appeal of the Christian Higher Education Year in 1950. This appeal was for a total of $6,000,000 and was of special benefit to colleges of the United Lutheran Church. The Philadelphia Seminary received only $195,547 as its share — 72% of it from the Ministerium of Pennsylvania, 20% from the United Synod of New York and New England, 8% from the Pittsburgh Synod.[13]

Another source of income, continuing through the years, was the Women's Auxiliary, organized in 1939 at the suggestion of a number of women in Philadelphia who were interested in the seminary. Within a few years many women in the supporting synods were enrolled — over 6,000 by 1945, over 17,000 by 1960 — and in the course of the years between 1939 and 1964 a total of about $250,000 was contributed to the seminary, most of it for renovations or other improvements on the campus.[14] The following, in the order of their succession, were presidents of the organization: Mrs. F. Eppling Reinartz, Mrs. Theodore K. Finck, Mrs. G. Elson Ruff, Mrs. Earl S. Erb, Mrs. S. White Rhyne, Mrs. George B. Ammon, Mrs. Arthur H. Getz, Mrs. Claude B. Wagoner. The success of these women incited some men to form a similar organization, called Men of Mount Airy Seminary, in 1948. Since then about $100,000 was gathered, especially for the maintenance and improvement of the seminary property, under the leadership of the following presidents: John H. Schul, Peter P. Hagan, and Leonard F. Ashford.[15] The Alumni Gift Fund, later called the Living Endowment Fund, continued to be gathered annually by the Alumni Association, for a few years in cooperation with the Men of Mount Airy Seminary but as a rule independently of this organization. Annual receipts of $1,500 to $4,000 were gathered under the leadership of the following presidents since 1938: W. Karl Hemsath, Ernest J. Hoh, Bela Shetlock, Gustav K. Huf, W. Chester Hill, Theodore L. Fischer, Fred E. Ringham, Jr., Oswald Elbert, and John J. Ziegler, Jr.

Legacies, generally added to the endowment of the seminary unless otherwise designated, also helped to ease financial pressure. Among these were bequests of $12,000 in 1944 from the estate of Miss Emma Schmauk of Lebanon, Pa.; of $7,700 in 1947 from the estate of Mr. J. Harvey Wattles, of Pittsburgh; of $10,000 in the same year from the estate of Mrs. Anna C. Robertson, of Philadelphia; of $75,000 in 1951 from the estate of Mrs. L. Elizabeth Nax, of Philadelphia; of $10,000 in 1952 from the estate of the Rev. John A. Weyl, of New York City; of $10,000 in 1953 from the estate of Mamie G. Longaker; of $10,000 in 1954 from the estate of Mrs. Coe K. Stough and of $9,000 in the same year from the estate of Mr. David D. Fritch; of $26,000 in 1956 from the estate of Cora Fretz and of $18,000 in the same year from the estate of Mary A. M. Schnepel; of $30,000 in 1959 from the estate of Mrs. S. Frederick Telleen, of New York City; of $74,000 in 1960 from the estate of Mr. Francis O. Ritter, of Allentown, Pa., and of $26,800 in the same year from the estate of Mrs. Emma R. Binnix; of $52,000 in 1962 from the estates of the Rev. and Mrs. John C. Fisher, of Philadelphia; of $10,000 in the same year from the estate of Mr. Harry R. W. Rahn; and also of $10,000 from the estate of Mr. Peter P. Hagan. Besides, in 1961 the seminary received from Messrs. Otto F. and Theodore A. Wiedemann, of Center Square and Norristown, Pa., a gift of twenty-eight acres in nearby Plymouth Township, Pa., which was valued at about $84,000.[16]

Between 1938 and 1963 the undergraduate enrollment registered a general but not a uniform increase. Hardly had the size of the student body recovered from the effects of the economic depression when World War II brought about another decline. There were 98 undergraduates during the academic year 1940-41 but only 61 in the year 1946-47. Some who had matriculated were given leaves of absence to enlist in the armed forces.[17] More who intended to apply for admission to the seminary interrupted their education to serve in the army, navy, or air force. After the war the enrollment quickly increased again to 100 in 1949, to 150 in 1951, and to 165 in 1957. There the undergraduate enrollment leveled off. During this whole period the standards of admission were made increasingly rigid. In 1940 six applicants were refused admission, and by 1954 only 54 of the total of 85 applicants were admitted.[18] The faculty could afford to be stricter in its requirements not only because the demands placed on the ministry were greater than they had been before but also on account of the limitations in existing dormitory and classroom space. The truth of the matter is that the seminary could not have accommodated as many as it did if it had not been for the fact that increasing numbers of students were married.

The marriage of undergraduates was quite uniformly frowned upon before World War II. In 1930 the faculty had formally expressed its opinion on the matter: "The marriage of students during their course (a) is not consistent with the demands of true self-respect because of the inability of the student to provide a home; (b) it tends to interfere with the development of an esprit de corps among the students; (c) it tempts the students to frustrate one of the purposes of marriage, viz., the establishment of a home."[19] This attitude persisted among some members of the faculty, and the earlier, paternalistic practice of reserving the right to grant or refuse a student permission to marry continued to be observed by President Reed to 1944. Thereafter all that was required was that a student report any change in his status during his seminary course. Many of the war veterans who now began to resume their studies (almost a fourth of the students in 1946 were veterans) were already married when they entered the seminary, and it became the increasing practice of others to marry during their course. By 1950 about half of the undergraduates were married, and after 1960 there was only a slight decline in the number.

It was inevitable that the question should be raised whether special housing should be provided for married students. The decision was negative "in view of the present financial condition of the seminary" and in view of the availability of apartments in the neighborhood of the seminary.[20] There is little doubt that married couples enjoyed much more independence and comfort by not being compelled to live in dormitories for married students. In any case, the fact that they lived off the campus relieved the pressure for dormitory space.

Undergraduates continued to come in largest numbers from church-related colleges, especially in the constituent synods. Muhlenberg, Wagner, and Thiel still headed the list, but while these colleges had formerly accounted for more than 75% of the students, they now came to represent only 40% of the enrollment. After World War II between 45 and 65 colleges and universities were represented in the student body, and the students came from many more states than before. Moreover, there were always some foreign students to contribute to the cosmopolitan character of the academic community. From time to time a few women, notably such as were in training for the female diaconate, were enrolled as part-time students. This was in keeping with the somewhat oblique action of the board of directors in 1948 that "there is no reason to oppose the admission, in exceptional cases, of women who are graduates of accredited colleges to some courses at the seminary." Not until 1962 was the charter of the seminary changed in such a way as to make the admission of women as regular students possible.[21]

During World War II the seminary accelerated its academic program in keeping with the requirements of the selective service system of the federal government. A summer term was added, and this made it possible for students to complete their course of studies in two instead of three calendar years. In order to accommodate students whose work was accelerated in college, too, the curriculum was so arranged as to permit their admission in March, July, or November and their graduation in February, June, or October. The most obvious consequence of such acceleration from July, 1944, to June, 1946, was that the average age of graduates was reduced from about 26 to about 24. A less apparent

Navy Trainees During World War II

but not less real consequence, in the opinion of the faculty, was that the students were deprived of the leisure to ponder and to mature intellectually. Certainly the members of the faculty were made aware of their own loss of sustained periods of time for creative research and study. During the two years of acceleration the seminary participated in the Navy V-12 program for the training of chaplains. Twenty-three navy trainees from the United Lutheran Church, the Augustana Church, the Evangelical Lutheran Church, and even the Lutheran Protestant Conference pursued the regular course of studies and were distinguishable from other students only by their uniforms.[22]

To meet the requirements of the selective service system, pretheological students began to be registered in 1941,[23] and this added to the paper work imposed on the office staff. In the same year a medical program was introduced according to which students had the free services of a physician and received prescribed medicines without charge. This program was introduced by the seminary to supplant the generous treatment formerly given to students by Lankenau Hospital. Ten years later a voluntary medical insurance program was added at an annual fee of $15.00, and in 1963 a Blue Cross-Blue Shield student medical plan was substituted.[24] Like everything else, the fees charged to students increased. No tuition was charged before 1954 but the so-called contingent or general fee rose to $100 a year in 1942, to $150 in 1955, and to $270 in 1962. A dormitory use fee of $70 was added in 1955 and raised to $120 by 1960. Meanwhile the cost of board in the refectory rose from $193.50 a year in 1942 to $456.00 a year in 1960. When the refectory's long-time matron Mrs. Agnes

Vansant retired in 1956, the Slater System took over. The increase in the cost of meals was not brought about by this change so much as by the rise in the cost of food and labor. In fact, the operating costs of the seminary as a whole almost tripled since World War II.[25]

In 1945 an orientation program was introduced for entering students and extended over several days before the formal opening of the academic year. Nine years later vocational and personality tests were required of entering students. In 1938 it was found that 50% of the incoming students were from the top third of their college classes. By 1943 this figure dropped to 40%, and in 1959 the academic average of entering students was computed to be 2.47 out of a possible 4.00. The apparent decline in academic rating probably reflected stiffer college standards; at all events, it was by no means below the national average of students of theology.

When the number of married students increased during and after World War II, Professor Hoh arranged occasional programs for the wives, and this led to the organization of a Wives' Club, which met regularly for discussion and fellowship. Missionary interest among the students continued to be fostered by the Heyer Commission, as it was now called, which annually raised $400 or $500 for special projects in India, Liberia, Japan, Malaya, Argentina, Puerto Rico,

Basketball Team

British Guiana, Tanganyika, etc. Occasional receptions and teas were held in faculty homes, but the less formal coffee breaks which the students arranged for themselves were undoubtedly even more productive of social fellowship.[26] For recreation and exercise students turned to tennis, basketball, volleyball, touch football, and badminton.

There was a gradual but observable change in the attitudes of most students. The earlier acquiescence in the status quo was shaken during the great economic depression,[27] when students began to be more aware of the kind of world in which they were living, and World War II increased their restlessness and their dissatisfaction with answers to questions they were no longer asking. Increasingly, students became preoccupied with social problems and the relevance of the Christian life to them. They struggled to understand the teaching of the church in the light of modern scientific and philosophical ideas. They took more seriously the results of an historical and literary criticism of the Bible and inquired about the consequences of this for the Christian faith. What was characteristic of all of these students was that they were no longer content with an appeal to authority. The increasingly dominant tendency was to question and to challenge the heritage from the past.

To be sure, there were also students who ignored the questions which were troubling most of their contemporaries, and there were others who sought refuge in ecclesiastical, doctrinal, or liturgical tradition. As early as 1935 the Rev. Augustus Steimle, D.D., referred to a minority that "finds satisfaction and joy by clothing its devotions in the ancient habiliments of formalism and treasures every outward manifestation in worship which has some historical precedent as the true means of approach to God." Of such romanticism President Charles M. Jacobs curtly said, "We believe that this is a mistaken emphasis and do not encourage it."[28] It grew, however, without encouragement from the faculty, and more than twenty years later even President Emeritus Reed was constrained to declare, "Its weakness lies in its emphasis on externalities, its extreme formalism, the constant necessity which rests upon it to explain its occult practices and to differentiate them from the practices of unevangelical churches, and the general lack of missionary spirit which remains satisfied with maintaining services of meaning and beauty for the few 'insiders.'" In the long run neither admonitions "to hold to middle ground" nor cautions to observe "good taste" met the issue.[29]

During the period after 1938 as well as during the preceding period there was experimentation and change in the chapel program. The time for daily Matins was altered several times, but 10 a.m. was the usual hour. In 1944 and again in 1953 Vespers were added, sometimes twice and sometimes four times a week, in response to requests "from a number of students."[30] At the urging of President Reed the long custom of celebrating the Lord's Supper in the chapel about four or five times a year (in addition to such access to the sacrament as

Seminary Choir in 1959

118

was available elsewhere on Sundays) was altered by the innovation of voluntary weekly communion on Thursday mornings. This did not prove to be generally satisfactory for a variety of reasons. In 1957 President Bagger therefore reduced the observance to every other week, and three years later the faculty decided to return to a frequency comparable with that which had obtained before 1944.[31] These changes were attended by extensive discussions among students and members of the faculty. Some of the latter were simultaneously engaged in the study of parallel questions raised in various parts of the church,[32] and it became increasingly evident that the arbiter in matters of this kind must ultimately be an understanding of man's total relation to God in and through the church and a recognition of the fact that the seminary is in the first instance a school and not a church.

There were also changes and experimentation in the curriculum. The former practice of separating graduation from admission to the degree of bachelor of divinity was discontinued. Beginning in 1942, the degree was conferred on graduation. The requirement of a thesis was tentatively dropped the same year, and in 1949 the comprehensive examinations given to Seniors were discontinued. In 1940 a period of supervised study and research, during which regular classes were suspended, was introduced. At first the period lasted two weeks in the fall of the year and later it was lengthened to four weeks and located between semesters. After ten years the experiment was given up on the ground that it was not of value to all students, and seminars were restored to the roster as electives. In 1959 an annual inter-seminary seminar was introduced, and academic credit was given to a limited number of participants selected from six seminaries in the Philadelphia area (Baptist, Moravian, United Church of Christ, Episcopal, and Lutheran). More important changes in the external structure of the undergraduate curriculum were made in 1958 after a long study by the faculty. The academic year was lengthened by a week, and the year was divided into three quarters (without the summer quarter) rather than two semesters. Most courses extended over more than one quarter, and so the common weakness of numerous splinter courses was avoided. In fact, the number of courses was reduced (by combining them in many cases), and they were arranged in a sequence which was intended to reflect the stages in a student's theological development. Insofar as teaching loads and the availability of classrooms permitted, large classes were divided into sections. Moreover, the faculty decided to require a knowledge of Greek for admission by the fall of 1965.[33]

Such changes were accompanied by a gradual tightening of academic standards, and students (generally in their first year) who were unable or unwilling to meet the requirements were dropped from the rolls. At the same time increased attention was given to field work. A program was first developed by Professor Hoh, and by the close of World War II every student was assigned during his first two years to a parish or a welfare institution as well as a practice teaching situation. As a rule the parish assignment was for weekends only, and the other assignments were for one or two afternoons a week. Hospitals, prisons, reformatories, settlements, homes for the aging, and other institutions were visited, and a limited number of students spent an additional summer under supervisors accredited by the Council for the Clinical Training of Theological Students. For eleven years, beginning in 1948, this program was continued under the direction of Professor Doberstein, who, like Professor Hoh before him, devoted only spare time to it. This was changed in 1959 with the calling of the Rev. John P. Stump as director of field work. In addition to service as a navy chaplain during World War II, Mr. Stump served parishes in Philadelphia, Pittsburgh, Brooklyn, and La Canada, Calif., and did graduate work in Union Theological Seminary. In 1963 he resigned to become a secretary for the board of theological education of the Lutheran Church in America. He concurred in the judgment of the faculty that the arrangement of making the director of field work an administrative officer prevented a proper correlation of field work with the academic program of the seminary. Provision was accordingly made for an additional instructor in Practical Theology, special responsibility for field work was assigned to the whole teaching staff in the practical area, and an attempt was made to shift as much instruction in this area as feasible from the classroom to the field. To accommodate some of this instruction, at least one summer quarter was added to the requirements for graduation.[34]

The rationale underlying all these (and also projected additional) changes was expressed by the faculty in these terms: "(1) A theological seminary is a community of faculty and students whose task within the total mission of the church is the broad and inclusive one of providing theological leadership and guidance in the church under the Word of God. (2) Basic to this task is the education of men primarily for the parish ministry and also for specialized ministries which have become vital to the church's life. It includes also the education of lay men and women for specific tasks in the church so that they, too, may be better prepared to be the church in the world. (3) In this context the aim is, briefly stated, to help students toward a fuller understanding and appropriation of the Gospel and to a greater effectiveness in its communication. . . . Therefore, it is essential to provide the kind of community life most favorable to the realization of this aim. (4) This total orientation requires that the seminary be more than a training institution. As an institution of higher learning in a context of universal knowledge, it is properly a place for critical and creative study and research in all areas of the church's concern . . . . (5) The aim and purpose of theological education also requires a living dialogue between the church and the world. This is essential because the Gospel is always addressed to a particular situation. Christians must employ constantly changing forms in order to be true to their unchanging Lord . . . ."[35]

Austerities connected with World War II, notably the rationing of gasoline, caused some retrenchment in the program of the graduate school. In 1942 graduate classes were concentrated on one day (Thursday mornings and afternoons), and this emergency measure was continued for more than two decades, except in the case of graduate students who devoted their full time to study, on account of the statistical reduction in teaching loads in the face of expanding undergraduate and graduate enrollments. The number of graduate students dropped over 30% during the war and was also reduced by the imposition of larger fees.[36] However, after the war there was again a fairly steady growth. The annual enrollment exceeded 100 after 1958, and the proportion of non-Lutherans grew from 19% to 34%. The academic offerings were strengthened by the introduction of seminars in 1954 and of more rigid standards for dissertations. After the death of Charles M. Jacobs in 1938 the administration of the graduate school was temporarily placed in the hands of a committee of the faculty. In 1943 Professor Nolde was made dean of the graduate school and served in this capacity until 1962, when a committee again took care of administrative matters temporarily.[37]

Regulations governing graduate fellowships were liberalized in 1958,[38] and the following served as fellows between 1938 and 1964: Luther F. Schlenker, Joseph L. Schantz, George Mack, Donald R. Pichaske, Charles J. Harris, Whitson Seaman, Theodore A. Hartig, John A. Kaufmann, John D. Newpher, Robert J. Goeser, Robert E. Bornemann, Celo V. Leitzel, Arvid E. Anderson, John Reumann, Robert C. Brecheisen, James A. Harrison, H. George Anderson, Norman P. Melchert, Charles P. Sigel, Ernest R. Walek, Foster R. McCurley, Jr. In addition to the courses offered in the graduate school, members of the faculty gave an annual series of extension lectures in New York, Albany, and

Rochester, N. Y., from 1944 to 1953 and at Thiel College in Greenville, Pa., from 1948 to 1953.[39] The pastors' convocation continued to be held on the campus during Easter week of every year under the auspices of the Alumni Association.

In the light of the greatly increased enrollment of graduate and under-graduate students the enlargement of the faculty was modest and tardy. In 1939, when the economic depression was yielding place to preparation for war, a member of the board of directors declared, "If the seminary had had a budget in the last few years, it would not have dared to elect as many men to its faculty as it has seen fit to call. We have a larger faculty than we are justified in main-taining."[40] Considerations of economy prevented increase in the size of the faculty until after World War II. Meager provision was made for an additional professor in 1952, when Mr. and Mrs. Peter P. Hagan endowed a professorship of "applied Christianity" by adding $10,000 to a previous gift of $30,000 for a lectureship.[41] In 1960 the Women's Auxiliary of the seminary began to gather $100,000 for another professorship, in honor of Luther D. Reed, and it was anticipated that the endowment would be completed by 1964.[42] While before World War II the number of professors remained at seven, after the war there were eight professors who gave their full time to teaching, and there were also three, four, or five instructors and assistant professors, besides several part-time teachers.[43]

The increase in salaries was as modest and tardy as the increase in personnel. From 1864 to 1913 the salary of a professor was $1,800. The increase to $2,000 in 1913 was inadequate to meet the higher cost of living during and following World War I, and so a bonus of $300 and then $400 was given annually from 1918 to 1920 "in view of the increased expenses." Salaries were advanced to $2,750 in 1920, to $3,300 in 1923, and to $3,600 in 1926. In 1932, during the economic depression, salaries were reduced to $3,240, and the cuts were not restored until 1943. In 1948, after the cost of living had almost doubled again, salaries were raised to $4,350.[44] Since that time substantial increases were

Faculty in 1939. Front row, left to right: Frederic W. Friday (registrar), Russell D. Snyder, Henry Offermann, Luther D. Reed, Emil E. Fischer, O. Frederick Nolde. Back row: Luther F. Schlenker (fellow), Paul J. Hoh, George R. Seltzer, Theodore G. Tappert, Joseph W. Inslee (fellow), Charles M. Cooper

made. Provision for sabbaticals was first made in 1958, originally for one semester or one quarter, and then for two quarters and a summer.[45] Secretarial help, often quite limited, began to be provided for faculty members in 1951.[46] Retirement of a professor at the age of 70 was permitted after 1920, but not required until 1944; since 1962 a professor was given the option of retiring at age 65 instead of 70.[47] A statement on tenure was adopted by the board of directors in 1960. Long before this members of the faculty were encouraged to participate in learned societies connected with their disciplines.[48] Many of them were also active participants in the Conference of Lutheran Professors of Theology, held annually since 1927 for professors in the United Lutheran Church and since 1943 for professors in all Lutheran churches in the United States and Canada.

The theology taught in the seminary during the quarter of a century between 1938 and 1964 may be characterized as historical in its orientation, but not in the sense in which this had been true before. The ecclesiastical heritage continued to be respected but it was no longer looked upon as normative. On the one hand, this heritage was not seen in the same light as before. It was subjected to re-examination, and earlier views about it were in certain respects altered. This applies not only to the immediate heritage of the Lutheran Church in the United States but also to the larger Reformation tradition, and indeed to the whole Christian past, including the Scriptures themselves. On the other hand, the heritage of the past was adapted to the needs of the changing world. Not only did it become clearer that the form of every teaching and practice of the past was conditioned, but 'the need for a more conscious address by the church to people of a new age was also recognized. The seminary participated in the revived interest in theology which was generally characteristic of this period. Its teaching was influenced in various ways by the Luther renaissance, by new biblical studies, by existentialism, by the ecumenical movement, by new social awareness. The faculty was stimulated by its close acquaintance with European as well as American thought, but it remained no less Lutheran in its confessional position. A brief review of the careers of the members of the faculty will support this general characterization.

The first in chronological order among those whose major teaching falls in this period is O. Frederick Nolde.[49] Born in Philadelphia in 1899, he was graduated from Muhlenberg College and the Philadelphia Seminary, where he also did graduate work. He served for three years as pastor of Grace Church in Wyndmoor, a suburb of Philadelphia, while he pursued graduate studies in Education at the University of Pennsylvania (Ph.D.). In 1925 he was made instructor, in 1928 assistant professor, and in 1931 professor of Christian Education in the Philadelphia Seminary. At the same time, from 1925 to 1943, he was part-time instructor, assistant professor, and lecturer in Education at the University of Pennsylvania. It was under his direction that seminary students began to engage in practice teaching in a released-time school. Until World War II most of Professor Nolde's writing was in the field of education. Besides occasional articles, he wrote The Department of Christian Education in the Theological Seminary (1929), Guidebook in Catechetical Instruction (1932), Yesterday, Today, and Tomorrow (1933), eight small texts for leadership training in collaboration with Paul J. Hoh (1934-37), and Truth and Life (1937).

During World War II, moved by concern about the troubled world situation, Dean Nolde turned his attention in a new direction. He became a member of the Commission on a Just and Durable Peace of the Federal Council of Churches, in 1943 was secretary of the Princeton International Round Table, in 1944 was appointed executive secretary of the Joint Committee on Religious Liberty, and in 1945 was selected as an associate consultant to the United States delegation to the United Nations Conference convened in San Francisco. In 1946 he was made director of the Commission of the Churches on International Affairs and two years later became associate general secretary of the World Council of Churches with the portfolio of international affairs. These activities made increasing demands on Dean Nolde's time. He was given a few short-term leaves by the seminary, and from 1949 to 1953 he was assisted in his undergraduate courses by an instructor, the Rev. Celo V. Leitzel.[50] After 1953, with the exception of one year, Dean Nolde limited his teaching to the graduate school, where his courses dealt with international problems, world order, human rights, the ecumenical movement, etc. In 1962 he was placed on indefinite leave. In addition to the drafting of countless policy statements and the publication of a score of articles for scholarly journals and symposia in his later years, he wrote *Christian World Action* (1942), *Power for Peace* (1946), and *Freedom's Charter* (1949). He received degrees of D.D. and LL.D. from Muhlenberg College in 1932 and 1946, of L.H.D. from Wittenberg College in 1952, of Litt.D. from Temple University in 1957.

Russell D. Snyder was the second member of the teaching staff in this period. Born in Berrysburg, Pa., in 1898, he was a graduate of Muhlenberg College and the Philadelphia Seminary. He did graduate work in the latter, and also in English Literature in the University of Pennsylvania (A.M.). For three years he was pastor of St. Peter's Church in Shepherdstown, W. Va., and for four years he was pastor of the Church of the Incarnation in Philadelphia. In 1931 he was elected professor in the seminary. The long illness and then the death of Professor Seegers compelled Professor Snyder to teach Practical Theology for several years before he was able to return to the teaching of the

Faculty in 1946. Front row, left to right: Theodore G. Tappert, Luther D. Reed, Paul J. Hoh, Charles M. Cooper. Second row, left to right: George R. Seltzer, O. Frederick Nolde. Third row, left to right: Elmer E. Zieber, Russell D. Snyder. Fourth row, left to right: Robert E. Bornemann (fellow), Martin J. Heinecken, John A. Kaufmann

New Testament and ancient Church History, for which he had originally been called.[51] With an interruption of only two years, he was a member of the Board of Publication of the United Lutheran Church from 1932 to 1958, and in 1949 he was made a member of Lankenau Hospital's board of trustees. For many years a popular lecturer in summer assemblies, he was the author of the treatment of I Corinthians in H. C. Alleman, ed., *New Testament Commentary* (1936), and wrote *The Book of Life* (1950) and *Jesus: His Mission and Teaching* (1959), the former also translated into Spanish and the latter into Telegu. In addition he contributed a few articles to church journals and a symposium and had several sermons published. In 1932 he received the degree of D.D. from Muhlenberg College.

Paul J. Hoh has already been mentioned as president of the seminary. His early death limited his teaching in the seminary to fifteen years. Born as the son of a minister in Reading, Pa., in 1893, he was a graduate of the University of Pennsylvania and the Philadelphia Seminary. After serving pastorates in Bethlehem, Pa., Wildwood, N.J., and Philadelphia, Pa., he was an editor of textbooks for religious education from 1930 to 1937 under the United Lutheran Church's parish and church school board. He was responsible for the "Christian Life Course" and for a pioneer series of leadership texts. He served for a term as a member of the commission of adjudication and for a term on the board of foreign missions of the United Lutheran Church. In 1937 he was called to the seminary as professor of Practical Theology. During World War II he spent his spare time as a panel member of the Philadelphia district of the War Labor Board. He was the co-author of eighteen educational texts, wrote a score of articles for theological journals, and was the author of *Little Children, Come Unto Me* (1927), *The Faith of Our Day* (1939), *Two Minutes with God* (1940), and *Parish Practice* (1944). Professor Hoh was widely known as a popular preacher, and his pastoral counsel was often sought. He died in 1952 after serving as president of the seminary the last seven years of his life. He received the degree of D.D. from Muhlenberg College in 1939 and of LL.D. from Upsala College in 1946.

The next according to seniority was Theodore G. Tappert. The son of a minister, he was born in 1904 in Meriden, Conn., and was a graduate of Wagner College and the Philadelphia Seminary. He did graduate work in the latter school and in History at Columbia University (A.M.) and the University of Pennsylvania and was assistant pastor for about two years in Trinity Church, Staten Island, N. Y. After serving as instructor in the seminary from 1931 to 1936, he was made assistant professor and, on the death of Charles M. Jacobs in 1938, professor of Church History. For twelve years he was a member of the board of publication and for six years a member of the committee on church papers of the United Lutheran Church, and he was a participant in interdenominational as well as denominational study commissions. For six years he was a member of the executive board of the Ministerium of Pennsylvania, since 1952 a member of the board of the Luther-Gesellschaft, since 1957 a member of the board of directors of the Foundation for Reformation Research, and a past president of the American Society for Reformation Research. Besides editing *The Lutheran Quarterly,* he was editor of *The Lutheran World Review* (1948-50) and department editor of the *New Schaff-Herzog Encyclopedia of Religious Knowledge* (2 supplementary vols., 1955). He contributed articles to a half-dozen other encyclopedias, about sixty articles to theological journals, and chapters to a dozen symposia. He translated H. Sasse's *Here We Stand* (1938), and with J. W. Doberstein he edited and translated *The Journals of Henry Melchior Muhlenberg* (3 vols., 1942-1958). He was the author of *The Church Through the Ages* (1941), *Our Neighbors' Churches* (1954), *Luther's Spiritual Counsel* (1955), and *The Lord's Supper* (1961). In

Faculty in 1954. Left to right: Edmund A. Steimle, John Reumann, George R. Seltzer, Robert E. Bornemann, John A. Kaufmann, Theodore G. Tappert, Elmer E. Zieber, John W. Doberstein, Henry H. Bagger, Erich F. Voehringer, O. Frederick Nolde, Luther D. Reed, Russell D. Snyder, Martin J. Heinecken

addition, he collaborated on a new edition of *The Book of Concord* (1959). He received degrees of D.D. from Wagner College in 1938, Luther Seminary in St. Paul in 1956, and the University of Western Ontario in 1959 and the degree of Litt.D. from Muhlenberg College in 1943.

Charles M. Cooper followed in chronological order. Born as the son of a minister in Lima, Ohio, in 1909, he was graduated from Harvard University and the Philadelphia Seminary. After serving as assistant pastor in the Church of the Holy Trinity, Akron, Ohio, for three years, he was called to the seminary in 1936 as an instructor in the Old Testament. In 1941 he was promoted to the rank of assistant professor and in 1945 was elected professor. During these years he completed his graduate studies in Semitics at Dropsie College in Philadelphia (Ph.D.). In addition to a half-dozen articles in learned journals, he contributed to the *Westminister Study Bible* (1948), wrote on Deuteronomy in the *Old Testament Commentary* (1948), edited by H. C. Alleman and E. E. Flack, contributed to the *Uniform Lesson Commentary* in 1954 and 1957, and was the author of *The Psalms in Life* (1959). He had taught Old Testament in the seminary for eighteen years when, in 1953, he was elected president of the Ministerium of Pennsylvania. After eight years in this office he became president of the Pacific Theological Seminary in Berkeley, Calif., in 1961. He received the degree of D.D. from Muhlenberg College in 1954.

Martin J. Heinecken was also the son of a minister and was born in 1902 in Sugar City, Col. A graduate of Wartburg College and of Wartburg Theological Seminary, Dubuque, Iowa, he did his graduate work in Philosophy at the University of Minnesota and the University of Nebraska (Ph.D.). For seven years he was pastor of churches of the American Lutheran Church in Ashland, Wis., and Hebron, Neb. He taught briefly in Immanuel College, Australia, and part-time in Hebron Junior College in Nebraska before joining the faculty of Wagner College in 1939, where he taught Religious Studies. Six years later, in 1945, he was elected professor in the Philadelphia Seminary and taught Systematic Theology. A member at various times of a number of denominational and interdenominational study conferences and commissions (on the ministry, on marriage and divorce, on social responsibility, on Holy Communion, on economic life, on confirmation, etc.), he was often called upon to deliver public lectures and also served on the board of parish education of the United Lutheran Church and of the Lutheran Church in America. The author of about thirty articles in theological journals and in several symposia, he also wrote *Basic Christian Teachings* (1949), *Truths We Live By* (1949), *The Moment Before God: An Interpretation of Kierkegaard* (1956), *Christ Frees and Unites* (1957), *God in the Space Age* (1959), *Beginning and End of the World* (1960), and *The Meaning of the Cross* (1962). He received the degree of Litt.D. from Muhlenberg College in 1959 and of LL.D. from Wartburg College in 1961.

George R. Seltzer was born in Lebanon, Pa., in 1902. A graduate of Muhlenberg College and the Philadelphia Seminary, he was pastor of St. Paul's Church in Hartford, Conn., from 1928 to 1937. During these years he pursued graduate studies in Church History in the Hartford Seminary Foundation (Ph.D.), where he also served for a time as a member of the library staff. In 1937, at a time when Professor Reed's health seemed to be especially precarious, Dr. Seltzer was appointed assistant professor in the Philadelphia Seminary. He devoted only part of his time to the teaching of Liturgics, his special interest, until 1945, when he was elected professor upon President Reed's retirement.[52] Since courses in Liturgics and Church Art did not comprise a full teaching load, Professor Seltzer as a matter of fact continued to teach a course in Church History until 1956. After 1940 he was given charge of chapel services, and for a few years he was director of the student choir. Ever since 1930 he had been a member of liturgical and music committees of the United Lutheran Church, and he was an active member of the joint commission which produced the *Service Book and Hymnal* (1958). Since 1962 he was a member of the commission on worship of the Lutheran Church in America.

John W. Doberstein was born in 1905 in Marinette, Wis., and was graduated from Thiel College and the Philadelphia Seminary. There as well as in the University of Pennsylvania he did some graduate work. From 1932 to 1943 he was pastor of the Church of the Good Shepherd in Philadelphia and of Grace Church in Norristown, Pa., after which he served for four years as chaplain and head of the department of Religion in Muhlenberg College. Since 1960 he was a member of the board of publication of the United Lutheran Church and then of the Lutheran Church in America. He was elected professor in the Philadelphia Seminary in 1947 and taught Homiletics and Pastoral Theology. He compiled many books of prayers for a variety of circumstances and individuals: *On Wings of Healing* (1942), *Student Prayers* (1947), *We Bow our Heads* (1949), *Minister's Prayer Book* (1960), and *A Lutheran Prayer Book* (1960). He was an indefatigable translator from the German, having put into English Dietrich Bonhoeffer's *Life Together* (1954), K. Schubert's *The Dead Sea Community* (1959), H. Girgensohn's *Teaching Luther's Catechism* (2 vols., 1959-60), and Eberhard Mueller's *Conversation on Faith* (1961). He translated a dozen books by theologian-preacher Helmut Thielicke, ranging from *The Waiting Father* (1959) and *How the World Began* (1961) to *Voyage to the Far East* (1962) and *Encounter with Spurgeon* (1963). He also selected and translated a volume of sermons for *Luther's Works* (1959) and collaborated with T. G. Tappert in the publication of *The Journals of Henry Melchior Muhlenberg* (3 vols., 1942-1958) and H. Boehmer's *Road to Reformation* (1946). He received the degrees of Litt.D. from Muhlenberg College in 1943 and D.D. from Thiel College in 1961.

Edmund A. Steimle, the son of a minister, was born in 1907 in Allentown, Pa. He was graduated from Princeton University and the Philadelphia Seminary and also did graduate work at the latter school and in English Literature at the University of Pennsylvania (A.M.). He was pastor of the Church of Our Saviour in Jersey City, N. J., for five years and of the University Lutheran Church in Cambridge, Mass., for twelve years. In 1952 he was elected professor in the Philadelphia Seminary, where he taught Homiletics for nine years. In 1955

Faculty in 1963. Front row, left to right: Martin J. Heinecken, Russell D. Snyder, Henry H. Bagger, John W. Doberstein, Theodore G. Tappert. Second row, left to right: Erich F. Voehringer, William H. Lazareth, John Reumann, George R. Seltzer. Others, left to right: John A. Kaufmann, Henry H. Scherer, Richard W. Lundin, John P. Stump, Victor I. Gruhn, Clarence L. Lee, Robert H. Bornemann, Charles P. Sigel

Professor Steimle began his career as a radio preacher with a series of sermons on the Protestant Hour, and he was also heard from pulpits throughout the country. A volume of his sermons, *Are You Looking for God?* (1957), was published, and many of his sermons were distributed in leaflets to his radio audiences. In 1961 he succeeded Paul E. Scherer as professor of Homiletics in Union Theological Seminary, New York. He received the degrees of D.D. from Wagner College in 1950, of Litt.D. from Muhlenberg College in 1957, and of LL.D. from Roanoke College in 1960.

Erich F. Voehringer was born in 1905 in Ghana, Africa, where his father was a merchant. He studied in Tübingen University, in Germany, and was graduated from the Philadelphia Seminary. He did graduate work in Religion at the University of Pennsylvania (A.M.) and in Anthropology at the University of

Berlin (Ph.D.). For five years he was assistant pastor in the Deaconess Mother-house in Philadelphia, served as missionary on the Gold Coast in Africa from 1933 to 1941 under the Bremen Mission, was pastor of Tabor Church in Philadelphia from 1943 to 1946, and was associate secretary of the World Council of Christian Education from 1946 to 1953. In 1954 he returned to the Philadelphia Seminary as professor of Christian Education and Missions and showed special interest in audio-visual methods and equipment. He was the author of *It Depends on You: a Study of Christian Missions (1961)*.

John H. P. Reumann, the son of a minister, was born in Easton, Pa., in 1927. A graduate of Muhlenberg College and the Philadelphia Seminary, he did his graduate work in the same seminary and in Greek at the University of Pennsylvania (Ph.D.), and he also spent a year at Cambridge University. For a few years he engaged in part-time pastoral work. In 1951 he was appointed instructor and in 1954 assistant professor in the Philadelphia Seminary, where he was made professor of the New Testament in 1959. Since 1960 he was a member of the board of trustees of Muhlenberg College. He wrote several articles for learned journals and in 1961 was made associate editor of *The Journal of Biblical Literature*. He was the author of *Four Centuries of the English Bible* (1961) and in 1963 began to serve as general editor of a series of short studies on the Bible called "Facet Books."

William H. Lazareth was born in New York City in 1928 and was graduated from Princeton University and the Philadelphia Seminary. He did his graduate work in Union Theological Seminary and Columbia University (Ph.D.), in addition to study in Germany and Sweden. From 1955 to 1959 he was instructor in Systematic Theology in the Philadelphia Seminary. In 1959 he was appointed assistant professor and in 1962 he was elected professor. The special area of Systematic Theology for which Professor Lazareth was responsible was Ethics, although not in disjunction from Dogmatics. He was a participant in several denominational and interdenominational commissions and study conferences, especially such as dealt with social questions. Since 1962 he was a member of the board of social ministry of the Lutheran Church in America. In addition to several articles in theological journals and two symposia, he wrote *Luther on the Christian Home* (1960), *Man: in Whose Image* (1961), and, with M. F. Garhart, *Helping Children Know Doctrine* (1963).

Robert H. Bornemann was born in 1923 in Willoughby, Ohio. He was graduated from Wittenberg College and the Philadelphia Seminary. His graduate work in biblical studies was done in the Philadelphia Seminary, Princeton Theological Seminary, and Dropsie College in Philadelphia (Ph.D. candidate). From 1950 to 1953 he was pastor of the Church of the Atonement in Asbury Park, N. J. On the resignation of Professor Cooper in 1953 he was appointed assistant professor of the Old Testament and in 1962 he was promoted to the rank of associate professor.

Richard W. Lundin was born in Kearney, Neb., in 1923. He was graduated from Midland College in Fremont, Neb., and from the Philadelphia Seminary. During World War II he saw active duty in the United States Navy as a lieutenant (j.g.). From 1951 to 1962 he was pastor of St. John's Church in Easton, Pa., and from there he was called to the seminary in 1962 as associate professor of Homiletics, succeeding Professor Steimle.

Clarence L. Lee, the son of a minister, was born in 1929 in Rochester, Minn. He was graduated from St. Olaf College and from Luther Theological Seminary in St. Paul, Minn., both schools of the American Lutheran Church. After 1955 he did graduate work in Church History in Harvard Divinity School

(Th.D. candidate) while serving as stated supply in a congregation in Roxbury, Mass. In 1958 he was appointed instructor and in 1963 action was taken to promote him to the rank of assistant professor of Church History in the Philadelphia Seminary.

There were other members of the teaching staff who served for shorter periods of time. The Rev. Edward T. Horn III was assistant professor of Practical Theology from 1943 to 1946, combining his work in the classroom with the administrative tasks of registrar and office manager; he resigned to become pastor of Trinity Church, Philadelphia (Germantown).[53] The Rev. John A. Kaufmann was lecturer in English Bible from 1946 to 1952, and his instruction was added to his work as registrar until his administrative tasks demanded all his time. During the academic year 1955-56 Professor Martin Schmidt, then of Berlin, Germany, was guest lecturer in Church History, and during the year 1959-60 the Rev. Terence Y. Mullins was guest lecturer in New Testament. In 1958 the Rev. Norman K. Bakken was appointed instructor in the biblical area and remained in this position until 1962, when he was called to teach in Northwestern Theological Seminary, Minneapolis. He was succeeded by the Rev. Victor I. Gruhn, who was called for a two-year term in 1962. The Rev. Charles P. Sigel was also appointed instructor in the biblical field in 1961. In addition to these, there were many special lecturers who gave an occasional course — from the Rev. Fred S. Blank, who gave a course in the Rural Church in 1950-51, to Professor Paul E. Scherer, who returned in 1961-62 to give a course in Homiletics.

When Mr. Robert Schurig died in 1938, voice culture was temporarily assigned to the instructors in Homiletics and Liturgics. In 1939 the services of Mr. G. Marston Haddock were employed, and from 1940 to his death in 1955 the Rev. Elmer E. Zieber was instructor in voice culture. He also became director of the student choir and introduced choir tours in 1950. In 1955 John H. Duddy, Jr., Mus. D., organist and choir director in Trinity Church, Norristown, Pa., was appointed part-time instructor in voice while Professor Bornemann directed the choir.[54]

In 1949 *The Lutheran Church Quarterly,* published jointly by the Philadelphia and Gettysburg seminaries, was merged with *The Augustana Quarterly* and a projected theological journal of the former American Lutheran Church. The ownership of the merged journal was vested in all the seminaries of the churches connected with the National Lutheran Council.[55] Professor Tappert, who was editor of the old quarterly from 1938 to 1949, became editor of the new *Lutheran Quarterly* in 1953. Meanwhile the *Philadelphia Seminary Bulletin* continued to be published regularly, with a more appropriate format since 1944 and with Registrar John A. Kaufmann as editor since 1946. In 1938 it was decided to publish a new edition of the *Biographical Record.*[56] After an interruption caused by World War II and numerous additional delays and postponements, the projected publication finally appeared in connection with the observance of the centennial of the seminary.

The library played an increasingly important role in the intellectual life on the campus, and the renovations which were made in the building increased its attractiveness and efficiency. In addition to several archives, the collection grew to 80,000 volumes. The budget for the purchase of books and periodicals was increased and further enlarged by gifts from the Sealantic Fund, Inc. A notable addition was the gift of a large collection of Luther medals from the Rev. Otto L. Schreiber, Ph.D., of Kingston, N. Y.[57] On the resignation of Miss Winifred V. Eisenberg in 1949 the long outdated arrangement of having a professor serve as director of the library was abolished and supplanted with a library com-

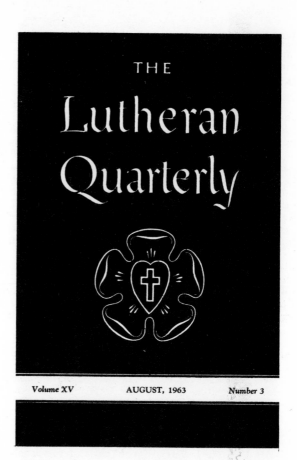

THE

Lutheran

Quarterly

Volume XV   AUGUST, 1963   Number 3

mittee.[58] Miss Margaret J. Hort was appointed librarian and served with great competence for eleven years. She was succeeded in 1960 by the Rev. Henry H. Scherer, Ed.D., who had previously served on the staff of the Midland College library in Fremont, Neb. As for other members of the library staff, by 1964 Mrs. D. Hildenbrand had served thirty years, Mrs. K. Willoughby twenty years, and the Rev. Karl Schild eighteen years.

As in the period before 1938, so in the period after this year, there was discussion of seminary merger. Although earlier attempts to unite Hartwick Seminary with the Philadelphia Seminary had failed, the former became a victim of the economic depression and ceased to exist. In 1939 a special board-faculty committee of the Philadelphia Seminary entered into negotiations with the board of education of the United Synod of New York and New England in the hope of defining the relation of the synod to the seminary and of perpetuating the name of Hartwick in theological education. The latter was not achieved on account of reluctance in New York, but after three years of discussion it was agreed that the two professors of the Ministerium of New York and of the New York and New England Synod should henceforth be elected by the United Synod of New York and New England and not, as formerly, by the Ministerium of Pennsylvania after nomination in New York. It was also agreed that the United Synod of New York and New England should have increased representation on the board of directors in return for increased annual appropriations.[59] As a result of these agreements

the synod entered upon a period of larger support of and more fruitful cooperation with the seminary.

Two decades later, in 1958, the board of directors of the Philadelphia
Seminary once again invited the board of the Gettysburg Seminary to enter jointly
upon consideration of the desirability and feasibility of a merger of their two
schools. For several years committees of the two boards not only met and discussed the proposed consolidation but also engaged a firm of consultants to make
"an objective study of the sociological, educational, economic, and ecclesiastical
aspects of the entire territory of the seven supporting synods, and of the two
seminaries as well, against the background of the whole question of theological
education in the East." The consulting firm of Booz, Allen, and Hamilton recommended after its study that "merger at a new urban and university-oriented site
is the solution which could mean the greatest degree of meaningful stewardship
of Lutheran resources." The substance of this recommendation was endorsed
by both the faculty and the board of the Philadelphia Seminary. When the board
of directors of the Gettysburg Seminary countered with a proposal to merge the
schools at Gettysburg, the negotiations ended in a stalemate inasmuch as this
site did not provide either urban or university orientation.[60]

The unhappy conclusion of the conversations with Gettysburg confronted
the Philadelphia Seminary in its centennial year with the necessity of answering
a number of critical questions: Should new buildings be erected on the existing
site or should the seminary relocate? What kind of university relationship should
be sought, and with which of several possible universities? Who should be chosen
as president to provide vigorous leadership for the years that lie ahead? As early
as 1956 plans had begun to be formulated to launch a centennial appeal for
$1,475,000. At that time it was proposed to use the funds that might be raised to
double the endowment of the seminary and undertake a modest construction program. In view of the discussion of merger with Gettysburg and the possibility of
relocation, plans were held in abeyance and the appeal was postponed from 1962
to 1964.[61] The pattern was familiar.

Gunnar Knudsen, Chairman of the Board
of Directors at the Seminary's Centennial

The century of the seminary's history accordingly approached its close
with unresolved questions. However these might be answered, it seemed certain
that, for better or worse, the seminary was on the threshold of a new era. Change
was not new to the seminary. The outward appearance of the campus, not to speak
of the appearance of the faculty, had not remained the same over the years. The
teaching of the seminary in 1964 was not identical with that in 1864 or that in

131

1914 either in method or in content. To deplore this would be a denial of growth in the apprehension of the Word of God and a refusal to address this Word to a changing world. What remained constant through the century, however, was the seminary's concern with the understanding and communication of the gospel and the seminary's service to the church and its ministry.

Appendix: Statistical Studies

By JULES J. AUGER

THE FOLLOWING STUDY was based on data sheets mailed to living alumni of the Lutheran Theological Seminary at Philadelphia in 1960, together with the *Philadelphia Seminary Biographical Record,* published in 1923. The categories were determined by the availability of information on the returned biographical sheets and, where possible, were extended back to 1865 by using the *Biographical Record*. The figures used to establish numbers and percentages were based solely on these two sources. The resulting figures were distorted to some degree by two factors: (1) The returned questionnaires were more numerous in some classes than others, and (2) in many cases some questions were not answered with information specific enough to be of value. It should be stated at the outset that no attempt was made to correct these distortions because it was felt that the resultant figures would be sufficiently valid to indicate honest trends and tendencies. The graphs and table reflect figures which were constant and complete enough to give an accurate picture of the situation. Where the available information was not consistent, accurate, or significant enough to justify charting, impressions of trends are summed up in writing.

The categories which have been charted begin with the number of graduates from the seminary in each class (graph No. 1). This is the only figure which extends to 1963. A definite upward trend is noted throughout. In 1945 and 1953 the figures reach highs of 70 and 63 respectively, due to the accelerated programs undertaken during World War II. Three graduations were held during each of these years.

In graph No. 2 the average age at graduation in a class every fifth year was determined and the result charted. A surprisingly even graph line is depicted with a class average of 25.2 years of age as the low and an average of 28 years as the high. The average age over the 95 years is 26.3 years at the time of graduation.

To observe factors in the backgrounds of seminary alumni, an attempt was made to study the occupations of fathers of seminary graduates. The number of those whose fathers were clergymen (information was available back to 1865) is shown on graph No. 3. In addition, an endeavor was made to classify, from the

133

questionnaires only, the lay backgrounds of fathers of alumni in such categories as labor, agriculture, professions (other than clerical), trade, merchant, etc. After all of the figures were inspected, it was felt that the results of this study were not accurate enough to be charted. This was due not only to the possibility of error in making the arbitrary decisions necessary for many borderline cases, but also to the fact that this particular category was left unanswered in many of the questionnaires. Generally speaking, those categories which contained the largest number of lay occupations were laborer and white collar worker, in which clerks, managers, and now professional office workers were included. Surprisingly, there was only a small but fairly consistent number of men whose fathers were employed in agriculture. The professional category (doctors, lawyers, educators) remained relatively small throughout.

The next study in the background of our alumni was to find the number of men who were alumni of Lutheran church-related colleges (graph No. 4). At first an attempt was made to determine the number of men from church-related colleges in general, but it was necessary to drop this due to the obscured denominational relations which some colleges and universities have had in the past or now have. Church affiliations are often hidden and, for all practical purposes, non-existent. The percent of men from Lutheran church-related colleges has always been high and has only recently declined a bit. It was interesting to note the shift from school to school as the history of the seminary unfolded. In the early years many men came from Gettysburg College or Capital University. Then, in the 1880's, Gettysburg dropped from the picture and Thiel, Muhlenberg, and Wagner Colleges were the major sources of our students. The trend of men from Muhlenberg in particular continued to be very heavy until recent years, when men from non-church-related schools began to appear in greater number.

In tabulating the schools attended and the degrees earned by our graduates, it was found that many did graduate work, and a good number earned master's degrees and some earned doctor's degrees. To chart this out, however, would not be quite valid due to the lack of consistent and accurate information available from the questionnaires. In addition, a major problem is encountered with the difference in degree requirements in past situations at various schools. More specific information is needed before an accurate picture can be established. An interesting observation is that the majority of men who have gone on to earn graduate degrees came to the seminary with degrees from non-church-related colleges.

From a study of the type of colleges attended by alumni, we turned to the subjects in which alumni majored during their undergraduate years. As the undergraduate "major" is a phenomenon of education of more recent years only, the figures for this statistical table (No. 1) begins with the Class of 1921. Again, there is some distortion of figures because a number of men did not indicate a college major on their questionnaires. However, the numbers of indicated majors were totaled and percentages were drawn on the basis of those totals with the feeling that the trends were significant and valid enough to be of interest. The majors were tallied separately and then grouped for purposes of charting. The Social Science grouping includes sociology, political science, economics, social sciences, and finance. The category marked "other" includes such subjects as speech, drama, and the like. The remaining categories speak for themselves.

The majors which increased substantially in recent years are history, philosophy, and sociology. English has been the most consistent major throughout. In the last few years there has been a marked tendency toward a diversification of background study; that is, there are many more kinds of majors now in an entering class than there were 15 years ago.

The final category for which there is a graph is that which reflects the number and percentage of men who were married upon entering or who married during their years at the seminary (graph No. 5). These figures were taken from every fifth class until 1930, and then were taken from each class. The fluctuation is great, but the trend has been toward marriage before or during seminary years.

As this study proceeded, certain patterns of behavior with relation to date of marriage became clear. Until the early 1940's, the great majority of men married immediately or within six months of their graduation from seminary. In the war years the majority of those who married did so at the end of their Middle year. By the 1950's most of the men who were married in seminary were married before entering. This pattern, generally speaking, has continued.

In connection with marriage, a sampling was taken every five years for the denominational background of the wife prior to her marriage. This proved to be insignificant, however, as the vast majority of the wives had Lutheran backgrounds with relatively few backgrounds scattered throughout the other major Protestant denominations.

It was thought that perhaps there might be significant trends in other areas, such as academic positions held by alumni, foreign mission posts held, or military service experience, but these areas did not prove to be important enough for comment. It was not the purpose of this study to undertake an exhaustive statistical project. Rather, it was intended to point to trends and tendencies which might give some picture of the men who were educated in the Philadelphia Seminary.

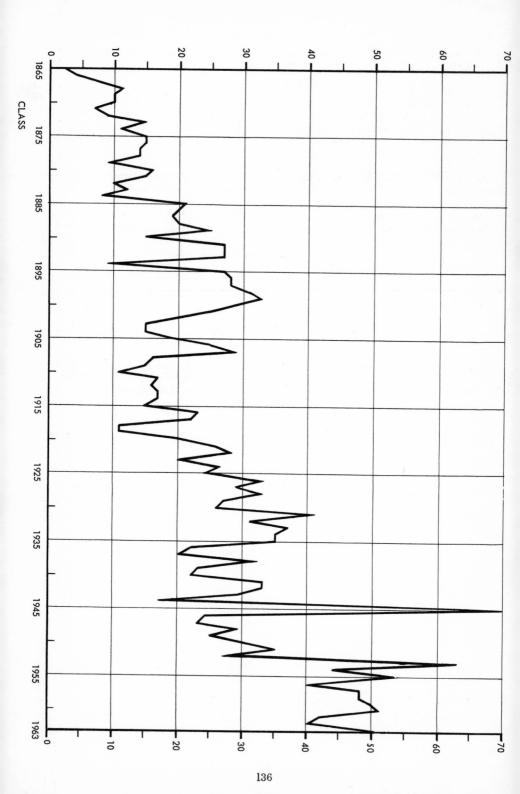

CLASS

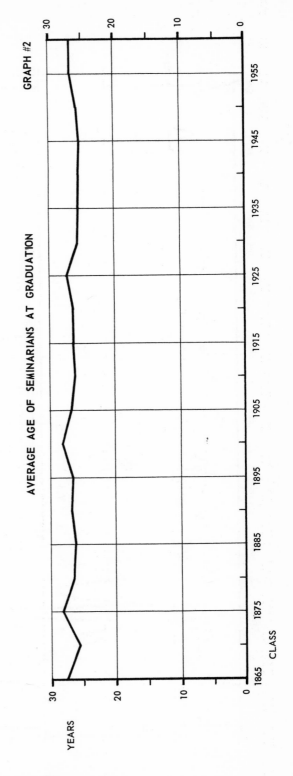

AVERAGE AGE OF SEMINARIANS AT GRADUATION

GRAPH #2

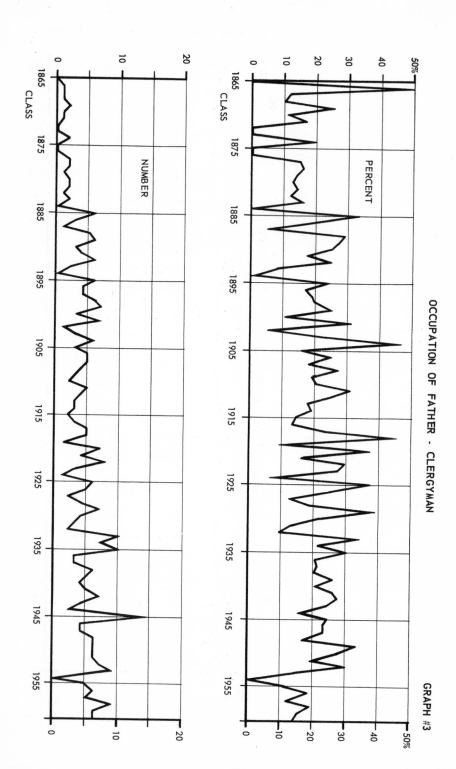

OCCUPATION OF FATHER - CLERGYMAN

GRAPH #3

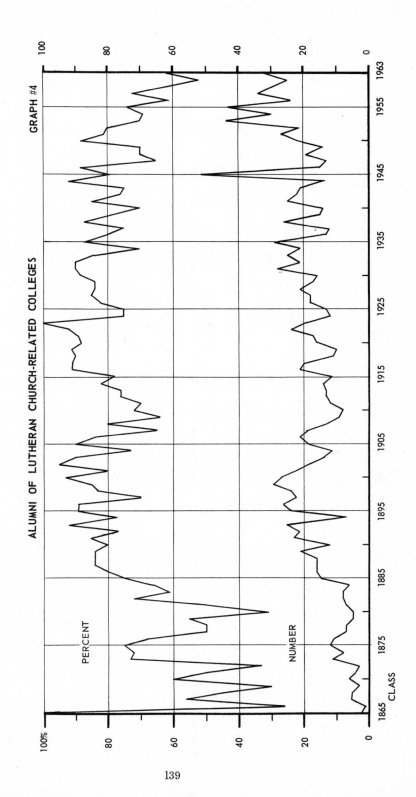

ALUMNI OF LUTHERAN CHURCH-RELATED COLLEGES

GRAPH #4

PERCENTAGE OF COLLEGE MAJOR SUBJECT

MAJOR	1921	1922	1923	1924	1925	1926	1927	1928	1929	1930	1931	1932	1933	1934	1935	1936	1937	1938	1939	1940
English	50	38	10	10	30	34	25	37	23	17	23	23	23	16	46	24	26	24	17	17
Languages - Modern & Classical	50	0	30	30	24	7	25	35	23	34	36	41	36	10	3	8	8	19	12	17
History	0	25	10	20	7	0	0	7	17	23	12	0	4	16	3	30	8	24	12	17
Philosophy and Religion	0	37	0	10	0	26	25	0	7	0	4	0	14	5	15	0	17	16	29	34
Education and Psychology	0	0	40	10	16	13	0	0	7	8	0	18	14	16	23	0	8	3	6	5
Arts and Music	0	0	0	10	0	13	9	0	17	8	14	0	9	10	7	8	8	7	12	0
Social Sciences	0	0	0	0	7	7	0	14	0	0	0	0	0	22	3	17	0	0	0	5
Natural Sciences and Math	0	0	0	10	0	0	0	0	0	8	0	6	0	5	0	0	0	7	6	5
Others	0	0	0	0	16	0	0	0	0	8	0	0	0	0	0	0	8	0	0	5

MAJOR	1941	1942	1943	1944	1945	1946	1947	1948	1949	1950	1951	1952	1953	1954	1955	1956	1957	1958	1959	1960
English	15	24	12	20	23	13	29	22	5	12	25	20	18	14	22	4	19	21	13	15
Languages - Modern & Classical	33	32	16	20	24	21	29	8	11	3	3	11	5	4	7	7	2	4	8	2
History	26	20	16	28	18	0	16	16	12	16	19	11	24	23	26	16	19	21	16	15
Philosophy and Religion	15	8	28	20	23	47	39	38	50	50	29	26	32	32	16	25	21	21	23	23
Education and Psychology	0	4	8	6	3	0	0	0	0	5	3	16	3	2	7	16	6	2	0	0
Arts and Music	7	0	12	0	3	6	0	0	5	0	3	0	0	0	0	7	0	4	3	4
Social Sciences	4	4	4	0	5	13	11	12	5	5	9	8	11	14	14	18	21	23	24	20
Natural Sciences and Math	0	0	4	6	1	0	0	0	0	0	9	8	11	6	4	0	12	4	10	6
Others	0	8	0	0	0	0	5	4	12	0	0	0	3	2	4	7	0	0	6	4

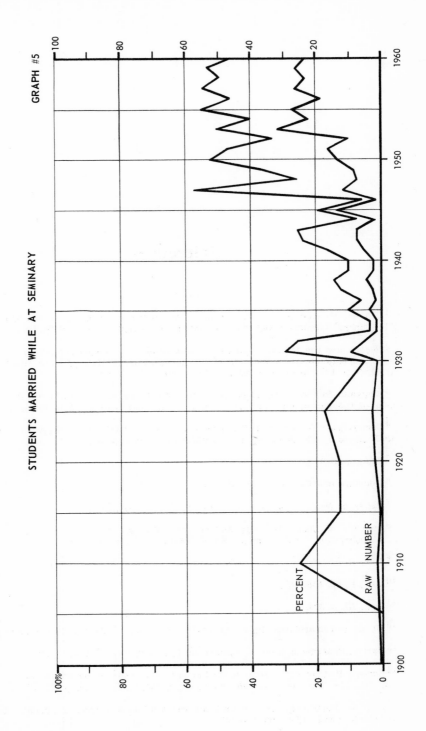

STUDENTS MARRIED WHILE AT SEMINARY

GRAPH #5

References

Chapter I

[1] Charles H. Glatfelter, "The Colonial Pennsylvania German Lutheran and Reformed Clergyman," typescript doctoral dissertation, Johns Hopkins University, 1952, pp. 88-92.

[2] *Nachrichten von den vereinigten Deutschen Evangelisch-Lutherischen Gemeinen in Nord-America,* edited by W. J. Mann and W. Germann, 2 vols. (Philadelphia and Allentown, 1886, 1895), II, p. 197. Hereinafter referred to as *Hallesche Nachrichten.*

[3] Benjamin Sadtler, "The Education of Ministers by Private Tutors Before the Establishment of Theological Seminaries," in *The Lutheran Church Review,* XIII (1894), pp. 167-183.

[4] *Documentary History of the Evangelical Lutheran Ministerium of Pennsylvania, 1748-1821,* edited by Adolph Spaeth et al. (Philadelphia, 1898), p. 281.

[5] *Ibid.,* pp. 3-23.

[6] Indenture in archives, PM95, Z24.

[7] *Hallesche Nachrichten,* II, p. 628; *Documentary History,* p. 107.

[8] *Journals of Henry Melchior Muhlenberg,* edited and translated by T. G. Tappert and J. W. Doberstein, 3 vols. (Philadelphia, 1942-1958), II, pp. 181, 295.

[9] *Ibid.,* II, p. 318.

[10] *Ibid.,* II, pp. 586, 587.

[11] *Ibid.,* III, p. 369.

[12] Manuscript in archives, PM95, A1772-74, pp. 83-86. Cf. *Documentary History,* p. 145.

[13] Carl F. Haussmann, *Kunze's Seminarium* (Philadelphia, 1917), pp. 5-80.

[14] Edward P. Cheyney, *History of the University of Pennsylvania* (Philadelphia, 1940), pp. 124, 130, 133; Haussmann, *op. cit.,* pp. 80-84; *Hallesche Nachrichten,* II, p. 794.

[15] Charles Mampoteng, "The Lutheran Governors of King's College," in *Columbia University Quarterly,* XXVII (1935), pp. 436-453.

[16] *Hallesche Nachrichten,* II, pp. 787, 788, 791.

[17] *Catalogue of the Governors, Trustees, and Officers . . . of Columbia College . . . from 1754 to 1870* (New York, 1871), p. 23.

[18] The judgment of Professor Miller, of Princeton, recorded by Samuel S. Schmucker, *The American Lutheran Church* (Springfield, Ohio, 1851), pp. 34, 35.

[19] Henry H. Heins, *Throughout All the Years: The Bicentennial Story of Hartwick* (Oneonta, N. Y., 1946); John W. Schmitthenner, "The Origin and Educational Contribution of Hartwick Seminary," typescript doctoral dissertation, New York University, 1934; "Protocoll der Amerikanischen Gesellschaft zur Beförderung des Christentums und der Erkenntnis unter den Teutschen in Amerika," pp. 49-87, manuscript in archives; William Hull, "A Valuable Historical Document," in *The Lutheran Church Review,* XVII (1898), pp. 517-549.

[20] *Documentary History,* p. 195.

[21] *Ibid.,* p. 193.

[22] *Minutes and Letters of the Coetus of the German Reformed Congregations in Pennsylvania, 1747-1792* (Philadelphia, 1903), pp. 403, 404.

[23] Frederic S. Klein, *The Spiritual and Educational Background of Franklin and Marshall College* (Lancaster, 1939), p. 30.

[24] *Ibid.,* p. 24.

[25] *Ibid.,* pp. 32-64.

[26] C. Elvin Haupt, *Emanuel Greenwald* (Lancaster, Pa., 1889), pp. 26, 27.

[27] *Documentary History,* pp. 344, 345, 357, 370, 381, etc.

[28] *Kurzer Bericht . . . Reise-Prediger betreffend* (Philadelphia, 1808), pp. 5, 6.

[29] B. H. Pershing, "Paul Henkel, Frontier Missionary," in *The Lutheran Church Quarterly,* VII (1934), pp. 125-151.

[30] Willard D. Allbeck, "John Stough, Founder of Ohio Lutheranism," in *The Lutheran Quarterly,* XII (1960), pp. 25-43.

[31] E. Theodore Bachmann, *They Called Him Father* (Philadelphia, 1942).

[32] M. Diehl, *Biography of Rev. Ezra Keller* (Springfield, Ohio, 1859).

[33] G. E. Hagemann, *Friedrich C. D. Wyneken, Pioneer Lutheran Missionary* (St. Louis, 1926).

[34] *Documentary History,* pp. 280, 533.

[35] *Minutes,* Pennsylvania Ministerium, 1840, pp. 28, 29.

[36] Bodo Heyne, "Ueber die Anfänge kirchlicher Fürsorge für die ausgewanderten evangelischen Deutschen in Nordamerika," in Ernst Schubert, ed., *Auslanddeutschtum und evangelische Kirche,* Jahrbuch 1933 (München, 1933), pp. 54-75.

[37] Donald H. Yoder, "Lutheran-Reformed Union Proposals, 1800-1850," in *Bulletin,* Theological Seminary of the Evangelical and Reformed Church, Lancaster, Pa., XVII (1946), pp. 39-77.

[38] Klein, *op. cit.,* pp. 99-120.

[39] F. W. E. Peschau, tr., *Minutes of the Evangelical Lutheran Synod of North Carolina from 1803 to 1826* (Newberry, S. C., 1894), p. 28.

[40] *Documentary History,* p. 376.

[41] Jacob L. Morgan et al., *History of the Lutheran Church in North Carolina* (1953), p. 57.

[42] *Documentary History,* pp. 517, 522.

[43] The text of the "proposed plan" in *ibid.,* pp. 542-544.

[44] Adam Stump and Henry Anstadt, eds., *History of the . . . Synod of West Pennsylvania* (Chambersburg, Pa., 1925), pp. 68-93.

[45] Harry J. Kreider, *History of the United Lutheran Synod of New York and New England,* Vol. I (Philadelphia, 1954), pp. 62-84.

[46] Abdel Ross Wentz, *History of the Gettysburg Theological Seminary* (Philadelphia, 1926), pp. 90-105.

[47] *Ibid.,* pp. 137-145; Samuel G. Hefelbower, *The History of Gettysburg College* (Gettysburg, 1932), pp. 3-67, 301, 302.

[48] Henry E. Jacobs, "The Ideals of 1748 and their Realization," in *The Lutheran Church Review,* XLII (1923), p. 220.

[49] Wentz, *op. cit.,* pp. 133, 134.

[50] *Minutes,* Pennsylvania Ministerium, 1835, pp. 11, 12, 16, 17; 1837, pp. 17, 18.

[51] J. G. Morris in *Indicator,* published by the Indicator Association of the Lutheran Theological Seminary, Philadelphia, V (1885), pp. 13, 14.

[52] *Minutes,* Pennsylvania Ministerium, 1842, pp. 15, 21.

[53] Paul H. Buehring, "Wilhelm Schmidt, Founder of the Columbus Seminary," in *Lutheran Quarterly,* VII (1955), pp. 348-357.

[54] *Minutes,* Pennsylvania Ministerium, 1843, pp. 20, 21; 1844, p. 28; 1845, pp. 19, 24; 1847, p. 24; C. Spielmann, *Abriss der Geschichte der evangelisch-lutherischen Synode von Ohio u.a. Staaten* (Columbus, 1880), pp. 106-130; David B. Owens et al., *These Hundred Years: The Centennial History of Capital University* (Columbus, 1950), pp. 9-25.

[55] *Minutes,* Pennsylvania Ministerium, 1843, p. 12.

[56] *Ibid.,* 1846, p. 19.

[57] *Ibid.,* 1845, pp. 16, 23, 29; 1846, pp. 26, 29; 1847, pp. 19, 20, 29, 37; 1848, pp. 22, 23; 1849, pp. 22, 24-34, 42, 43.

[58] *Ibid.,* 1850, p. 19; 1851, pp. 15, 16; Hefelbower, *op. cit.,* pp. 159-161.

[59] *Minutes,* New York Ministerium, 1836, pp. 19, 20; 1839, p. 9.

[60] *Ibid.,* 1851, p. 30.

[61] *Minutes,* Pennsylvania Ministerium, 1852, pp. 13, 17; 1853, pp. 17-19. Italics in original.

Chapter II

[1] T. G. Tappert, "Die Anpassung der Lutherischen Kirche Europas an die amerikanische Umgebung," in *Zeitschrift für systematische Theologie,* XVII (Berlin, 1940), pp. 151-184.

[2] Georg von Bosse, *Ein Kampf um Glauben und Volkstum* (Stuttgart, 1920), p. 79; P. A. Peter and W. Schmidt, *Geschichte der Allgemeinen Evang.-Lutherischen Synode von Ohio* (Columbus, 1900), p. 8.

[3] "Vorschlag an die Synode," in *Evangelisches Magazin*, I (Philadelphia, 1811), p. 2.

[4] "Zuruf an die deutschen protestantischen Kirchen in Nord-Amerika," in *ibid.*, II (1813), p. 67.

[5] J. Nicum, *Geschichte des Ev.-Luth. Ministeriums vom Staate New York* (Reading, Pa., 1888), pp. 199-248.

[6] *Minutes*, Pennsylvania Ministerium, 1861, pp. 22-25, 34-36; 1862, p. 25.

[7] *The Lutheran and Home Journal*, II (Philadelphia, 1861), p. 81.

[8] Engelbert Peixoto in *Lutherische Kirchenzeitung*, V (Pittsburgh, 1843), p. 78.

[9] *Ibid.*, IV (1841), no. 25. Cf. Wilhelm Löhe and J. F. Wucherer, eds., *Kirchliche Mitteilungen*, I, no. 5 (Nördlingen, 1843), p. 2.

[10] *Lutherische Kirchenzeitung*, V (1842), p. 13.

[11] E.g., *Hallesche Nachrichten*, II, p. 623.

[12] *Journals of H. M. Muhlenberg*, II, pp. 180, 387; III, p. 427.

[13] Harry J. Kreider, *History of the United Lutheran Synod of New York and New England, 1786-1860* (Philadelphia, 1954), pp. 41-45.

[14] Joh. Aug. Probst, *Die Wiedervereinigung der Lutheraner und Reformirten* (Allentown, Pa., 1826), p. 80.

[15] Quoted in Vergilius Ferm, *The Crisis in American Lutheran Theology* (New York, 1927), pp. 101, 102.

[16] P. Anstadt, *Life and Times of Rev. S. S. Schmucker* (York, 1896), p. 63.

[17] Abdel Ross Wentz, *History of the Gettysburg Theological Seminary* (Philadelphia, 1926), p. 101.

[18] S. S. Schmucker, *Elements of Popular Theology*, 1st edition (Andover, 1834), p. 41.

[19] Cf. William E. Hall, "The Formation of the Tennessee Synod," in *The Lutheran Quarterly*, VI (1954), pp. 57-63.

[20] On the last see, e.g., H. Shelton Smith, R. T. Handy, and L. A. Loetscher, eds., *American Christianity: an Historical Interpretation with Representative Documents*, Vol. II (New York, 1963), pp. 92-105.

[21] *The Evangelical Review*, I (Gettysburg, 1849-50), pp. 78, 120, 457, 458.

[22] *Ibid.*, I, p. 15.

[23] Wentz, *op. cit.*, pp. 157-165.

[24] *Lutherische Hirtenstimme*, quoted in W. H. T. Dau, *Ebenezer* (St. Louis, 1922), p. 113. See *Minutes*, General Synod, 1845, p. 49.

[25] *Minutes*, Ministerium of Pennsylvania, 1840, p. 12; 1845, p. 23; 1852, p. 25; 1853, pp. 16, 31, 32. Charles F. Schaeffer's report to the synod is published in *The Evangelical Review*, V (1853), pp. 189-213.

[26] Cf. Ferm, *op. cit.*, pp. 185-235.

[27] *Minutes,* Pennsylvania Ministerium, 1856, pp. 22, 23, 27, 28.

[28] *Minutes,* Pittsburgh Synod, 1856, p. 28.

[29] *Minutes,* New York Ministerium, 1856, pp. 33, 34; 1858, p. 30; 1859, pp. 23, 24.

[30] *Minutes,* Pennsylvania Ministerium, 1859, p. 37.

[31] E.g., *ibid.,* 1859, p. 10.

[32] Quoted from *Evangelisches Magazin,* 1811, in William B. Sprague, *Annals of the American Lutheran Pulpit* (New York, 1869), p. 74.

[33] *Lutheran Observer,* I, new series (1834), p. 186.

[34] E. W. Hutter, *Eulogy of the Life and Character of Rev. Benjamin Kurtz* (Philadelphia, 1886), p. 58.

[35] R. Weiser, *The Mourner's Bench* (Bedford, Pa., 1844), p. 18. Cf. David H. Bauslin, "The Genesis of the New Measure Movement in the Lutheran Church in This Country," in *The Lutheran Quarterly,* XL (1910), p. 373.

[36] Cf. Frank H. Seilhamer, "The New Measure Movement among Lutherans," in *The Lutheran Quarterly,* XII (1960), pp. 140, 141.

[37] *Journal,* Franckean Synod, 1844, p. 7.

[38] *Minutes,* Allegheny Synod, 1843, p. 38.

[39] *Minutes,* East Pennsylvania Synod, 1843, pp. 12, 13.

[40] *Minutes,* Ohio Synod, 1832, pp. 20, 21.

[41] *Verhandlungen,* Pennsylvania Ministerium, 1836, p. 13.

[42] M. Diehl, *Biography of Rev. Ezra Keller* (Springfield, Ohio, 1859), p. 237.

[43] *Minutes,* Pennsylvania Ministerium, 1848, p. 20; 1860, p. 18. Cf. *Lutherische Zeitschrift,* V (Allentown, 1862), p. 69.

[44] E.g., S. E. Ochsenford and O. E. Pflueger, eds., *Jubilee Memorial Volume of the Danville Conference of the . . . Ministerium of Pennsylvania* (Lebanon, Pa., 1898), pp. 91, 92, 99, 100, 103, 105, 139, 153, 171, 183, 186.

[45] *Minutes,* New York Ministerium, 1854, pp. 22, 36, 37; 1859, p. 29.

[46] J. Kohler in *First Free Lutheran Diet in America: Essays, Debates, and Proceedings,* 1877, edited by H. E. Jacobs (Philadelphia, 1878), p. 175.

[47] *Minutes,* Pennsylvania Ministerium, 1849, p. 30; 1851, p. 27; 1852, pp. 24-27; 1853, pp. 23-27; 1854, pp. 24-30.

[48] *Ibid.,* 1853, p. 43; 1854, pp. 21, 23, 30.

[49] *Ibid.,* 1855, pp. 23, 24, 46-50.

[50] Wentz, *op. cit.,* pp. 174, 175.

[51] *Minutes,* Pennsylvania Ministerium, 1857, p. 40; 1858, p. 24; cf. 1859, p. 49.

[52] *Ibid.,* 1858, pp. 22, 27; 1859, pp. 24, 25, 32; 1860, pp. 24, 25.

[53] *Ibid.,* 1862, p. 39; 1863, p. 26; *Lutherische Zeitschrift,* VI (1863), p. 92. Cf. Wentz, *op. cit.,* pp. 176-180.

[54] *Minutes,* Pennsylvania Ministerium, 1859, pp. 10, 24, 25, 30.

[55] *Ibid.,* 1853, p. 14; 1857, p. 12; *Minutes,* New York Ministerium, 1855, p. 27.

[56] *Lutherische Zeitschrift,* III (1860), p. 135; cf. VII (1864), p. 53.

[57] *Minutes,* Pennsylvania Ministerium, 1851, pp. 5, 20, 27, 38; 1853, pp. 6, 31, 52; 1854, p. 36; 1861, pp. 47-55.

[58] *Ibid.,* 1861, pp. 48, 49.

[59] *Minutes,* New York Ministerium, 1861, p. 50.

[60] *Lutherische Zeitschrift,* VII (1864), p. 60.

[61] *Minutes,* Pennsylvania Ministerium, 1860, pp. 11, 12.

[62] *Ibid.,* 1860, pp. 22, 30; 1861, pp. 39, 40; 1862, p. 30.

[63] *Ibid.,* 1864, pp. 10, 11.

[64] Gordon W. Ward, Jr., "The Formation of the Lutheran General Synod, South, During the Civil War," in *The Lutheran Quarterly,* XIII (1961), pp. 132-154.

[65] Cf. Adolph Spaeth, *Charles Porterfield Krauth,* 2 vols. (New York and Philadelphia, 1898, 1909), II, pp. 127-170.

[66] P. Anstadt, *op. cit.,* pp. 339, 340.

[67] C. F. Heyer et al., "Historical Account of the Origin and Progress of the Lutheran Seminary of Philadelphia," manuscript, pp. 2, 3.

[68] *The Lutheran Observer,* Jan. 20, 1865, pp. 1, 2.

[69] *Lutheran and Missionary,* III (Philadelphia, 1864), p. 166. Also in *The Lutheran Observer,* Aug. 26, 1864, p. 2.

[70] *Minutes,* Pennsylvania Ministerium, 1864, pp. 35-37, 42, 43, 47, 76, 80-82.

[71] *The Lutheran and Missionary,* III (1864), p. 166.

[72] Wentz, *op. cit.,* pp. 188, 189; *Minutes,* Pennsylvania Ministerium, 1865, pp. 9, 13, 21, 23.

[73] *The Lutheran Observer,* Sep. 2, 1864, p. 2; Sep. 23, 1864, p. 2; Oct. 7, 1864, p. 2.

[74] S. E. Ochsenford, ed., *Documentary History of the General Council* (Philadelphia, 1912), pp. 59-151.

[75] *Minutes,* New York Ministerium, 1866, p. 20.

Chapter III

[1] Board Minutes, manuscript, I, pp. 11, 12, 14, 15; Faculty Minutes, manuscript, I, p. 12.

[2] *Addresses Delivered at the Installation of the Professors of the Theological Seminary of the Evangelical Lutheran Church, Philadelphia* (Gettysburg, 1865).

[3] Faculty Minutes, I, 7-9.

[4] *Indicator,* IX (1889), p. 21. Cf. Adolf Spaeth, *Wilhelm Julius Mann, ein deutsch-amerikanischer Theologe* (Reading, Pa., 1895), p. 218.

[5] C. F. Heyer et al., "Historical Account of the Origin and Progress of the . . . Seminary at Philadelphia," manuscript, p. 12.

[6] Board Minutes, I, pp. 15, 20; *Minutes,* Pennsylvania Ministerium, 1864, p. 79; 1865, p. 28.

[7] *Verhandlungen,* New York Ministerium, 1862, p. 39; 1865, p. 14.

[8] *Ibid.,* 1865, pp. 26, 28.

[9] J. Nicum, *Geschichte des Ministeriums vom Staate New York* (Reading, Pa., 1888), pp. 252-254.

[10] *Verhandlungen,* New York Ministerium, 1872, p. 30.

[11] *Ibid.,* 1871, pp. 28, 45, 66-68.

[12] *Ibid.,* 1872, pp. 28-31, 62, 63; 1889, p. 31; Board Minutes, I, pp. 67-72, 74-77.

[13] *Verhandlungen,* New York Ministerium, 1873, pp. 21-23; 1874, pp. 21, 22, 43; 1879, p. 31; 1894, p. 47.

[14] Board Minutes, I, p. 43; Minutes of Central Executive Committee, manuscript, p. 13.

[15] Faculty Minutes, I, pp. 17-19.

[16] *Ibid.,* I, 19, 21-31, 40-42, 70, 71, 84, 85.

[17] *Ibid.,* I, p. 86; Minutes of Central Executive Committee, pp. 44-46, 66, 68-72, 75; *Minutes,* Pennsylvania Ministerium, 1868, pp. 18, 28, 29; 1869, p. 23; 1871, p. 18; 1872, p. 13; 1873, p. 23.

[18] Minutes of Central Executive Committee, manuscript, pp. 41, 56, 57, 80-83, 109, 110, 114, 118, 126; Faculty Minutes, I, pp. 33, 34; II, pp. 14-16; *The Lutheran and Missionary,* XII (1873), p. 74.

[19] Board Minutes, I, p. 10; Minutes of Central Executive Committee, pp. 1-49; Heyer et al., *op. cit.,* p. 4.

[20] *Minutes,* Pennsylvania Ministerium, 1867, pp. 20, 49; 1870, pp. 18, 19; Board Minutes, I, p. 33.

[21] *Minutes,* Pennsylvania Ministerium, 1875, p. 19.

[22] Board Minutes, I, pp. 153, 163, 190, 193, 195, etc.

[23] *Verhandlungen,* New York Ministerium, 1874, p. 22; 1875, pp. 55, 97; 1876, p. 36; 1877, p. 30; 1880, p. 51.

[24] Faculty Minutes, I, pp. 39, 88.

[25] *Ibid.,* II, p. 274.

[26] Heyer et al., *op. cit.,* pp. 21, 40, 64-70; Minutes of Central Executive Committee, pp. 91-94, 101; Board Minutes, I, pp. 130, 131.

[27] Minutes of Central Executive Committee, pp. 19, 25-27, 29, 30, 36, 46, 50, 53, 59, 60, 99-101, 105, 106, 117-120; Faculty Minutes, I, pp. 32, 33, 36, 40, 41, 101-104, 109, 110, 185, 188; II, p. 139; III, pp. 105, 107; Board Minutes, I, pp. 24, 26, 36, 42, 120, 121; Heyer et al., *op. cit.,* pp. 50, 51, 55, 62, 64, 82.

[28] *Minutes,* Pennsylvania Ministerium, 1865, p. 75 (Art. V, sec. 1).

[29] *Ibid.,* 1871, p. 18; 1873, pp. 22, 23.

[30] Faculty Minutes, I, p. 121.

[31] Minutes of Central Executive Committee, 22, 23, 27, 37; Faculty Minutes, I, p. 180; II, pp. 195, 196; "Rules and Regulations for the Government of the Theological Seminary," 1864, manuscript, pp. 4, 9.

[32] Faculty Minutes, I, pp. 99-103, 106, 112, 113, 180; II, pp. 48, 172, 235, 236, 287, 288; III, pp. 44-46, 57, 58; Minutes of Central Executive Committee, pp. 73, 74; Heyer et al., *op. cit.,* pp. 42, 58; *Indicator,* IX (1889), p. 31.

[33] Faculty Minutes, II, pp. 7, 8, 13, 16, 37-43; Minutes of Central Executive Committee, 84-86; Board Minutes, I, pp. 48, 73, 82; Heyer et al., *op. cit.,* pp. 25-29; *Indicator,* VIII (1889), supplement.

[34] Heyer et al., *op. cit.,* p. 35.

[35] Board Minutes, I, p. 55, insert p. 2; Minutes of Central Executive Committee, p. 25; Faculty Minutes, II, pp. 111-119, 123-127; III, pp. 84-86; Heyer, et al., *op. cit.,* pp. 45-49; Minutes of Alumni Association, manuscript, I, pp. 154, 167, 190, 195, 199, 207, 214, etc.

[36] "Rules and Regulations for the Government of the Theological Seminary," 1864, pp. 3, 7; Faculty Minutes, I, pp. 59, 60, 135, 154, 203, 204, 222, 223; II, pp. 169, 170, 176, 201, 238, 240, 243, 269, 302, 310; III, pp. 6, 140; Board Minutes, I, pp. 29, 39.

[37] Faculty Minutes, I, pp. 10, 22, 57; *Minutes,* Pennsylvania Ministerium, 1881, p. 34.

[38] Faculty Minutes, I, pp. 93, 114, 235; II, pp. 7, 83, 96, 162; III, p. 153; *Verhandlungen,* New York Ministerium, 1877, pp. 29, 30; *Minutes,* Pennsylvania Ministerium, 1869, p. 23; 1872, p. 15; 1877, p. 25; 1878, p. 22; *Indicator,* I (Sept. 1881), p. 4 et passim; Heyer et al., *op. cit.,* pp. 44, 52, 53.

[39] Faculty Minutes, I, pp. 57-59, 80, 102, 260, 261; II, p. 272.

[40] Heyer et al., *op. cit.,* pp. 59, 63, 65, 86, 87; Faculty Minutes, I, pp. 105, 109, 136; Board Minutes, I, pp. 47, 54, 55, 125, 179, 192; Harriet R. Spaeth, *Life of Adolph Spaeth* (Philadelphia, 1916), p. 134.

[41] *Minutes,* Pennsylvania Ministerium, 1865, p. 71 (Constitution, Art. IV, sec. 6).

[42] Faculty Minutes, I, pp. 1, 2, 11, 69, 72; *Catalogue of the Theological Seminary,* 1869, p. 11; 1873, p. 12; 1877, p. 12; 1881, p. 12; 1884, p. 12.

[43] Adolph Spaeth et al., *Memorial of Charles F. Schaeffer* (Philadelphia, 1880).

[44] Heyer, et al., *op. cit.,* pp. 59, 60.

[45] Faculty Minutes, I, pp. 1, 68, 130, 198, 241, etc.; Board Minutes, I, p. 57. Cf. Constitution, Art. IV, sec. 4.

[46] Abdel Ross Wentz, *History of the Gettysburg Theological Seminary* (Philadelphia, 1926), pp. 178, 179; George H. Gerberding, *Reminiscent Reflections of a Youthful Octogenarian* (Minneapolis, 1928), p. 43.

[47] Henry E. Jacobs, "Memoirs," unpublished typescript, pp. 54, 55.

[48] *Indicator,* VII (1888), p. 55.

[49] Adolph Spaeth, *Charles Porterfield Krauth,* 2 vols. (New York and Philadelphia, 1898, 1909).

[50] *Ibid.,* II, pp. 301-303.

[51] T. E. Schmauk, quoted in *ibid.*, II, p. 144.

[52] H. E. Jacobs, "Memoirs," p. 186 (Part II, chap. 3).

[53] *Ibid.*, p. 173.

[54] *Indicator,* I, no. 3 (Nov, 1881), pp. 5, 6; Jacobs, *op. cit.,* p. 186.

[55] Spaeth, *Charles Porterfield Krauth,* II, pp. 314-321.

[56] William A. Lambert, "The Confession and the Church," in *The Lutheran Quarterly,* XLIII (1913), pp. 226-236.

[57] C. P. Krauth, *The Conservative Reformation and its Theology* (Philadelphia, 1871), pp. 165, 186.

[58] S. E. Ochsenford, ed., *Documentary History of the General Council of the Evangelical Lutheran Church in North America* (Philadelphia, 1912), p. 137. Cf. Krauth, *op. cit.,* pp. 167-200.

[59] Faculty Minutes, I, pp. 55, 57-62; Board Minutes, I, pp. 16, 17.

[60] Adolph Spaeth, *Memorial of William Julius Mann* (Philadelphia, 1893), p. 23; A. Spaeth, *Wilhelm Julius Mann,* pp. 125, 126.

[61] Spaeth, *Wilhelm Julius Mann,* pp. 34, 36.

[62] Faculty Minutes, II, pp. 133, 202, 265, 313; III, pp. 117, 124; Minutes of Central Executive Committee, p. 73.

[63] Emma T. Mann, *Memoir of the Life and Work of William Julius Mann* (Philadelphia, 1893), pp. 123-128; Spaeth, *Wilhelm Julius Mann,* pp. 218, 219, 223.

[64] Gerberding, *op. cit.,* pp. 48-52.

[65] W. J. Mann, *Lutheranism in America* (Philadelphia, 1857), pp. 18-101; Spaeth, *Memorial of W. J. Mann,* pp. 28-30, 40-47.

[66] Spaeth, *Wilhelm Julius Mann,* pp. 59-67, 163-167, 201-213.

[67] H. E. Jacobs, "Memoirs," p. 184 (Part II, chap. 3).

[68] W. M. Horn, *In Memoriam G. F. Krotel* (New York, 1907).

[69] Henry E. Jacobs, "In Memoriam Charles William Schaeffer, " in *The Lutheran Church Review,* XV (1896), pp. 369-381.

[70] Faculty Minutes, II, pp. 271, 309; III, pp. 3, 17, etc.

[71] *Ibid.*, II, pp. 5, 6; IV, pp. 49-53; Gerberding, *op. cit.,* pp. 43, 44.

[72] *Minutes,* Pennsylvania Ministerium, 1865, p. 71; 1883, p. 35; Board Minutes, II, p. 39.

[73] Faculty Minutes, I, pp. 76, 79, 99, 128, 173, 178, 216.

[74] Minutes of Central Executive Committee, pp. 47, 55, 73; Board Minutes, I, pp. 39, 55, 64; Faculty Minutes, I, pp. 204, 206, 233, 256.

[75] Faculty Minutes, I, p. 171; III, p. 73; *Minutes,* Pennsylvania Ministerium, 1867, p. 47; *Verhandlungen,* New York Ministerium, 1880, p. 50; *Indicator,* V (1886), p. 68.

[76] Quoted in *Indicator,* IX (1889), p. 32.

[77] Board Minutes, I, pp. 19, 21, 31, 32, 36, 41, 54, 96; Heyer et al., *op. cit.*, pp. 13, 32, 33; *Minutes,* Pennsylvania Ministerium, 1865, p. 14; Emma Mann, *op. cit.,* p. 186.

[78] Faculty Minutes, I, pp. 19-21, 96; Board Minutes, I, p. 23.

[79] Board Minutes, I, pp. 45, 120; Faculty Minutes, II, p. 273; IV, pp. 118, 174, 179; Heyer et al., *op. cit.,* p. 34.

[80] *Minutes,* Pennsylvania Ministerium, 1883, pp. 48, 49; Heyer et al., *op. cit.,* pp. 75-77.

[81] *Indicator,* VII (1888), p. 35; VIII (1888), p. 14; IX (1889), pp. 84, 113; Minutes of Alumni Association, I, pp. 29, 50, 57.

[82] Board Minutes, I, pp. 26, 49, 120, 126, 147, 155, 156, 195, 196; Faculty Minutes, III, pp. 5, 19; Minutes of Central Executive Committee, p. 123; *Indicator,* III (1883), pp. 5, 41; IV (1884), p. 17.

[83] Faculty Minutes, III, pp. 76, 107.

[84] Minutes of Alumni Association, I, pp. 63, 67, 72, 80, 89, 116, 137, 147, 156; Faculty Minutes, III, p. 35.

Chapter IV

[1] Edward P. Cheyney, *History of the University of Pennsylvania* (Philadelphia, 1940), pp. 257, 261.

[2] C. F. Heyer et al., "Historical Account," manuscript, pp. 74-76.

[3] *Indicator,* IX (1889), p. 31; *Minutes,* Pennsylvania Ministerium, 1882, p. 48.

[4] *Minutes,* Pennsylvania Ministerium, 1882, pp. 12, 48, 49.

[5] Heyer et al., *op. cit.,* pp. 70, 71, 78, 79, 84; *Minutes,* Ministerium of Pennsylvania, 1883, pp. 47, 48; Board Minutes, II, pp. 147, 148, 151, 152, 154, 155; Faculty Minutes, III, pp. 97, 103, 150, 151; letter, William H. Staake to H. E. Jacobs, Apr. 16, 1915, manuscript, PJ 17, E 1, Vol. 3.

[6] Board Minutes, III, p. 131; Faculty Minutes, IV, p. 65.

[7] Heyer et al., *op. cit.,* p. 84.

[8] S. F. Hotchkin, *Ancient and Modern Germantown, Mount Airy, and Chestnut Hill* (Philadelphia, 1889), pp. 363-376; *Philadelphia Seminary Bulletin,* Apr. 1917, pp. 18-20; *The Seminarian,* Feb. 1938, pp. 11-15; H. E. Jacobs, "Memoirs," pp. 218, 219 (Part II, chap. 6); *Catalogue of the Mount Airy Agricultural Institute* (Philadelphia, 1849), p. 6.

[9] Jacob Fry, "A Quarter-Century of Changes at the Seminary," in *Seminary Bulletin,* June 1917, pp. 6-8; H. E. Jacobs, "Memoirs," p. 231 (Part II, chap. 9), p. 259 (chap. 12).

[10] Hotchkin, *op. cit.,* pp. 416, 495, 496.

[11] *Indicator,* VI (1886), p. 28.

[12] *Verhandlungen,* Ministerium of New York, 1886, pp. 42, 43; 1887, p. 25; 1888, p. 30; 1889, p. 22; 1890, p. 28; 1891, p. 29, etc.

[13] Board Minutes, I, pp. 223, 225, 226; II, p. 95; Faculty Minutes, IV, pp. 20-22; *Indicator,* IX (1889), pp. 46, 47.

[14] Board Minutes, II, pp. 4, 182-185; *Catalogue*, 1891, pp. 5, 6; *Indicator*, VIII (1889), p. 86.

[15] Board Minutes, I, p. 186.

[16] *Indicator*, IX (1889), p. 30.

[17] Board Minutes, I, p. 195.

[18] *Ibid.*, I, p. 217; II, p. 94; Minutes of Executive Committee, I, pp. 3-5; Harriet R. Spaeth, *Life of Adolph Spaeth* (Philadelphia, 1916), p. 126.

[19] Board Minutes, I, p. 226; II, pp. 103, 104, 109, 110, 121; Minutes of Executive Committee, I, pp. 19, 40.

[20] Board Minutes, II, pp. 61, 111, 112; Faculty Minutes, IV, pp. 81, 100.

[21] Minutes of Executive Committee, I, p. 7; Faculty Minutes, III, pp. 160, 232, 290; Albert W. Shumaker et al., *History of the Lutheran Church of the Ascension, Mount Airy, Philadelphia* (Philadelphia, 1940), pp. 13-29.

[22] Board Minutes, II, pp. 136, 141, 168, 196; Minutes of Executive Committee, I, pp. 7, 10, 34-36, 38, 40, 41; Faculty Minutes, III, pp. 309, 310, 314; IV, p. 46; *Indicator*, VIII (1889), p. 104; *Seminary Bulletin*, June 1917, pp. 6-8; Dec. 1917, pp. 8, 9; H. E. Jacobs, "Memoirs," pp. 272, 273 (Part II, chap. 14); *Catalogue*, 1894-95, p. 15; 1903-04, p. 17.

[23] Board Minutes, II, pp. 115, 117-124, 162, 163, 178; Minutes of Executive Committee, I, pp. 23, 24, 187, 231, 232; Faculty Minutes, IV, p. 201; Shumaker et al., *op. cit.*, pp. 30-33.

[24] Board Minutes, II, pp. 9, 35, 51; Faculty Minutes, III, pp. 176, 179, 215, 276, 324; IV, pp. 39, 40, 65, 68, 77, 108, 132, 150, 208, 385, 387, 578, 581, 583; *Indicator*, V (1885), p. 106; IX (1889), pp. 82, 84; IX (1890), pp. 120, 129.

[25] Faculty Minutes, IV, p. 141; Board Minutes, II, pp. 147, 154, 221.

[26] Board Minutes, II, pp. 112, 126, 133, 135, 140, 149, 168, 169, 172, 218; Faculty Minutes, III, p. 174; Heyer et al., *op. cit.*, p. 97; *Indicator*, IX (1889), p. 117.

[27] Faculty Minutes, IV, pp. 224, 245, 261; Board Minutes, II, pp. 180, 182, 183, 185, 188; Luther D. Reed, "Early History of the Krauth Memorial Library," typescript, 1948; Luther D. Reed, "A Benefactor of the Church: B. Frank Weyman," in *The Lutheran Church Review*, XXXVIII (1919), pp. 291-298.

[28] *Catalogue*, 1906-07, pp. 17-19; 1908-09, pp. 25-27; Board Minutes, II, pp. 193, 194; III, pp. 89, 120-124; Minutes of Executive Committee, I, pp. 159, 172-195; Carrie W. Williams, "A History of the Krauth Memorial Library," typescript thesis for master's degree in Library Science, Drexel Institute, 1952.

[29] Board Minutes, II, pp. 124, 193, 200-202; Minutes of Executive Committee, I, p. 26; Faculty Minutes, IV, pp. 227, 262; *Verhandlungen*, New York Ministerium, 1907, p. 60.

[30] Board Minutes, I, p. 192; Minutes of Executive Committee, I, p. 77; Faculty Minutes, IV, p. 166.

[31] Faculty Minutes, IV, p. 66; Minutes of Executive Committee, I, pp. 25, 153, 179.

[32] Heyer et al., *op. cit.*, p. 98; *Indicator*, IX (1890), p. 156; letter, W. G. Griffith, Esq., to H. E. Jacobs, May 19, 1895, manuscript PJ 17, E 1, Vol. 1.

[33] Faculty Minutes, IV, p. 220.

[34] Board Minutes, I, pp. 190, 193, 195, 205, 207, 208, 210, 213, 216; *Verhandlungen*, New York Ministerium, 1892, pp. 1-12 (appendix).

[35] *Verhandlungen*, New York Ministerium, 1883, p. 45.

[36] *Ibid.*, 1891, pp. 37, 38.

[37] *Ibid.*, 1894, pp. 50, 62; 1895, pp. 50, 51.

[38] H. E. Jacobs, "Memoirs," pp. 256, 257 (Part II, chap. 12).

[39] Faculty Minutes, IV, 36-43, 45, 48, 80, 81; Minutes of Executive Committee, I, p. 15.

[40] Board Minutes, II, pp. 131, 137; *Verhandlungen,* New York Ministerium, 1897, pp. 39-42.

[41] *Verhandlungen,* New York Ministerium, 1897, pp. 40-44, 50, 51, 55, 56; 1900, pp. 22-24, 68, 72; 1901, p. 66; 1903, p. 59; 1904, pp. 23, 45, 50; 1905, pp. 25, 58, 62, 63, 67; 1906, pp. 20, 29, 51, 52, 55.

[42] *Ibid.*, 1882, p. 30.

[43] Nicum, *op. cit.*, pp. 332-337.

[44] Ochsenford, *op. cit.,* pp. 474, 477, 478, 486, 487.

[45] Board Minutes, II, p. 129; *Report of the Executive Committee,* 1910, p. 11; cf. *Verhandlungen,* New York Ministerium, 1908, p. 69; 1909, p. 40.

[46] Faculty Minutes, III, pp. 80, 83, 90, 100, 102, 103, 120, 121, 208, 209; Wilhelm F. Herrmann, "The Kropp Lutheran Seminary," typescript S.T.M. thesis, Lutheran Theological Seminary, Philadelphia, 1938; Wilhelm Jentsch, "Die Bedeutung des Predigerseminars Eben Ezer in Kropp für die Lutherische Kirche in Nordamerika," in G. Werner, ed., *Lutherische Kirche in Bewegung* (Erlangen, 1937), pp. 144-153.

[47] *Catalogue,* 1884, p. 11; Board Minutes, I, pp. 125, 129, 225; II, p. 142.

[48] Heyer et al., *op. cit.,* pp. 81-83, 88, 89, 90-93; Minutes of Alumni Association, I, pp. 163, 164; II, p. 74; Faculty Minutes, IV, p. 98; *Verhandlungen,* New York Ministerium, 1905, p. 50; 1906, pp. 59-61.

[49] *Minutes,* United Lutheran Church in America, 1930, pp. 396, 397; P. Puls, "Das Kropper Predigerseminar," in *Der Lutherischer Herold,* Nov. 28, 1942, pp. 10, 11.

[50] Faculty Minutes, IV, p. 332.

[51] *Verhandlungen,* New York Ministerium, 1894, pp. 27, 66; 1906, pp. 51, 52; 1907, pp. 25, 26, 47.

[52] Samuel Trexler, *Crusaders of the Twentieth Century* (New York, 1926), pp. 28-36.

[53] *Minutes,* Pennsylvania Ministerium, 1903, pp. 77, 78; *Verhandlungen,* New York Ministerium, 1903, pp. 43-45, 58, 59; *Minutes,* Pittsburgh Synod, 1903, p. 29; *Minutes,* New York and New England Synod, 1903, p. 14; Board Minutes, II, pp. 163, 165, 170.

[54] Board Minutes, II, pp. 171, 173, 174, 225; Faculty Minutes, IV, pp. 193-195, 214, 215.

[55] Faculty Minutes, III, pp. 245-247, 252.

[56] *Ibid.*, II, p. 102; Faculty Minutes, IV, p. 32.

[57] Board Minutes, I, p. 6 (insert); II, p. 105; Minutes of Central Executive Committee, pp. 128, 129; Abdel Ross Wentz, *History of the Gettysburg Theological Seminary* (Philadelphia, 1926), pp. 249, 250.

[58] Board Minutes, I, pp. 112, 217.

[59] *Minutes,* Pennsylvania Ministerium, 1896, pp. 46-48; 1897, pp. 63-65; 1898, pp. 65, 66; 1899, pp. 80-82.

[60] Faculty Minutes, IV, p. 130.

[61] Cf. Wentz, *op. cit.*, pp. 275, 276, 356, 359, 360; Roland H. Bainton, *Yale and the Ministry* (New York, 1957), p. 199.

[62] Faculty Minutes, II, p. 57; IV, pp. 84, 108, 127, 128, 145, 199.

[63] *Ibid.,* III, p. 292.

[64] *Ibid.,* IV, p. 9.

[65] Constitution, Art. V, sec. 2, in *Minutes,* Pennsylvania Ministerium, 1865, p. 73; Bylaws, II, 10 (1894), in Board Minutes, II, p. 35; Faculty Minutes, III, pp. 225, 284; IV, 319, 320, et passim.

[66] Board Minutes, I, pp. 29, 67, 98, 102; II, pp. 67, 68, 167, 218; Faculty Minutes, III, p. 187; *Minutes,* Pennsylvania Ministerium, 1909, p. 72.

[67] Board Minutes, I, pp. 184, 226; II, pp. 64, 66, 77, 78, 141, 149; Minutes of Executive Committee, I, pp. 5, 31, 92, 93, 180, 284; Faculty Minutes, III, p. 227; IV, pp. 98, 216, 218, 307, 309, 329, 351, 388, 409, 553.

[68] Board Minutes, II, pp. 95, 168, 178, 184; III, p. 253; Minutes of Executive Committee, I, pp. 5, 6; Faculty Minutes, III, pp. 256, 261; IV, pp. 5, 210, 211, 240, 243-246, 276, etc.; *Verhandlungen,* New York Ministerium, 1889, p. 57.

[69] Board Minutes, I, pp. 184, 212, 221; II, pp. 49-57, 222; III, pp. 103-113; Minutes of Executive Committee, I, pp. 66, 74, 127; Faculty Minutes, I, p. 115; III, p. 186; IV, pp. 2, 30, 59, 358.

[70] Harriet R. Spaeth, *Life of Adolph Spaeth* (Philadelphia, 1916).

[71] H. E. Jacobs, "Memoirs"; *Seminary Bulletin,* Oct. 1932, pp. 1-3; H. Offermann et al., "In Memoriam Henry Eyster Jacobs," in *The Lutheran Church Quarterly,* VI (1933), pp. 1-31, 220-224.

[72] *Verhandlungen,* General Council, 1870, pp. 17, 18; 1875, pp. 10, 58; 1876, pp. 54, 55; 1877, p. 61; 1878, p. 33.

[73] Minutes of Executive Committee, I, p. 128.

[74] Board Minutes, V, pp. 153, 175, 204, 225. On his eightieth birthday a "Festschrift" was published in his honor: J. A. W. Haas et al., *Theological Studies* (Philadelphia, 1924).

[75] H. E. Jacobs, "Memoirs," p. 249 (Part II, chap. 11).

[76] Cf. Benjamin Lotz, "Henry Eyster Jacobs in Retrospect," in *The Lutheran Church Quarterly,* XVII (1944), pp. 382-393.

[77] Board Minutes, I, pp. 197, 198; II, pp. 96, 100; IV, pp. 117, 143; Faculty Minutes, III, pp. 230-232; IV, p. 60; H. E. Jacobs, "Memoirs," pp. 233, 234 (Part II, chap. 9); Jacob Fry, *The History of Trinity Lutheran Church, Reading, Pa.* (Reading, 1894), pp. 216-279; A. Shumaker et al., *op. cit.,* pp. 27-39.

[78] J. Fry, *The Pastor's Guide* (Philadelphia, 1915), preface.

[79] Faculty Minutes, IV, p. 481.

[80] J. Fry, *Elementary Homiletics* (Philadelphia, 1901), pp. 32, 33.

[81] J. Fry, *The Pastor's Guide,* pp. 53, 75, 97.

[82] S. E. Ochsenford, ed. *Muhlenberg College* (Allentown, 1892), pp. 209-212; H. E. Jacobs, "George Frederick Spieker," in *The Lutheran Church Review,* XXXII (1913), pp. 864-871; H. E. Jacobs, "Memoirs," pp. 72, 73 (Part II, chap. 10), 95, 96 (Chap. 11), 252-255 (chap. 12); *Minutes,* Pennsylvania Ministerium, 1865, p. 9; 1866, p. 13; 1894, pp. 57, 58.

[83] Cf. G. F. Spieker, "The Negative Criticism of the Old Testament," in *The Lutheran Church Review,* XII (1893), pp. 335-348.

[84] Board Minutes, III, pp. 190-193; Faculty Minutes, IV, pp. 452-454.

[85] Faculty Minutes, III, pp. 228, 239, 240, 254, 307; IV, p. 222.

[86] Board Minutes, I, pp. 194, 198, 200-202, 208, 209; manuscript letters of J. Fry to H. E. Jacobs, Mar. 11, 1892, and J. A. Seiss to H. E. Jacobs, Mar. 10, 1892, and Aug. 24, 1892, in archives.

[87] Faculty Minutes, III, pp. 241, 268, 270, 272; IV, pp. 106, 107, 109, 215, 216, 438; Board Minutes, I, pp. 208, 211; II, pp. 106, 110, 129, 135, 136, 142, 170, 178, 226; G. Everett Arden, *The School of the Prophets: History of Augustana Theological Seminary* (Rock Island, 1960), pp. 211, 226; James A. Montgomery, "In Memoriam Albert T. Clay," in *Journal of the American Oriental Society,* XLV (1925), pp. 289-300.

[88] Ochsenford, *op. cit.,* p. 12.

[89] Faculty Minutes, III, pp. 170, 175-177; IV, 154, 155, 180, 189-191, 254, 292-295; *Minutes,* Pennsylvania Ministerium, 1892, pp. 1-24, appendix; 1903, pp. 161, 162; *Verhandlungen,* New York Ministerium, 1884, 1-19 (appendix); "Concerning the Dogma of Predestination," in *The Lutheran Church Review,* XI (1884), pp. 223-236.

[90] Minutes of Alumni Association, I, pp. 137, 197, 201, 209, 215; II, pp. 34, 35, 40, 59, 68, 77, 115; Faculty Minutes, IV, pp. 151-154.

Chapter V

[1] Minutes of Executive Committee, I, pp. 153, 154, 161-163; III, pp. 75-80, 219, IV, pp. 2, 42, 65, 95, 159; *Minutes,* Pennsylvania Ministerium, 1912, pp. 50-53.

[2] *Verhandlungen,* New York Ministerium, 1916, p. 63.

[3] *Ibid.,* 1910, pp. 42, 60, 72, 73; 1911, pp. 25, 26, 62, 63, 66, 67; 1912, pp. 21, 22; 1916, p. 53; 1917, p. 40; 1918, p. 59; 1919, pp. 30, 48, 49; 1920, p. 41; 1927, p. 38.

[4] Board Minutes, VI, p. 293. Cf. synodical minutes, passim.

[5] Faculty Minutes, IV, pp. 370, 371; Board Minutes, III, p. 19.

[6] *Verhandlungen,* New York Ministerium, 1908, pp. 60, 80; 1909, pp. 24, 41, 43, 44, 46, 47; 1910, pp. 20, 21; 1911, p. 25; Faculty Minutes, IV, pp. 334, 346-350; Board Minutes, II, pp. 230-232; *Minutes,* Pennsylvania Ministerium, 1910, pp. 12, 13, 46-48.

[7] Board Minutes, III, pp. 14, 24-30, 37, 38, 74, 88, 89, 113, 130, 131, 185, 186, 277, 278; Minutes of Executive Committee, I, pp. 123-125; Faculty Minutes, IV, pp. 357, 358, 371, 379; *Proposed Reconstruction of Departments, Chairs, and Courses of the Lutheran Theological Seminary,* Sept. 1910; *Minutes,* Pennsylvania Ministerium, 1911, pp. 11-18.

[8] Board Minutes, III, pp. 32, 43-47, 134-138, 207; Minutes of Executive Committee, I, pp. 134, 142, 143, 154, 155, 185-187, 193, 196, 201, 225, 239; Faculty Minutes, IV, pp. 437-441, 455, 467; "Charles A. Schieren," in *The American Lutheran Survey,* Mar. 29, 1915, pp. 37, 38; *Minutes,* Pennsylvania Ministerium, 1913, pp. 6-12.

9 Board Minutes, III, pp. 138, 139, 155, 184, 216, 267, 271-276, 290; Faculty Minutes, IV, p. 541.

10 Board Minutes, IV, pp. 126, 153, 253, 295, 296; V, pp. 6, 7, 12-14, 27, 29-34, 37, 53, 83, 117, 153, 175, 204, 225, 285, 331; Faculty Minutes, V, pp. 120, 129, 130; *Seminary Bulletin,* June 1920, pp. 1, 2; June 1926, pp. 4-7; Dec. 1926, pp. 1-5; June 1927, p. 14.

11 Board Minutes, I, p. 223; Faculty Minutes, V, p. 262.

12 Minutes of Alumni Association, I, pp. 117, 126, 146, 158; Faculty Minutes, IV, pp. 178, 318, 321, 333, 358, 389, 391-393; Board Minutes, I, pp. 56, 220, 221; *Minutes,* Pennsylvania Ministerium, 1910, pp. 50, 51.

13 Minutes of Executive Committee, I, pp. 134, 154, 155, 185-187, 193, 196, 198-201; Board Minutes, III, pp. 134-138, 140-153, 166; Faculty Minutes, IV, pp. 391-393, 411-421; *Minutes,* Pennsylvania Ministerium, 1913, pp. 9-11.

14 C. M. Jacobs, "The Graduate School in our Philadelphia Seminary," in *The Lutheran Church Review,* XXXIII (1914), pp. 120-125.

15 Board Minutes, IV, pp. 7, 8, 31, 33, 254, 268, 269; Minutes of Executive Committee, I, pp. 294-296; II, pp. 6, 7, 107. 294-296; *Seminary Bulletin,* Dec. 1923, pp. 5, 6.

16 Faculty Minutes, IV, pp. 574-576; V, p. 6; Board Minutes, IV, pp. 51, 291.

17 Board Minutes, IV, pp. 103-230.

18 *Ibid.,* II, p. 106; III, pp. 227-230, 292; IV, pp. 7, 22, 52, 93-95; Minutes of Executive Committee, I, p. 296; II, pp. 5, 6; Faculty Minutes, IV, pp. 470, 471, 568, 589-591; *Minutes,* Pennsylvania Ministerium, 1914, pp. 48, 57.

19 Faculty Minutes, V, pp. 345, 352, 353, 367.

20 *Ibid.,* I, p. 5.

21 *Ibid.,* IV, p. 257.

22 *Ibid.,* IV, p. 257; VI, pp. 240, 241; Board Minutes, IV, p. 175; Minutes of Executive Committee, II, p. 82.

23 *Minutes,* Pennsylvania Ministerium, 1910, p. 49; Minutes of Executive Committee, I, pp. 170, 177-179, 181, 269, 292; Board Minutes, II, pp. 208, 212, 216, 222; III, pp. 17, 46, 50, 51, 57, 82-84, 102, 114, 158-160, 205, 248, 256; IV, pp. 69, 70, 77, 82, 117, 179, 260, 271, 287, 296; V, pp. 130, 150, 179, 180, 353, 355.

24 Board Minutes, IV, pp. 36, 39, 111, 112, 117, 143, 234, 256, 259; *Seminary Bulletin,* Dec. 1919, pp. 1, 2; June 1923, pp. 1, 2; *Catalogue,* 1925-26, p. 33.

25 Board Minutes, II, pp. 196, 198; IV, pp. 100, 108, 187, 190, 213; V, p. 179; *Seminary Bulletin,* Dec. 1919, pp. 1, 2; June 1926, p. 3; *Minutes,* Pennsylvania Ministerium, 1914, p. 47; *Verhandlungen,* New York Ministerium, 1913, pp. 47, 66; 1914, pp. 23, 34-38; 1915, pp. 28, 60.

26 Board Minutes, IV, pp. 36, 39, 55, 93, 107, 165, 178, 238.

27 *Ibid.,* IV, pp. 27, 32, 40, 56; V, p. 417; *Seminary Bulletin,* Oct. 1917, pp. 4-6; Apr. 1949, p. 3; Dec. 1937, pp. 5-8.

28 Board Minutes, V, pp. 39a, 175.

29 *Seminary Bulletin,* Apr. 1921, pp. 1-8; June 1922, pp. 1-6.

30 Board Minutes, IV, pp. 225, 251, 266, 271, 288, 289; V, pp. 64, 66, 91-94, 146, 147, 197; *Seminary Bulletin,* June 1923, pp. 2, 3; June 1924, pp. 2-4; Oct. 1925, p. 14; Dec. 1930, p. 2.

[31] Faculty Minutes, V, pp. 80-84, 165, 179; Board Minutes, IV, pp. 95, 187-189, 229, 265; Abdel Ross Wentz, *History of the Gettysburg Theological Seminary* (Philadelphia, 1926), p. 278.

[32] *Minutes,* United Lutheran Church in America, 1926, p. 541; 1928, pp. 405, 406; Board Minutes, V, pp. 60, 61, 102, 107-115; *Seminary Bulletin,* Apr. 1929, p. 2; June 1929, pp. 1-5; Henry H. Bagger, "The Problem of Our Theological Seminaries," in *The Lutheran Church Quarterly,* I (1928), pp. 336-345.

[33] Board Minutes, V, pp. 142, 143, 176; *Minutes,* Alleghany Synod, 1929, pp. 35, 37, 49; Maryland Synod, 1929, pp. 33-40; Pennsylvania Ministerium, 1929, pp. 146-152, 262; Pittsburgh Synod, 1929, p. 90; Susquehanna Synod, 1929, pp. 59, 79; West Pennsylvania Synod, 1929, pp. 47-56.

[34] *Minutes,* United Lutheran Church, 1932, pp. 71, 453, 454.

[35] *Minutes,* United Synod of New York and New England, 1931, p. 145; 1932, p. 165; 1933, pp. 86, 87, 118, 120; 1934, pp. 118, 175; 1935, p. 89; Board Minutes, V, pp. 258, 259.

[36] *Seminary Bulletin,* Oct. 1933, p. 10.

[37] Board Minutes, IV, pp. 114-116, 142; V, pp. 8, 16; VI, p. 422; Minutes of Executive Committee, II, pp. 68, 73.

[38] Board Minutes, IV, pp. 29, 30, 42, 81, 82, 92, 95, 115, 165, 166, 182, 190, 205, 226, 227; V, pp. 57, 96, 132, 148, 180, 195, 224, 350, 365; *Seminary Bulletin,* Apr. 1922, p. 7; Dec. 1927, pp. 8, 9; April 1929, p. 10; Dec. 1929, p. 6; June 1932, p. 23; Dec. 1935, p. 1.

[39] Cf. T. G. Tappert et al., "Lutherans in the Great Economic Depression," in *The Lutheran Quarterly,* VII (1955), pp. 145-154.

[40] Board Minutes, V, p. 206.

[41] *Seminary Bulletin,* Oct. 1932, pp. 25-27; Board Minutes, V, pp. 269, 285, 290, 343, 353, 356, 375, 394.

[42] Board Minutes, VI, p. 25.

[43] *Ibid.,* IV, pp. 251, 254, 256; V, pp. 56, 168.

[44] S. E. Ochsenford, ed., *Documentary History of the General Council of the Evangelical Lutheran Church in North America* (Philadelphia, 1912), pp. 316, 318, 487; Faculty Minutes, IV, pp. 432, 433, 482-492, 513; Board Minutes, IV, p. 33, 174, 194, 254, 278.

[45] Board Minutes, V, p. 82.

[46] Faculty Minutes, V, p. 259; VI, p. 96; Board Minutes, V, pp. 95, 98.

[47] Faculty Minutes, V, p. 68; Board Minutes, IV, p. 297.

[48] Faculty Minutes, V, pp. 48, 49; *Seminary Bulletin,* Oct. 1918, pp. 8, 9.

[49] *Catalogue,* 1917-18, pp. 12-15; Faculty Minutes, V, pp. 25, 26, 34, 50, 51, 73, 79; *Seminary Bulletin,* Oct. 1917, p. 14; Apr. 1918, p. 12; June 1918, p. 12; Oct. 1918, pp. 15, 16; Dec. 1918, pp. 5, 6; Oct. 1919, pp. 7-9.

[50] Faculty Minutes, V, pp. 44-46, 48, 56; Board Minutes, IV, p. 104; *Catalogue,* 1918-19, pp. 12, 13; *Seminary Bulletin,* Oct. 1918, pp. 5, 6.

[51] Board Minutes, V, pp. 138, 198, 233, 267, 321, 322, 432; Faculty Minutes, VI, pp. 87, 90, 93, 94, 117, 118, 130, 192, 231, 267, 271, 302.

[52] *Minutes,* Pittsburgh Synod, 1935, p. 27.

[53] Faculty Minutes, IV, p. 328; V, pp. 125, 347; Board Minutes, III, p. 101; *Seminary Bulletin,* Oct. 1916, p. 8; Dec. 1916, pp. 13, 15, 16; Dec. 1917, pp. 14, 15.

[54] Board Minutes, III, pp. 99, 100; IV, p. 283; Faculty Minutes, IV, pp. 523, 552, 553; V, p. 319.

[55] Board Minutes, V, pp. 33, 56, 270, 322, 330; Faculty Minutes, V, pp. 356, 365, 400; *Seminary Bulletin,* Dec. 1927, p. 8; Dec. 1928, pp. 7, 8.

[56] Faculty Minutes, V, pp. 50, 88, 248, 252, 266, 289, 290, 355, 380; VI, pp. 77, 79, 140, 240, 247; Board Minutes, III, pp. 95, 96, 111; IV, p. 195; *Minutes,* Pennsylvania Ministerium, 1912, pp. 42, 43; *Seminary Bulletin,* Oct. 1916, p. 16; Oct. 1925, p. 23; Dec. 1931, p. 1; Dec. 1932, p. 11; Apr. 1933, p. 2; *Catalogue,* 1916, pp. 16, 17.

[57] Faculty Minutes, IV, pp. 396, 398; V, pp. 22, 24; Board Minutes, III, p. 96; *Order of Service for the Admission of Students,* leaflet, 1912; for its source see Hugh Benson, ed., *Prayers, Public and Private, being Orders and Forms of Public Services . . .* compiled, written or translated by Edward White Benson (London, 1900), pp. 28-39.

[58] Faculty Minutes, IV, pp. 472, 548; Minutes of Executive Committee, I, pp. 114, 115; Board Minutes, III, pp. 10-13, 41, 42, 61, 93, 94, 100, 101, 104; IV, p. 102; V, pp. 6-8; *Catalogue,* 1918-19, pp. 14-18; 1919-1920, pp. 20-26; *Minutes,* Pennsylvania Ministerium, 1912, pp. 41-47, 54; *Seminary Bulletin,* June 1919, pp. 12-20; Apr. 1922, p. 5.

[59] Faculty Minutes, V, p. 318; Board Minutes, IV, pp. 292-294.

[60] Faculty Minutes, V, pp. 184, 185, 245, 297, 318; VI, pp. 126, 129; Board Minutes, V, p. 325.

[61] Board Minutes, IV, p. 196.

[62] *Catalogue,* 1926-27, pp. 18-21; *Inaugural Address of President Charles M. Jacobs* (Philadelphia, 1927).

[63] Cf. C. Umhau Wolf, "Present Trends in Lutheran Seminary Training," in *The Lutheran Church Quarterly,* XV (1942), pp. 67-75.

[64] Robert L. Kelly, *Theological Education in America: A Study of 161 Theological Schools in the United States and Canada* (New York, 1924), pp. 72, 73, 89.

[65] Cf. Board Minutes, IV, p. 195; *Seminary Bulletin,* Apr. 1922, p. 7.

[66] Cf. Faculty Minutes, IV, p. 594.

[67] Letter to C. P. Krauth, 1848, in Adolph Spaeth, *Charles Porterfield Krauth,* 2 vols. (New York and Philadelphia, 1898, 1916), I, p. 183.

[68] Cf. Henry Offermann, "The Church, the Seminary, and the Study of Theology," in *The Lutheran Church Quarterly,* XVIII (1945), pp. 10-18.

[69] Board Minutes, V, pp. 38, 144, 369, 415; VI, p. 12.

[70] Luther D. Reed, "Henry Offermann," manuscript, 1953.

[71] For the full texts of this and other student parodies of the 1930's, see archives.

[72] George W. Sandt, *Theodore Emanuel Schmauk* (Philadelphia, 1921); Henry E. Jacobs, "Dr. Schmauk and the Seminary," in *The Lutheran Church Review,* XXXIX (1920), pp. 213-219.

[73] Sandt, *op. cit.,* pp. 189, 190.

[74] Faculty Minutes, IV, pp. 532-535; Board Minutes, III, pp. 285-287.

[75] Luther D. Reed, "At Eventide: Recollections and Reflections," 1959, unpublished typescript.

[76] Henry Offermann, "Charles M. Jacobs: Teacher, Scholar, Theologian," in *The Lutheran Church Quarterly,* XII (1939), pp. 74-81; *Seminary Bulletin,* Apr. 1938, pp. 1-5; Oct. 1938, pp. 4-7.

[77] *Inaugural Address of President Charles M. Jacobs* (Philadelphia, 1927), pp. 11-17; cf. C. M. Jacobs in *The Ministry and the Sacraments,* ed. Roderic Dunkerley (New York, 1937), pp. 138-145.

[78] *Seminary Bulletin,* Dec. 1936, pp. 1-5.

[79] Faculty Minutes, V, pp. 218, 219, 223, 285; *Seminary Bulletin,* Dec. 1922, pp. ,2; Oct. 1924, p. 8.

[80] Cf. his "Theses on the Holy Scriptures" in Ochsenford, *op. cit.,* pp. 398-405.

[81] Emil E. Fischer, "Inaugural Address," in *The Lutheran Church Review,* XXXIX (1920), p. 467.

[82] *Seminary Bulletin,* Dec. 1936, pp. 7-10.

[83] Minutes of Alumni Association, II, pp. 212, 233, 234, 237, 238, 260; Faculty Minutes, V, pp. 116, 118, 146, 147, 172, 197, 240, 329, 337, 352, 359, 360, 369; Board Minutes, V, pp. 39, 51, 53, 59, 250, 251; *Seminary Bulletin,* June 1927, pp. 11, 12.

[84] Board Minutes, III, pp. 289, 290; IV, pp. 6, 13, 22; *Seminary Bulletin,* Oct. 1916, pp. 1-4.

[85] Faculty Minutes, IV, pp. 19, 299; Board Minutes, III, pp. 74, 217, 221, 230; Minutes of Alumni Association, II, 87-90, 93, 99, 105, 110-112, 114, 121-124, 135, 160, 161.

[86] *Seminary Bulletin,* June 1937, p. 17.

[87] Board Minutes, IV, pp. 12, 37, 40, 147, 160, 180, 221, 229; V, p. 236; Faculty Minutes, V, pp. 28, 31, 32, 69, 115, 158, 214, 301; *Seminary Bulletin,* June 1917, pp. 1,2; Oct. 1922, pp. 11-13; June 1933, p. 15.

[88] Faculty Minutes, IV, p. 402; Board Minutes, IV, p. 199; V, pp. 34, 180, 181; Minutes of Executive Committee, I, p. 167.

Chapter VI

[1] Board Minutes, VII, pp. 3, 137; VIII, p. 369; X, pp. 27-30; *Seminary Bulletin,* Apr. 1948, p. 3; June 1952, p. 2; June 1957, p. 2; Oct. 1957, p. 3.

[2] Board Minutes, VII, pp 62-65, 203-206, 210, 249, 256, 325, 346, 347; VIII, pp. 195-207, 509; *Seminary Bulletin,* Oct. 1947, p. 1.

[3] *Seminary Bulletin,* special issue 1953, p. 2.

[4] Board Minutes, VIII, pp. 195-207, 277.

[5] Report of Elwyn A. Smith and Robert Tobias, Feb. 10, 1959, in Board Minutes, X, pp. 180-192; cf. XI, p. 91.

[6] Board Minutes, VI, pp. 320, 321, 371, 384, 387.

[7] *Ibid.,* VIII, pp. 103, 105, 107, 233-241, 259-265; *Seminary Bulletin,* Dec. 1962, pp. 1, 2.

[8] Board Minutes, V, p. 422; VI, pp. 24, 26, 393, 394, 399; Faculty Minutes, VI, pp. 182, 230; *Seminary Bulletin,* June 1945, p. 3; Aug. 1945, pp. 2, 7.

[9] Board Minutes, VII, pp. 10-16; VIII, pp. 313, 314, 363; Faculty Minutes, VII, pp. 124-126, 129, 130; *Seminary Bulletin,* Aug. 1945, pp. 3-6; Feb. 1952, p. 1; Apr. 1952, p. 3.

[10] Board Minutes, VIII, pp. 317, 321, 325, 371; XI, p. 188; *Seminary Bulletin,* Feb. 1952, p. 1; June 1952, p. 1; Dec. 1952, pp. 1, 2; Dec. 1961, p. 1.

[11] Board Minutes, VII, p. 81; X, pp. 151-156; *Minutes,* Pennsylvania Ministerium, 1945, pp. 83, 84; *Seminary Bulletin,* June 1943, p. 1.

[12] Board Minutes, VI, pp. 140-143, 198, 199, 291, 320; VII, pp. 9, 60, 107, 173, 297, 369; *Minutes,* Pennsylvania Ministerium, 1945, pp. 83, 84.

[13] Board Minutes, VII, p. 369; VIII, pp. 3, 7, 513; *Minutes,* United Lutheran Church, 1948, pp. 353-357; 1952, p. 745; 1954, pp. 912, 913.

[14] Board Minutes, VI, pp. 3, 27, 34, 78, 80-86, 145, 162, 254, 280, 398; VII, pp. 125, 126; *Seminary Bulletin,* June 1950, pp. 3, 4; L. D. Reed, "At Eventide," unpublished typescript, pp. 238-255.

[15] Board Minutes, VII, p. 277; VIII, pp. 107, 245, 295, 387, 541.

[16] Board Minutes, VII, pp. 18, 250, 266; VIII, pp. 227, 247, 283, 303, 379, 441, 529; IX, pp. 4, 7, 52, 186; X, p. 104; XI, pp. 2, 21, 35, 38, 89, 90, 136; *Seminary Bulletin,* 1944-63, passim.

[17] Cf. Faculty Minutes, VII, p. 25; Board Minutes, VI, p. 346.

[18] Faculty Minutes, VIII, p. 1; Board Minutes, VI, pp. 8, 149, 211; IX, p. 26.

[19] Faculty Minutes, V, pp. 394, 396; VI, pp. 21, 23, 47.

[20] Board Minutes, VIII, pp. 55, 57, 59.

[21] *Ibid.,* VII, pp. 105, 117, 331, 337, 348, 363; X, p. 178; XI, pp. 163, 181; *Minutes,* Pennsylvania Ministerium, 1962, pp. 112, 113.

[22] Faculty Minutes, VII, p. 10; Board Minutes, VI, pp. 214, 288, 302, 362, 363, 366, 388, 389, 397, 423, 424; VII, pp. 33, 86, 87, 128; *Seminary Bulletin,* Apr. 1944, p. 8; Oct. 1944, p. 4; Oct. 1945, p. 8.

[23] Board Minutes, VI, pp. 214, 261.

[24] Faculty Minutes, VI, p. 280; Board Minutes, VI, pp. 148, 151, 152; VIII, pp. 99, 111; *Seminarian,* May 1, 1963, pp. 1, 4.

[25] Board Minutes, VI, pp. 285, 286; VIII, pp. 219, 339; IX, pp. 28, 30, 108, 112, 187, 202; X, p. 89; *Seminary Bulletin,* Dec. 1954, p. 4; June 1960, p. 2; June 1962, p 3.

[26] Faculty Minutes, VII, pp. 193, 196; Board Minutes, VI, pp. 28, 57, 150, 429; VII, p. 67; IX, p. 181; X, p. 240.

[27] Cf. Board Minutes, V, pp. 268, 323.

[28] A. Steimle in *The Lutheran Church Quarterly,* VIII (1935), p. 295, and *Seminary Bulletin,* June 1935, pp. 5, 6; Board Minutes, V, p. 324. Cf. David L. Scheidt, "The High Church Movement in American Lutheranism," in *The Lutheran Quarterly,* IX (1957), pp. 343-349; Lloyd M. Wallick, "The Society of St. Ambrose," in *ibid.,* XIII (1940), pp. 297-301.

[29] Reed, *op. cit.,* pp. 341, 352.

30 Faculty Minutes, VII, pp. 14, 55, 190.

31 *Ibid.,* VII, p. 14; VIII, pp. 56, 114, 151, 152, 202, 203, 208-213; IX, pp. 11-14, 19; cf. Board Minutes, XI, pp. 129-132.

32 Cf. "Externals of Worship," in *Minutes,* Ministerium of Pennsylvania, 1936, pp. 211-214; "The Holy Communion and its Use," in *ibid.,* 1956, pp. 73-77, 121; "Corporate Communions," in *Minutes,* United Lutheran Church, 1954, pp. 1019-1023; "The Sacraments of the Altar and its Implications," in *ibid.,* 1960, pp. 918-934.

33 Faculty Minutes, VI, pp. 276, 277, 287, 307, 316, 317, 334, 340; VII, p. 94; VIII, pp. 179, 180, 183; IX, pp. 79-81; Board Minutes, VI, pp. 104, 148, 150, 161, 197, 198, 213, 261, 289; X, p. 112; *Seminary Bulletin,* Apr. 1950, p. 1; Apr. 1958, p. 1; Oct. 1958, p. 2; Apr. 1959, p. 2; Feb. 1963, p. 2.

34 Minutes of Alumni Association, III, p. 67; Board Minutes, IX, pp. 245-253; X, pp. 110, 153; Faculty Minutes, IX, pp. 96, 97, 100-103; *Seminary Bulletin,* Apr. 1938, p. 10; Dec. 1944, p. 4; Aug. 1946, pp. 3, 4; Feb. 1951, p. 2; June 1956, pp. 3, 4; Dec. 1956, p. 1; Feb. 1960, p. 1; Dec. 1961, p. 2; Apr. 1962, p. 2; Apr. 1962, p. 2; Dec. 1962, p. 3.

35 Faculty Minutes, VIII, pp. 31, 32; IX, pp. 24-28, 105-111; Board Minutes, XI, pp. 133, 134, 170-173.

36 Board Minutes, VI, pp. 150, 290; *Seminary Bulletin,* June 1942, pp. 1, 2; Dec. 1960, p. 1; June 1961, p. 3.

37 Faculty Minutes, VI, p. 229; VIII, pp. 157, 205; IX, pp. 33, 84-88; Board Minutes, VI, pp. 78, 364; *Seminary Bulletin,* June 1954, p. 4; Feb. 1962, p. 4.

38 Faculty Minutes, VIII, p. 91; Board Minutes, X, p. 173.

39 Board Minutes, VI, pp. 287, 372, 425; VII, p. 364; VIII, p. 445; Faculty Minutes, VIII, p. 156; *Seminary Bulletin,* Dec. 1943, p. 4; Feb. 1945, p. 3; Feb. 1949, p. 3.

40 Board Minutes, VI, p. 65.

41 Board Minutes, VII, p. 327; VIII, pp. 277, 289, 291, 301; *Seminary Bulletin,* June 1952, p. 4.

42 Board Minutes, XI, p. 5.

43 Cf. the faculty's address to the board in 1953, in Faculty Minutes, VII, pp. 167-170; Board Minutes, VIII, pp. 299, 477-481.

44 Board Minutes, III, p. 136; IV, pp. 78, 82, 92, 120, 154, 155, 235; V, p. 10; VI, pp. 276, 277, 287, 301, 359; VII, pp. 279, 284.

45 Board Minutes, VIII, p. 509; X, pp. 26, 39, 113; Faculty Minutes, VIII, p. 122.

46 Board Minutes, VI, p. 426; VIII, p. 227; cf. VIII, pp. 103, 113.

47 *Seminary Bulletin,* June 1920, p. 2; June 1944, p. 7.

48 Board Minutes, XI, p. 23; Faculty Minutes, IX, p. 21.

49 Cf. *Current Biography,* Feb. 1947, pp. 34-36.

50 Board Minutes, VIII, pp 1-3, 53, 277, 283, 297, 469.

51 Board Minutes, V, pp. 184, 186, 325, 342, 369, 370.

52 *Ibid.,* V, pp. 369, 370, 416; VII, p. 152.

[53] *Ibid.,* VI, pp. 359, 370; VII, pp. 18, 20, 155, 156.

[54] Minutes of Executive Committee, VI, pp. 1, 10, 26, 30, 144, 152; Faculty Minutes, VI, p. 274; VIII, p. 18.

[55] Board Minutes, VII, pp. 209, 210, 218-220, 285, 364; VIII, pp. 11, 13, 171.

[56] Minutes of Alumni Association, III, pp. 7, 10, 15, 27, 30, 33, 34, 44; Board Minutes, VI, p. 214; XI, p. 3; *Seminary Bulletin,* Dec. 1941, p. 5.

[57] Board Minutes, VI, p. 428; VIII, p. 89; Faculty Minutes, IX, pp. 72, 73; Otto L. Schreiber, *Martin Luther and the Reformation in Numismatic Art: The Mount Airy Collection* (revised edition, 1960).

[58] Board Minutes, VIII, pp. 25, 27, 29.

[59] *Ibid.,* VI, pp. 34, 78, 95, 283, 302, 310-314, 372; *Seminary Bulletin,* June 1943, pp. 1-4.

[60] Board Minutes, X, pp. 97, 172, 195; XI, pp. 25, 36, 70, 118-126; Faculty Minutes, IX, pp. 24-28, 40-44, 47-51; *Seminary Bulletin,* Dec. 1958, p. 1; Feb. 1962, p. 1; Harry F. Baughman, "The Story of the Merger Negotiations," in *Gettysburg Seminary Bulletin,* May 1962, pp. 15-22; Booz, Allen, and Hamilton, *Planning Survey for Possible Merger* (1961).

[61] Board Minutes, IX, pp. 211, 213; X, p. 196; XI, pp. 85, 140.

Members of the Board of Directors, 1864-1964

The following abbreviations indicate the electing synod or board:

BTE   Board of Theological Education of the LCA
Car   Caribbean Synod of the LCA
EP   Eastern Pennsylvania Synod of the LCA
GC   General Council of the Evangelical Lutheran Church
LCA   Lutheran Church in America
NE   New England Synod of the LCA
NJ   New Jersey Synod of the ULCA or LCA
NY   New York Synod of the LCA
NYM   Ministerium of New York, GC or ULCA
NYNE   New York and New England Synod, GC or ULCA
Pitt   Pittsburgh Synod of the GC or ULCA
PM   Ministerium of Pennsylvania, GC or ULCA
SZ   Slovak Zion Synod of the LCA
ULCA   United Lutheran Church in America
UNY   United Synod of New York and New England, ULCA
WP   Western Pennsylvania-West Virginia Synod, LCA

Albrecht, Antonius C., 1884-93, 1902-14, PM
Armstrong, Ephraim, 1879-81, PM
Baden, Rev. J. H., 1875-87, NYM
Bagger, Rev. Henry H., 1942-52, PM
Baker, John R., 1870-77, PM
Bard, A. Raymond, 1934-37, PM
Beates, Henry, 1877-1903, PM
Beck, Rev. Alfred L., 1962- , NY
Beisler, Henry, 1939-46, UNY
Berger, John B., 1936-37, UNY
Berkemeyer, Rev. William C., 1962- , EP
Bert, Otto F. H., 1938-62, Pitt
Betz, William, 1947-52, 1955-59, UNY
Bittner, Frank D., 1895-1921, PM
Bock, Rev. Walter E., 1962- , NY
Bohlig, Frederick, 1942-45, UNY
Bohm, E., 1878-79, NYM
Bosch, Rev. Frederick H., 1920-29, NYM
Boschen, C. D., 1892-95, NYM
Boyer, D. S., 1895-98, PM
Brannick, Alvin P., 1962- , WP
Braun, William P. M., 1909-15, PM
Breinig, Alfred O., 1956-62, PM
Bremer, Rev. David H., 1956-62, PM; 1962- , EP
Bremer, Joseph A., 1894-1909, PM
Bremer, Lewis, 1864-65, PM
Brennecke, Rev. E., 1914-18, NYM
Brezing, Rev. Herman, 1934-41, UNY
Brighton, Ralph P., 1962- , NY
Brobst, Samuel K., 1864-71, PM
Brueckner, Rev. H., 1930-35, UNY
Bruns, John B., 1946-50, UNY; 1959-62, NJ
Buehrle, R. K., 1895-98, PM
Burkhalter, E., 1873-79, NYM
Chorley, H. C., 1886-92, PM
Colloday, Charles, 1883-85, PM
Cooper, Rev. Charles M., 1953-61, PM

Cornehlsen, Rev. Henry C., Jr., 1942-50, PM
Cousins, Windsor F., Esq., 1933-56, PM
Dangler, Jacob, 1908-14, 1917-22, NYM
Dash, G. Allan, Jr., 1950-56, PM
Daub, W. J., 1914-17, PM
Dewald, Rev. J. A., 1894-95, NYM
Diehl, T. H., 1879-1900, PM
Dinkey, James, 1864-65, PM
Dinkey, John F., 1917-30, NYNE
Doty, Kenneth B., 1955-61, UNY
Drehs, William S., 1943-62, PM
Early, Rev. John W., 1886-89, PM
Eck, William, 1922-24, NYM; 1939-42, UNY
Edwards, Rev. Francis R., 1952-57, PM
Ehrhart, Rev. Julius, 1873-79, NYM
Elbert, William, Sr., 1942-50, UNY
Endlich, J., 1865-68, PM
Endress, Henry, 1952-54, UNY
Erickson, Ernst S., 1938-39, 1960-62, UNY
Esser, Charles H., 1941-50, PM
Esterly, Rev. Franklin T., 1930-47, PM
Ettinger, George T., 1915-33, PM
Fegely, Jacob, 1889-1901, PM
File, John C., 1878-93, PM
Fischer, Rev. Emil E., 1945-59, PM
Fisher, Rev. John C., 1931-45, PM
Flath, Rev. G., 1878-79, NYM
FonDersmith, Charles A., 1903-09, PM
Freese, Earl, 1951-52, UNY
Fretz, Rev. Franklin K., 1926-41, PM
Frey, Rev. A. E., 1875-78, 1879-80, NYM
Frey, Rev. William E., 1922-24, Pitt
Fritch, D. D., 1905-31, PM
Fritch, Rev. George W., Jr., 1962- , EP
Fry, Rev. Jacob, 1879-91, PM
Fry, Rev. Franklin F., 1920-29, NYNE; 1929-33, UNY
Fry, S. Gross, 1865-75, PM

Gambier, Valentine, 1913-18, Pitt
Gebert, Rev. George, 1925-38, PM
Gebhardt, George M., 1953-62, PM
   1962- , EP
Geissenhainer, Rev. Augustus T., 1880-
   82, PM
Geissenhainer, Rev. Frederick W., 1864-
   79, PM
Geissenhainer, Hon. Jacob A., 1904-17,
   NYNE
Geissenhainer, Jacob, 1879-1904, PM
Geissinger, Rev. David H., 1879-94, PM
Geissinger, J. B., 1918-19, Pitt
Gerhard, Rev. Paul, 1963- , BTE
Gesler, Rev. A. U., 1943-46, Pitt
Gongaware, Rev. George J., 1912-13, Pitt
Grahn, Rev. Hugo, 1879-1903, PM
Greenwald, Rev. Emmanuel, 1867-79, PM
Greiner, G. F., Esq., 1919-30, 1932-38,
   Pitt
Greiner, John, Jr., 1925-29, 1931-47, PM
Groff, Henry C., 1941-55, PM
Guenth, Frederick, 1864-65, 1867-70, PM
Haas, Rev. John A. W., 1907-37, PM
Haas, Rev. George C. F., 1888-95, 1904-
   08, NYM
Hackman, Harry, 1961-62, NJ
Hagan, Peter P., 1928-54, PM
Hager, William H., 1909-47, PM
Hahn, Charles, 1881-84, PM
Hallock, Rev. Maynard C., 1961-62, PM
Hankey, Rev. William C., 1954-57, Pitt;
   1962- , WP
Harms, Rev. Henry W., 1943-49, PM
Harms, Rev. John Henry, 1920-28, 1938-
   47, PM
Hassold, Carl F. R., 1939-50, PM
Hassold, Frederick C., 1909-33, PM
Hauff, W., 1874-78, NYM
Hausman, Clarence B., 1953-55, NJ
Hawman, Alan M., Jr., Esq., 1955-62, PM
Heckel, F. W., 1869-72, PM
Heins, Gustavus, 1869-75, PM
Heischmann, Rev. John J., 1891-95, 1918-
   22, NYM
Heist, Rev. Paul W., 1940-43, 1946-47, Pitt
Hellwege, Rev. Adolph, 1910-12, PM
Henninger, Hon. James F., 1945-62, PM
Henry, Ray Y., 1963- , WP
Herold, F., 1864-65, PM
Hershey, Rev. Robert D., 1950-53, PM
Herstine, D., 1865-69, PM
Heyl, W. M., 1867-68, PM
Hill, Rev. Reuben, 1888-95, PM
Hill, W. F., 1921-31, Pitt
Hoffmann, Rev. Hugo W., 1908-14, NYM
Holthusen, Rev. Adolph H., 1935-41, UNY
Horine, Rev. John W., 1911-14, PM
Horine, Rev. Mahlon C., 1891-1909, PM
Horn, Rev. Edward T., 1901-12, PM
Horn, Rev. Edward T., III, 1937-43, UNY;
   1961-62, PM

Horn, Rev. Henry E., 1960-62, UNY
Horn, Rev. William M., 1955-62, PM
Houpt, Lewis L., 1864-84, PM
Ischinger, Rev. Robert H., 1936-49, PM
Jansen, William, 1937-39, 1960-62, UNY
Johnson, Roy H., 1935-62, Pitt
Jones, George M., Esq., 1925-43, PM
Jorgensen, Frederick H., 1950-53, NJ
Kaehler, Rev. Frank A., 1907-29, NYNE;
   1929-31, UNY
Katz, Rev. William L., 1933-36, 1937-52,
   PM
Kaufmann, L. W., 1906-08, NYM
Kavalek, Rev. Joseph, 1962- , SZ
Keiter, Rev. A. C. R., 1926-37, PM
Keiter, Rev. W. D. C., 1905-25, PM
Keller, Rev. Arnold F., 1947-57, 1958-61,
   UNY
Keller, Paul P., 1871-77, PM
Kidd, Rev. Samuel E., 1949-62, PM; 1962- ,
   EP
Kieffer, Rev. Norman E., 1946-54, 1957-
   59, Pitt
Kirsch, Rev. John A. W., 1929-32, UNY
Kirsch, Rev. Paul A., 1941-50, UNY
Klingensmith, Rev. Frank U., 1904-07,
   NYNE
Knisely, S. H., 1904-06, PM
Knudsen, Rev. Gunnar, 1949-62, PM;
   1962- , EP
Knudson, Harold W., 1962- , NE
Knudten, Rev. Edwin H., 1962- , NJ
Kohler, Rev. John, 1864-98, PM
Kracke, F., 1887-91, NYM
Krauch, Rev. Oscar, 1925-29, NYM
Kretschmann, Rev. Theodore W., 1912-21,
   PM
Krook, Hilding R., 1947-48, PM
Krotel, Rev. Gottlob F., 1873-75, NYM
Kuendig, Rev. J. J., 1864-65, 1873-75,
   1885-88, PM
Kunkelman, Rev. J. A., 1870-79, PM
Kunkelman, Rev. M. R., 1931-35, Pitt
Kurtz, Rev. Irwin B., 1914-33, PM
Kurtz, W. W., 1885-1905, 1906-08, PM
Laird, Rev. Samuel, 1865-67, 1883-1911,
   PM
Lane, Thomas H., 1903-09, Pitt
Langenstein, M., 1889-99, PM
Langsam, Walter C., 1950-52, UNY
Lehman, H., 1877-89, PM
Leicht, George A., 1888-92, NYM
Lessig, G. B., 1892-95, PM
Lindenstruth, Rev. L., 1909-30, PM
Livingston, Rev. Luther R., 1962-63, NE
Loew, Rev. Ralph W., 1951-62, UNY
Long, Rev. Alfred L., 1960-62, PM
MacIntosh, Rev. Aden B., 1928-40, PM
March, M. L., 1912-39, PM
Marsh, Thad N., 1963- , BTE
Marshall, J. W., 1930-35, Pitt
Mattes, Rev. John C., 1921-39, PM

Mattson, Rev. Earl R., 1962- , NY
Mayser, Rev. Frederick P., 1909-17, PM
Melhorn, Rev. Nathan R., 1918-45, PM
Meyer, Rev. J. Henry, 1943-47, UNY
Miller, Rev. C. Armand, 1914-18, PM
Miller, E. Augustus, Esq., 1893-95, 1900-22, PM
Miller, E. Clarence, 1901-44, PM
Miller, Rev. G. F., 1864-70, PM
Miller, Rev. George T., 1950-62, NJ
Miller, Rev. Harold S., 1945-62, UNY
Miller, Rev. Hermann F., 1940-42, PM
Miller, Rev. J. H., 1933-40, Pitt
Miller, J. Washington, 1889-1900, PM
Miller, Reuben B., 1875-88, PM
Moeller, George H., 1872-74, NYM
Mohr, Gloss K., 1902-31, PM
Moldenke, Rev. E. F., 1877-79, 1880-88, NYM
Moldenke, Richard, 1923-29, NYM; 1929-30, UNY
Moller, George H., 1898-1902, PM
Monroe, W. Frederick, 1898-1921, PM
Moser, Rev. Charles D., 1961-62, UNY
Mosser, J. K., 1894-1901, PM
Mosser, Robert K., 1941-47, UNY
Moyer, Rev. William O., 1961-62, PM
Mueller, Rev. George P., 1896-1901, PM
Muhlenberg, F. A., 1889-92, PM
Muhlenberg, H. H., 1864-68, PM
Muhlenberg, H. M., 1881-84, PM
Neff, C., 1879-81, PM
Nidecker, Rev. J. E., 1903-15, PM
Norton, Charles F., 1864-71, PM
Nutzhorn, Rev. Carl W., 1940-41, UNY
Oberly, Rev. Frank C., 1915-22, Pitt
Ochsenford, Rev. Solomon E., 1898-1904, PM
Odenwelder, A. J., Jr., 1937-52, PM
Offermann, Rev. Henry, 1907-10, PM
Olander, Rev. O. Karl, 1962- , NE
Opp, Charles B., 1899-1902, PM
Ortner, Rev. Elmer A., 1946-62, Pitt; 1962- , WP
Osterlund, O. W., 1935-50, PM
Paulson, Rev. Stephen M., 1916-17, PM
Pearson, Rev. Richard B., 1963- , NE
Peters, Rev. Hiram, 1893-94, PM
Petersen, Rev. C. F., 1887-91, NYM
Petersen, Rev. J. C. J., 1894-95, NYM
Pfatteicher, Rev. Ernst P., 1911-43, PM
Pfatteicher, Rev. Philip, 1875-1909, PM
Pflum, Rev. Henry J., 1941-45, UNY
Plitt, Rev. John K., 1879-86, 1895-98, PM
Potteiger, J. L., 1922-25, PM
Pretz, C., 1864-67, PM
Prigge, J. A., 1891-95, NYM
Querns, H. G. G., 1924-25, PM
Rabenold, Elwood M., Esq., 1920-29, NYNE; 1929-36, UNY
Rath, Rev. J. B., 1879-85, PM
Reed, Rev. Ezra L., 1879-86, PM

Rehrig, Rev. Wilson M., 1905-21, PM
Reichard, Clarence A., 1951-62, PM
Reinartz, Rev. F. Eppling, 1935-46, Pitt
Reinoehl, J., 1900-05, PM
Reno, Hon. Claude T., 1929-41, PM
Repass, Rev. Stephen A., 1894-1906, PM
Rhodes, Hon. Chester H., 1935-41, PM
Richards H. M. M., 1917-34, PM
Riter, Hon. Frank M., 1911-35, PM
Rodriguez, Rev. Jose D., 1963- , Car
Roehrs, Theodore, 1914-17, NYM
Romig, I. C., 1901-18, PM
Rommel, John, 1865-95, PM
Rosenberg, Rev. F. von, 1873-74, NYM
Ruff, Rev. G. Elson, 1945-55, PM
Ruperti, Rev. J., 1873-75, NYM
Rupp, Rev. J. C. F., 1924-33, Pitt
Sadtler, Samuel P., 1884-1923, PM
Sandt, C. Fleming, 1879-93, PM
Sandt, Rev. George Washington, 1904-31, PM
Schaack, Frederick, 1874-81, NYM
Schaeffer, Rev. William A., 1879-95, 1896-1908, PM
Schaeffer, Rev. William C., Jr., 1939-52, PM
Schaeffer, William L., 1868-75, PM
Scherer, Rev. Paul E., 1935-40, UNY
Schindel, Rev. Jacob D., 1895-1904, PM
Schmauk, B. F., 1875-78, PM
Schmauk, Rev. Theodore E., 1904-20, PM
Schmidt, Rev. Ernst, 1952-56, PM
Schmidt, F. R., 1879-89, PM
Schmidt, Frank H., 1947-54, PM
Schmitthenner, W. A., 1874-88, NYM
Schmucker, Rev. Beale M., 1864-88, PM
Schneider, Julius A., 1950-62, PM; 1962- , EP
Schwarzbek, William C., 1952-56, UNY
Seaman, Rev. William R., 1947-59, PM
Sedler, Arthur H., 1961-62, UNY
Seegers, Rev. John C., 1911-14, PM
Seiss, Rev. Joseph A., 1865-1905, PM
Semisch, William G., 1954-62, PM
Shaughnesy, Rev. John E., 1959-62, Pitt
Shearer, A. K., 1905-09, PM
Shepherd, G. Freemont, 1955-62, UNY; 1962- , NY
Shetlock, Rev. Bela, 1947-62, PM; 1962-63, EP
Sibole, Rev. Edward E., 1886-96, 1898-1904, 1905-11, PM
Simon, Burton C., 1918-21, PM
Sjauken, George S., 1941-45, UNY
Smith, Rev. J. Lawson, 1903-12, Pitt
Smith, Rev. Oliver P., 1886-1911, PM
Smith, Paul H., 1963- , BTE
Smith, Rev. R. Morris, 1913-15, Pitt
Soderlind, Arthur E., 1962- , NE
Spaeth, Rev. Adolph, 1871-73, PM
Spaeth, Rev. H. Douglas, 1915-20, PM
Spieker, Rev. George F., 1888-94, PM

Staake, Hon. William H., 1879-1909, PM
Stackel, William H., 1930-38, 1940-42, UNY
Steimle, Rev. Augustus, 1917-20, 1931-37, UNY
Steimle, Rev. Edmund A., 1941-52, UNY
Steinhaeuser, Rev. A. T. W., 1920-24, PM
Steinhaeuser, Rev. Jacob, 1904-05, PM
Stump, Rev. Joseph, 1911-16, PM
Steinkamp, William H., 1920-23, NYM; 1932-34, UNY
Stohlmann, A., 1881-87, NYM
Stoughton, Clarence C., 1945-50, UNY
Stover, William R., 1954-59, NJ; 1963- , BTE
Summers, Eric, 1962- , WP
Sunday, Rev. William F., 1932-35, UNY
Sutcliffe, Richard T., 1956-62, UNY
Tappert, Rev. Ernst A., 1920-31, Pitt
Tappert, Rev. Wilfried C. H., 1952-60, UNY; 1963- , BTE
Thompson, Edward, Esq., 1950-52, UNY
Tietzen, John H., 1873-74, NYM
Torres, Rev. Carlos A., 1962-63, Car
Trexler, B. F., 1868-69, PM
Trexler, Rev. Charles D., Jr., 1957-62, UNY
Trexler, H., 1864-67, PM
Trexler, M., 1893-94, PM
Ulrich, A. Stanley, 1879-86, PM
Ungerer, Heiby W., 1936-39, UNY
Urich, Rev. Frank M., 1922-51, PM
Vogelbach, Rev. J. T., 1864-82, PM
Wagner, George, 1872-75, PM
Wagner, Jacob, 1927-29, NYM; 1929-36, UNY
Wagner, Rev. John H., Sr., 1962- , NJ

Wagoner, Claude B., Esq., 1947-62, PM; 1962- , EP
Waidelich, Luther F., 1948-50, PM
Wallick Rev. Lloyd M., 1953-60, PM
Waltemade, Henry G., 1945-47, UNY
Wampole, Rev. J. F., 1879-86, PM
Wattles, J. Harvey, 1920-21, Pitt
Wattles, W. Warren, 1909-13, Pitt
Weber, Rev. Emil W., 1938-61, PM
Weidner, Revere F., 1882-83, PM
Weiskotten, Rev. Frederick W., 1879-1901, PM
Welden, Rev. C. F., 1864-75, PM
Welker, Louis, Jr., 1933-41, PM
Weller, Rev. Harvey A., 1902-26, PM
Wendel, Hugo, 1934-40, UNY
Wertz, Frank M., 1911-28, PM
Weyl, Rev. John A., 1922-25, NYM; 1929-30, UNY
White, Andrew J., 1963- , BTE
Whitteker, Rev. John E., 1912-21, PM
Wieboldt, Gustav, Esq., 1953-60, UNY
Wiedemann, Otto F., 1962- , EP
Wischan, Frederick, 1879-88, PM
Wohlsen, William, 1909-13, PM
Wuertz, Rev. Arnold A., 1962- , Car
Wulff, Martin, 1904-06, 1924-27, NYM
Yeckel, Herbert C., 1939-41, UNY
Zaun, Jacob, 1868-94, PM
Ziegenfuss, Rev. Samuel A., 1892-1911, PM
Zimmele, J. B., 1884-89, PM
Zimmerman, Rev. W. Russell, 1960-62, PM
Zinser, William E., 1903-08, PM
Zornan, Rev. John, 1962-, SZ
Zucker, Wolfgang M., 1962- , NJ
Zweizig, Rev. M. L., 1917-23, PM

Index